Person to Person
Peacebuilding, Intercultural Communication and English Language Teaching

LANGUAGES FOR INTERCULTURAL COMMUNICATION AND EDUCATION

Series Editors: Michael Byram, *University of Durham, UK* and Anthony J. Liddicoat, *University of Warwick, UK*

The overall aim of this series is to publish books which will ultimately inform learning and teaching, but whose primary focus is on the analysis of intercultural relationships, whether in textual form or in people's experience. There will also be books which deal directly with pedagogy, with the relationships between language learning and cultural learning, between processes inside the classroom and beyond. They will all have in common a concern with the relationship between language and culture, and the development of intercultural communicative competence.

All books in this series are externally peer-reviewed.

Full details of all the books in this series and of all our other publications can be found on http://www.multilingual-matters.com, or by writing to Multilingual Matters, St Nicholas House, 31–34 High Street, Bristol, BS1 2AW, UK.

LANGUAGES FOR INTERCULTURAL COMMUNICATION AND EDUCATION: 37

Person to Person Peacebuilding, Intercultural Communication and English Language Teaching

Voices from the Virtual Intercultural Borderlands

Amy Jo Minett, Sarah E. Dietrich and Didem Ekici

MULTILINGUAL MATTERS
Bristol • Jackson

DOI https://doi.org/10.21832/MINETT7086
Library of Congress Cataloging in Publication Data
A catalog record for this book is available from the Library of Congress.
Names: Minett, Amy Jo, author. | Dietrich, Sarah E., author. | Ekici, Didem, author.
Title: Person to Person Peacebuilding, Intercultural Communication and
   English Language Teaching: Voices from the Virtual intercultural
   Borderlands/Amy Jo Minett, Sarah E. Dietrich, Didem Ekici.
Description: Bristol, UK; Jackson, TN : Multilingual Matters, [2022] |
   Series: Languages for Intercultural Communication and Education: 37 |
   Includes bibliographical references and index. | Summary: "This book
   maps person to person peacebuilding as it intersects with, and is
   embedded in, intercultural communication. It foregrounds the voices and
   discourses of participants in an intercultural online service-learning
   project focused on peace through education in Afghanistan, primarily
   through synchronous English language tutoring"-- Provided by publisher.
Identifiers: LCCN 2021050238 | ISBN 9781788927086 (hardback) | ISBN
   9781788927079 (paperback) | ISBN 9781788927093 (pdf) | ISBN
   9781788927109 (epub)
Subjects: LCSH: English language—Study and teaching—Foreign speakers. |
   English language—Study and teaching—Afghanistan. | Intercultural
   communication—Cross-cultural studies. | Peace-building—Cross-cultural
   studies. Classification: LCC PE1128.A2 M5534 2022 | DDC 303.48/2—dc23/eng/20211123
LC record available at https://lccn.loc.gov/2021050238

British Library Cataloguing in Publication Data
A catalogue entry for this book is available from the British Library.

ISBN-13: 978-1-78892-708-6 (hbk)
ISBN-13: 978-1-78892-707-9 (pbk)

Multilingual Matters
UK: St Nicholas House, 31–34 High Street, Bristol, BS1 2AW, UK.
USA: Ingram, Jackson, TN, USA.

Website: www.multilingual-matters.com
Twitter: Multi_Ling_Mat
Facebook: https://www.facebook.com/multilingualmatters
Blog: www.channelviewpublications.wordpress.com

Copyright © 2022 Amy Jo Minett, Sarah E. Dietrich and Didem Ekici.

All rights reserved. No part of this work may be reproduced in any form or by any means without permission in writing from the publisher.

The policy of Multilingual Matters/Channel View Publications is to use papers that are natural, renewable and recyclable products, made from wood grown in sustainable forests. In the manufacturing process of our books, and to further support our policy, preference is given to printers that have FSC and PEFC Chain of Custody certification. The FSC and/or PEFC logos will appear on those books where full certification has been granted to the printer concerned.

Typeset by Nova Techset Private Limited, Bengaluru and Chennai, India.

Contents

Preface and Dedication: With and Without	ix
1 Introduction	**1**
The Chaos that Surrounds	1
The Purposes, Aims and Focus of This Book	3
Chapter Overview	4
The Backdrop: Landscapes of Conflict	5
Defining Peacebuilding	6
Person to Person Peacebuilding, Language Teaching, Peace Linguistics and Our Research	7
Person to Person Peacebuilding and Intercultural Communication	11
Peacebuilding and Intercultural Communication in Practice: The Example of International Educational Exchange Programs	13
Peacebuilding and Intercultural Communication: Theory and Empirical Research	15
Frameworks for Peacebuilding	18
Methods, Projects, Participants	22
Deductive Content and Critical Discourse Analysis	22
An Online Project with Afghan English Learners: Participants	26
Overview of Chapters	29
2 Understandings of Peacebuilding and Intercultural Communication	**32**
Introduction	32
Understandings of Peacebuilding	33
Research perspectives	33
Perspectives from practice	35
Peacebuilding in Practice: The UN Example	38
Understandings of Intercultural Communication Competence	39
Intercultural Communication Competence across Peacebuilding Levels	40

	The Personal Dimension of Peacebuilding and Intercultural Communicative Competence	41
	The Relational Dimension of Peacebuilding and Intercultural Communicative Competence	44
	The Structural Dimension of Peacebuilding and Intercultural Communicative Competence	47
	Conclusion	49
3	Context(s)	51
	Context(s) and Our Research	51
	Context 1: Afghanistan, history and the lives of our Afghan participants	54
	Context 2: US-based graduate TESOL programs and our participants	58
	Context 3: The virtual intercultural borderlands of online exchange	61
4	Person to Person Peacebuilding at the Personal Level	72
	The Personal Dimension of Peacebuilding	72
	Changes in Participants' Beliefs and Attitudes about Themselves: Resistance, Fear, Self-Confidence	75
	Changes in Participants' Beliefs and Attitudes about Others: Reconfiguring Perceptions, Out-Groups and In-Groups	81
	Changes in Participants' Beliefs and Attitudes about the World: Discursive Constructions of Afghanistan and Beyond	87
	Changes in Beliefs about Self, Others and the World	90
5	The Relational Dimension of Person to Person Peacebuilding	93
	The Growing Nature of Relationships through Dialogue	95
	Structuring Relationships: Starting from Similarities	96
	Structuring of Relationships: Embracing the Difference	102
	Closeness and Distance	105
	Use or Sharing of Power	107
	Maximizing Mutual Understanding: Empathy	110
	Resistance: Poorly Functioning Communication	113
6	Person to Person Peacebuilding at the Structural Level	115
	Participants' Understandings of the Causes and Effects of Conflicts	117
	Participants' understandings of the effects of conflict	117
	The demand for English as an effect of conflict	122
	Participants' Understandings of the Causes of Conflict	125
	Social actors and causes of conflict	125
	Differential access to resources: Technology	127

	Differential access to resources: English and 'native speakers'	129
	Conflict and societal norms	131
	Understandings of Inclusion, Decision Making and Means to More Broadly Include Voices	133
	Understanding How Structural Discourses Enable and Constrain Individuals and Groups	136
	Ways to Create Conditions and Relations that Contribute to Social Justice and Peace	138
	Resistance and the Structural Level of Person to Person Peacebuilding	142
	Conclusion	145
7	Fostering Person to Person Peacebuilding While Teaching Language and Intercultural Communication	146
	Reflection, Writing and the Reflective Practitioner	147
	Activities: Guided reflection, modeling, sharing	149
	Understanding Differential Access to Resources	152
	Activity: Access to resources	153
	Exploring Identity, Leveraging Peacebuilding	154
	Activities: Exploring identities	156
	Agency and Power	159
	Activities: Agency in the classroom and in the virtual intercultural borderlands	161
	Activities: Agency beyond the classroom, beyond the virtual intercultural borderlands	162
	Agency and Emotion	164
	Activities	164
	Concluding Remarks	166
Afterword: August 2021		169
References		170
Index		189

Preface and Dedication: With and Without

We write this note just before our book goes to press. It is late August 2021, almost exactly 20 years since the attacks of 9/11. With the withdrawal of US and international forces, Afghanistan has fallen to the Taliban. The number of Afghan refugees worldwide is skyrocketing; the local educational centers in Afghanistan have closed; the Taliban have asked women and girls to stay home (for their own safety, they say). The tutoring project has been suspended.

Thus, the context of this book and project has changed dramatically. We remind the reader that the voices in this book – those of Afghan students and US-based tutors – could speak, work, laugh, connect, learn and build peace, person to person, in the virtual intercultural borderlands of online exchange, *without* real fear of Taliban reprisals, *with* real hope for the future. The situation has changed dramatically, but the force and promise of the voices contained herein have not. While we are personally devastated, we are grateful we can share these voices with the world so that they can continue to inspire the need and desire to work for peace, and so that the world keeps watching and working toward basic human rights in Afghanistan. We continue to work for the evacuation and safety of our participants. Importantly, too, we continue to listen to these profound voices. We dedicate this book to those voices.

1 Introduction

The Chaos that Surrounds

'Rose,' Tutor of English as an additional language:

In light of the horrific events this weekend, I would like to touch on the impact this tutoring experience has and will have on me moving forward. As I was listening to the news and reading posts on the internet about the Orlando shootings connected to Islamic extremism, I could not help but reflect upon my brief but growing relationship with my tutee in Afghanistan. With so much hate and misunderstanding ... it is not only refreshing but overwhelmingly encouraging to know that it is still possible for two people from completely different walks of life to make a genuine connection despite the political/ideological chaos that surrounds. I am hopeful that someday we may focus our attention on building such positive relationships rather than condemning each other for our differences. (Rose, Summer 2016)

'Najibullah,' Afghan student:

[M]any of these [Afghan] students haven't had the experience to talk or communicate with a foreigner, like with an American or European, and in some areas, they are so religious ... they say bad things about you guys, honestly, but when students ... [are tutored] online with an American, then their idea changes, about you, they know that you are not bad, first, second, you're good [we laugh], they can share their happiness with you ... their mindset, ok, become positive, because when these students go home, he or she can share this experience to his family, to his mother, which is religious, to his father, which is religious, to his sister, and brothers, so it is not an effect on only one student, and the student, and his or her family, and his or her classmates. You have to add those too.

In these quotes we first meet Rose, a future teacher of English as an additional language (EAL),[1] who writes here of her experiences tutoring an adult learner of English who lives in Afghanistan. Their interactions took place online through videoconferencing, in a space we call the virtual intercultural borderlands. In this journal entry, as she responds to news of a shooting at a gay nightclub in the US state of Florida – in which 49 people died and 53 were injured – she refers directly to the 'political/ideological chaos that surrounds.' In her words, we see Rose place her growing personal connection with someone she describes as very different from herself within a broader context of conflict at a national and global level. In doing so, she evokes the power and potential future impacts of their intercultural interactions, suggesting that one on one relationships can not only lead to individual change but lay the groundwork for change at a 'political' or 'ideological' level. Put more simply, in Rose's words, we begin to see intersections between intercultural communication and person to person peacebuilding.

The second quote comes from an Afghan learner of English tutored online by a future teacher of EAL who was probably not unlike Rose. In Najibullah's words, too, we see the power and potential impact of intercultural interaction as he shares his perspectives on the value of Afghan English learners meeting online, one on one, with US-based tutors. Specifically, he remarks on the potency of direct contact between persons of different nationalities and 'mindsets': by such contact, we may come to realize that our intercultural counterpart is first 'not bad,' and second, perhaps, 'even good.' And what we learn from one another through such interactions we may share with our family and friends, who may share with *their* families and friends, and so on, in the process starting a counternarrative and new discourse chain (Bakhtin, 1984; Blackledge, 2005) which may push back against ideologies promoted by religious and political leaders alike.

The collaboration that brought Rose, Najibullah – and more than 70 other future EAL teachers – together with Afghan learners of English started with a conversation between the authors of this book. Our initial goal was relatively simple: to create opportunities for graduate students in teaching English to speakers of other languages (TESOL) to gain practical experience as part of their coursework. Inspired by the service-learning model (and, more recently, intercultural and international service learning; see Bamber, 2016; Rauschert & Byram, 2018), in which experiential education is linked to academic course goals, we designed a project in collaboration with an international community partner, a US-based nonprofit organization that focuses on peace in Afghanistan through education. Among other initiatives, this organization works with volunteer coordinators from across Afghanistan to pair students who want to practice English with volunteer tutors from across the globe.

For the project we explore in this book, the TESOL course instructor, the US-based director of coordination for the tutoring initiative, and local volunteers in Afghanistan worked together to pair each graduate student tutor with an adult Afghan learner of English. The pairs met over the course of a semester for weekly 90-minute tutoring sessions using videoconferencing; tutors and students were separated physically by a distance of over 7000 miles or 9000 kilometers. Many of the Afghan students did not have internet access in their homes and logged into their sessions from computers in educational centers and/or internet cafes. Tutors generally – although not all – participated from their homes. Given the time difference between Afghanistan and the US, most sessions for tutors were held before 8:30 in the morning or after 10:00 at night. As part of their coursework, the graduate students submitted six written journal entries in which they reflected on their tutoring experiences.

At the end of the first semester of this collaboration, we read the graduate students' reflections. Initially, we focused on what the tutors shared about teaching grammar, using technology and interacting online. Some reported feeling limited by only being able to see their students' faces; some expressed frustration at being unable to explain grammatical forms that to them just 'sounded right.' And then there were reflections like Rose's, which begins this chapter. Over and over, tutors described transformations they experienced, including their own shifting perceptions and prejudices, their evolving relationships with their Afghan counterparts and their growing insights into war, peace and the world around them. Compelled by their words and voices, we realized that we wanted to learn more. While the project continued with other groups of future EAL teachers and Afghan learners, we put out a call inviting former tutors and Afghan participants alike to share their thoughts on and experiences with the project in interviews. As our data grew, so did the references to peace and conflict in participant voices. Thus the research for this book began.

The Purposes, Aims and Focus of This Book

In this book, we map the discursive terrain and potential of person to person peacebuilding as it intersects with and is embedded in intercultural communication. Using deductive content and critical discourse analysis, we show how participants, both EAL tutors and Afghan learners of English, avail themselves of the unexpected affordance of building peace, person to person, as they meet and interact in what we call the virtual intercultural borderlands of online exchange. Ultimately, it is our aim in this book to provide teachers and teacher educators of language and intercultural communication with evidence of the power and potential of online exchange, particularly between students in conflict-affected countries, as well as with conceptual frameworks (Broome & Collier, 2012; Lederach, 2003) which can help teachers more deliberately leverage the communicative affordances of person to person peacebuilding, whether in the virtual intercultural borderlands of online exchange or in in-person classrooms.

As we explore the words and experiences of project participants, the following questions guide our research and analysis:

- In what ways do the discourses of intercultural interactants – US-based tutors and adult Afghan English learners – evidence change, actions and action possibilities that contribute to peacebuilding personally, relationally and structurally?

- How do participants' discourses evidence intersections between person to person peacebuilding and intercultural communication?
- How can teachers and teacher educators of language and intercultural communication help language learners and intercultural interactants more deliberately leverage the affordance of peacebuilding?

To answer these questions, we draw on analytical frameworks for peacebuilding developed by Lederach (2003) and Broome and Collier (2012) in conjunction with critical discourse analysis (Blackledge, 2005; Cruikshank, 2012; Fairclough, 1989, 2001, 2013; van Leeuwen, 2008; Wodak et al., 2009). As we explore the voices of US-based tutors of EAL and adult Afghan English learners as they write and talk about the tutoring project, themselves, each other, their interactions and their worlds, we examine three distinct but interconnected levels related to peacebuilding: the personal, the relational and the structural (Broome & Collier, 2012; Lederach, 2003). Lederach et al. (2007: 18) describe these levels or dimensions – in addition to a cultural dimension[2] – as sites of inexorable change as a result of social conflict. Accordingly, through analysis of participants' voices as gathered from interview transcripts and reflective writing, we seek discursive evidence of positive or 'preferred' change related to the personal, relational and structural levels of peacebuilding: change that points toward what Lederach (2003: 35) calls 'the horizon of the preferred future'; change that bodes the promise of less conflict, more peace. At the same time, we acknowledge the interdependence of these dimensions. To look at any one level solely is to sorely curtail understandings of the work of intercultural communication in peacebuilding – and peacebuilding in the work of intercultural communication.

It is our hope, finally, that the analyses we present and the implications thereof will add importantly to the limited but growing research into the peacebuilding prospects of intercultural communication and language teaching, particularly as they occur online through videoconferencing, in the virtual intercultural borderlands of online exchange. From these borderlands, we discovered in our participants' voices and discourses the unexpected affordance of peacebuilding, an affordance comprised of the accumulation and constellation of discursive indicators of peacebuilding which we find in and gather from the voices of tutoring project participants. These discursive indicators, in turn, provide us with ways to reimagine our work as language and intercultural communication educators, where person to person peacebuilding becomes an affordance we *deliberately* leverage in order to maximize opportunities for peace work at personal, relational and structural levels.

Chapter Overview

In this first chapter, we begin with a quick overview of the current landscapes of conflict, global and geopolitical – both the backdrop to our work and the motivation that propels us forward. We next provide the definitions of peacebuilding we use before examining how the three pivotal constructs we take up – peacebuilding, language teaching and intercultural communication – have been explored and operationalized in various combinations in previous research which both inform our work and make plain how our study is distinct. We conclude with details about the peacebuilding frameworks we use along with methods and participants before outlining the remaining chapters that make up the book.

The Backdrop: Landscapes of Conflict

We live in an age in which we hear devastating news on a daily basis: we are contending with catastrophic numbers of pandemic deaths, the dramas of a climate (environmental and political) undergoing dangerous change, ongoing war and acts of terrorism. We worry, therefore, that it may be too easy to become numb to or 'normalize' such devastation and violence. In terms of conflict specifically, we worry that the ability to look beyond or through the strife of others may lead us to an almost willful indifference to and 'othering' of those who endure conflict, making it possible to stay silent in the face of brutality, hegemony, inequity and injustice. As scholars and practitioners, teacher educators and language instructors and, most importantly, simply as humans and global citizens, we see a grave and urgent need for person to person peacebuilding, around the world and in our classrooms.

The current world order is one of disorder and terrible uncertainty. The global refugee crisis has reached historic proportions (Ritzen, 2016), with 68.5 million people having been forcibly displaced from their homes due to conflict. From this number, 25.4 million people are refugees, over half of whom are under the age of 18; 57% of these refugees are from South Sudan, Syria or Afghanistan (UNHCR, 2019). In the US, a former president worked ferociously to ban Syrian refugees and citizens of primarily Muslim countries from entering the country, to build a wall on the US/Mexico border and to separate immigrant children from their parents, brutal acts the effects of which will continue to haunt US foreign and domestic policy for years to come. Nor has the US been alone on its precarious path toward walls and isolationism: in Europe, too, 'populism' – with its anti-immigrant, Islamophobic underpinnings – has surged in the wake of Brexit, with recently 'opened' EU societies (Hungary, Poland) moving steadily toward becoming closed authoritarian states. 'Re-education' camps in China, the violence faced by the Rohinga in Myanmar, the kidnapping of school girls in Nigeria, an attack on a shopping mall in Kenya: daily we encounter reminders of the power and presence of conflict around the world. And as we have worked on this book, we have consistently been confronted with new instances of terrorism: a suicide attack on an educational center in Kabul in which at least 48 students and teachers lost their lives (August 2018); a mass shooting at a Pittsburgh Synagogue that caused 11 deaths (October 2018); 50 people killed praying in a mosque in New Zealand (March 2019); an attempted coup on the US Capitol building threatening a peaceful transfer of power (January 2021). Each incident reminds us of the urgent need for peacebuilding and for peace.

Defining Peacebuilding

To define what we mean by peacebuilding, we turn first to Lederach (1998), whose analytical framework shepherds our analysis throughout this book. He writes:

> [Peacebuilding is] a comprehensive concept that encompasses, generates, and sustains the full array of processes, approaches, and stages needed to transform conflict toward more sustainable, peaceful relationships. The term thus involves a wide range of activities that both precede and follow formal peace accords. Metaphorically, peace is seen not merely as a stage in time or a condition. It is a dynamic social construct. (Lederach, 1998: 20)

Lederach's emphasis here on 'the *full* array of processes, approaches, and stages needed to transform conflict' (emphasis added) is wide-ranging, inclusive, and creates meaningful space for the work of civil society actors and educators as well as UN peacekeepers, conflict mediators, soldiers, politicians, diplomats. And it creates space for peacebuilding such as we see between the participants in the tutoring project and whose voices we share in our research. We discuss this understanding of peacebuilding later in this chapter and in greater depth in Chapter 2.

In the meantime, we embrace here Lederach's (1998) comprehensive definition, as it also allows us to narrow our use of 'peacebuilding' to the more precise parameters of this study, which examines *person to person* peacebuilding. To explain: on its website, the community partner in the project we explore in this book describes itself as a 'people-to-people peacebuilding' initiative, a term that originates from the US Agency for International Development (USAID, 2011). The term has been used to describe projects in multiple contexts: in programs involving Israel and Palestine (Pundak, 2012); in conflict mitigation and reconciliation programs in Burkina Faso, Colombia, Ethiopia, Georgia, Honduras, Jamaica, Kenya, Kosovo, Macedonia, Mali, Niger and Senegal (USAID, 2018); and in Dili, Timor-Leste (Ingram *et al.*, 2015), to name but a few examples. The actual definition provided by USAID explains further:

> While there is no official or standardized definition of 'People-to-People' (P2P), most generally agree that it entails bringing together representatives of conflicting groups to interact purposefully in a safe space. … Projects in this arena address the prejudice and demonizing that

reinforces the perceived differences between groups and hinders the development of relationships between conflict parties. The aim is to create opportunities for a series of interactions between conflicting groups in the community to promote mutual understanding, trust, empathy, and resilient social ties. (USAID, 2011: 6–7)

From this definition, we find elements that are as appropriate for 'person to person' peacebuilding as they are for 'people-to-people': our participants are meeting in a 'safe space'; initial differences between participants are perceived as dramatic if not necessarily 'demonizing'; and, most importantly, their successful interactions depend on their abilities to understand each other, trust each other, empathize with each other and eventually develop social relationships which are resilient enough to withstand the inevitable flux and dynamism of human interaction. USAID's reference to 'community' can also certainly be understood as 'global community' – the nations and peoples of this world who are connected through technology and who are politically, socially and economically interdependent (see also Iriye, 2004). These definitions, then, provide the starting point for understanding how we use 'person to person peacebuilding' in this book.

Person to Person Peacebuilding, Language Teaching, Peace Linguistics and Our Research

Before we explain our frameworks and then share analyses of the discourses of US-based tutors of EAL and adult Afghan learners, we must first acknowledge the richness of previous studies which both inform our research as well as illuminate how our work is different. In 1990, the United Nations (UN) formally made the organization of TESOL a non-governmental organization (NGO) affiliated with the UN Department of Public Information, endowing it with the responsibility to help grow public understanding of the UN and its programs (TESOL & UN, 1990). As TESOL's first liaison to the UN, Larson (1992) subsequently pushed for teacher preparation programs to educate candidate teachers on the UN's primary points of focus, such as sustainable development, social justice, human rights and peace; she encouraged writers of TESOL materials to infuse these issues into curricula and texts, and she proposed that language teachers educate students as 'world citizens' who share the values and goals of the UN. Clearly, Larson regarded language teachers as uniquely prepared to spearhead the movement toward peace education, given their focus on and backgrounds in communications. So, too, Ashworth (1991), in concert with and simultaneous to Larson, centered her discussions on how TESOL as an organization should work to advance language rights, education and peace, arguing particularly for language teachers to focus on skills such as mediation, cooperation and negotiation. Ashworth further challenged TESOL to hold *itself* accountable to UN values and ethical standards, advocating, for example, for bilingualism and children's rights to their first language.

More recently, Kruger (2012: 20) explores in detail the relationships between peace education and the TESOL profession, distilling for us two approaches to pairing language and peace: by suffusing classroom teaching and curricula with peace principles ('non-violence, compassion, love, and reverence for all life'); and/or by teaching content related explicitly to peace, such as the catch-all 'global issues.' Additionally, Kruger (2012: 24), inspired by Gomes de Matos (2014), encourages TESOL professionals to teach and practice a 'linguistics of non-violence' (Gomes de Matos' term), explicitly teaching inclusive language that affirms diversity, for instance, and helping students recognize how language can humanize and dehumanize individuals. The end goal Kruger defines for TESOL courses integrating peace education is that learners develop both communicative competence and 'communicative peace,' an approach broadly defined as teaching language so as to: (1) spotlight connections between 'attitude, behaviour, and language'; (2) emphasize communication as both right and responsibility; and (3) help learners communicate 'for the good of humankind' (Gomes de Matos, 2014, as quoted in Kruger, 2012: 24). Kruger (2012: 24–25) goes on to extend these goals to teacher education as well, asserting that TESOL programs add whole courses devoted to peace education and theories of peace and conflict. Gkonou *et al.* (2021) agree, encouraging, for instance, language teacher educators to become versed in and then teach 'fundamental peace knowledge' and specific peacebuilding competencies, including 'ethnocultural empathy,' 'intercultural understanding,' 'emotion regulation' and 'cognitive flexibility' (Gkonou *et al.*, 2021: 66–83; see also Oxford *et al.*, 2021).

In other studies that fall under the umbrella of peacebuilding and English language teaching (ELT), we find multiple personal narratives of ELT teachers' journeys toward peacebuilding in their classrooms (Jakar & Milofsky, 2016; Medley, 2016; Oxford *et al.*, 2021), along with specific examples of and suggestions for integrating elements of peacebuilding into the curriculum (Allen, 2011; Dormer & Woelk, 2018; Jakar & Milofsky, 2016; Morgan & Vandrick, 2009; Oxford, 2013, 2014; Oxford *et al.*, 2021). As but two examples, conflict resolution and mediation skills have been used as primary content for English language and English for specific purposes curricula (see, for example, Jakar & Milofsky, 2016; Kennett, 2011; Rothman & Sanderson, 2018). We also find studies seeking to identify the impact of such courses on students. Rothman and Sanderson (2018: 61) conduct a qualitative study of a global issues course at a Japanese university, investigating how students reflected on identity and used language during class to generate 'more peace and constructive dialogues.' Like Larson (1990) and Ashworth (1991), Rothman and Sanderson (2018: 71) conclude that the integration of peace education with global issues and language education is 'a natural fit,' given how their students engaged with critical thinking, reflected on selves and developed awareness of 'the Other.'

Oxford (2013, 2014; Oxford *et al*., 2018, 2021) offers an expansive perspective on language, language teaching and peacebuilding through her 'Language of Peace Approach' (LPA). In Oxford's first book related to language and peace (Oxford, 2013: 3–23), she begins by sketching out tenets of peacebuilding, from accepting that peace is indeed possible, to recognizing that the language of peace exists in both word and image and is by no means simple. Oxford then endeavors to instruct us (as educators, researchers, students, activists or, feasibly, all of the above) on how we can use the language of peace to create harmony, from analyzing important peace documents in class, such as King's (1963) 'Letter from a Birmingham Jail,' to considering with students ways in which language creates discord and conflict, which she shares through examples that range from cyberbullying to genocide. Oxford *et al*. (2018: 11) build on these ideas in order to make explicit connections between the profession of TESOL and peacebuilding, encouraging practitioners in language and applied linguistics 'to become conscious, collaborative peacebuilders.' Here the authors ask us to adopt the values and definitions proposed by prominent figures in the arenas of peace and conflict studies, including Mahatma Gandhi, Martin Luther King, Jr., Mother Teresa, Galtung and Lederach, among others; they further advocate for the value of close linguistic analysis of communication, both peaceful and violent, in order to enrich peace communication (see also Gomes de Matos, 2014; Schäffner & Wenden, 1995; Wenden, 2007). Like Jakar and Milofsky (2016) and Kruger (2012), Oxford *et al*. (2018) proclaim, too, that we should integrate peace activities into language teaching and teacher education curricula. In Oxford *et al*.'s most recent (2021) edited volume, we thus encounter a multiplicity of peace activities for the language teacher and classroom along with an even more expansive exploration of the possibilities of peacebuilding and language education, including for instance: ways we can understand, apply and help our students apply peacebuilding for inner, interpersonal and intergroup peace (Gkonou *et al*., 2021); the role of 'revolutionary' peace and love in the construction of language teacher identities (Barcelos, 2021); and ways to utilize social justice pedagogies and critical language awareness in second language classrooms so as to promote and foster peacebuilding (Mahalingappa *et al*., 2021).

It is clear from multiple mentions of his name above that Gomes de Matos (2011, 2014) has inspired numerous TESOL professionals with constructs such as a 'linguistics of non-violence,' 'communicative peace' and 'applied peace linguistics.' He defines his version of 'peace linguistics' as interdisciplinary, with the broad goal of helping educational systems prepare 'human beings as peaceful language users' (Gomes de Matos, 2014: 186). To this end, he first plots the indicators of 'Nonviolent Communication' (NVC; see also Rosenberg, 2003) as a conflict resolution approach founded upon 'appreciation, compassion, conflict, feeling(s)/nonfeelings, judgments, needs, positive action, responsibility, and vocabulary (for feelings)' (Gomes de Matos, 2014: 187). In order to link these concepts with applied peace linguistics, Gomes de Matos situates the word 'communicative' before each term and then reimagines their nonviolent possibilities (Gomes de Matos, 2014: 187). He further breaks down the role of 'feelings' by drawing on Rosenberg's (2003) two lists of vocabulary for feelings based on whether or not 'needs' are being met: (1) 'positive feelings' (communicatively affectionate, appreciative, cheerful, free, friendly, good humored, loving, optimistic, peaceful, pleasant, tender and warm); and (2) 'negative feelings' (communicative anger, bitterness, despair, exasperation, hostility, impatience, irritation, pessimism, resentment, shock and wretchedness) (Gomes de Matos, 2014: 187). From this work, Gomes de Matos (2014: 188) raises important questions, asking: 'What violent vocabulary do we use not only about other human beings but about ourselves, and how can that be self-monitored? How can our condition of peaceful communicative creatures be improved in that respect?'

What we find of particular relevance from Gomes de Matos (2014) is his discussion of 'Appreciative Inquiry' (AI). As he explains, 'AI authors believe that "words create worlds" and that language has the power to create social change and reality' (Gomes de Matos, 2014: 189). In turn, he writes, we should seek out 'meaning making' in the words of 'interview data – stories, quotes, and inspirational highlights – for deeper interaction' (Gomes de Matos, 2014: 189). This is what we do in this book, as we explore participants' voices for evidence of peacebuilding through their interactions with one another. Additionally, Gomes de Matos describes how AI seeks to engender positive change, to articulate conditions for the 'liberation of power,' including 'the freedom to be heard,' the opposite of which is being silenced, 'the experience of the oppressed' (Gomes de Matos, 2014: 189), in language appropriately evocative of Freire's (1970) *Pedagogy of the Oppressed*. Finally, citing Whitney and Trosten-Bloom (2003), Gomes de Matos (2014: 189) lauds and articulates their meaning of 'power': 'the capacity to create, innovate, and positively influence the future' (Whitney & Trosten-Bloom, cited in Gomes de Matos, 2014: 189).

In each of these works above, we see intersections of peacebuilding and language teaching which hold promise for the TESOL profession in important ways: through specific curricular content and skills development; through adapting 'peace principles' in the classroom; through a linguistics of non-violence which helps us attend to how language can exclude or include, humanize or dehumanize. We are grateful for this work: indeed, to some extent, our use of critical discourse analysis (CDA) to examine participants' voices converges with and amplifies discussions of peace linguistics and critical language awareness (Gomes de Matos, 2014; Kruger, 2012; Mahalingappa *et al*., 2021; Oxford, 2013; Oxford *et al*., 2018, 2021), for, like Gomes de Matos (2014: 189), we believe 'words create worlds' and that 'language has the power to create social change and reality.'

To the richness of the works described above, we offer: (1) conceptual frameworks (Broome & Collier, 2012; Lederach, 2003) that allow us as teachers, researchers and teacher educators to analyze and thereby recognize discursive evidence of person to person peacebuilding; and (2) discussion, informed by our analysis of participant voices, of ways and means by which teachers and teacher educators can more deliberately leverage the affordance of peacebuilding when teaching language and intercultural communication, in person and online.

We say more about CDA later in this chapter, in the discussion of our methodology. We look next at existing research into intercultural communication and how it intersects with person to person peacebuilding, to continue to highlight how such research both informs our study and makes important space for the approach we take in this book.

Person to Person Peacebuilding and Intercultural Communication

We start this section with a caveat. Research on conflict resolution and transformation which intersects with intercultural communication spans a range of academic and professional areas, including studies regarding interpersonal relationships within families (e.g. Bystydzienski, 2011; Flanagan & Levine, 2010; Miike, 2017), educational settings and intercultural conflict (Davies, 2004; Deardorff, 2018; Landis *et al.*, 2004), intercultural conflict and international business (Carté & Fox, 2008; Okoro, 2013) and intercultural conflict in healthcare (Farini, 2008; Österberg & Lorentsson, 2011). In the fields of conflict resolution and mediation, researchers have contrasted Western techniques for mediation with Indigenous mediation methodologies (Mahan & Mahuna, 2017), explored mediation in cross-border economic conflicts (Kopka, 2017), and examined the impact of culture on transnational business relations (Hartl & Chavan, 2016). Gulliver's (1979) work *Disputes and Resolutions: A Cross-Cultural Perspective* may be the first to expressly link culture with conflict resolution and remains influential today, along with Avruch's more recent work on *Culture and Conflict Resolution* (1998, 2003, 2006). The prospects and promise of such analyses are exhilarating but also exhausting. By necessity, then, we limit ourselves here to studies that have brought together intercultural communication and *peacebuilding* (the specific word coined by Galtung [1975] and the specific focus of our research), even as we acknowledge that terms like 'conflict resolution' and 'conflict transformation' have at times been used interchangeably with 'peacebuilding' (Botes, 2003).

Like Broome and Collier (2012), we take the position that intercultural communication and person to person peacebuilding are interconnected by their very nature, yet these connections may be too often overlooked. In van Meurs and Spencer-Oatey's (2007: 99) words, these constructs are like the 'Bermuda Triangle,' and if they are not handled appropriately, 'hazardous conditions will emerge.' One such hazard of 'inappropriate' communication is misunderstanding, the consequences of which lead us to Ting-Toomey and Oetzel's (2001: 366) statement: 'Miscommunication often gives rise to escalatory conflict spirals or prolonged misunderstandings.' Bearing in mind the spirals and potential intractability and violence of conflict, we next seek to contextualize and distinguish our work by examining studies into intercultural communication and peacebuilding in existing literature.

Hahn (2018) presents a useful synopsis of 'communication for peacebuilding' which helps build a base understanding of our project in this book. She describes communication for peacebuilding as primarily the venture of intercultural communication scholars and practitioners seeking answers to broad but profound questions: What makes us get along? How do we put to rest problems when we disagree? She then proceeds to position the work of intercultural communication scholars as relevant before, during and after conflict (see also Lederach, 1998), with the end goal being a peace that endures. For success in any form at any level, she writes, peacebuilders through intercultural communication must confront systemic social problems (e.g. racism, religious intolerance) through education for all (and all ages), such that participants from all sides of a conflict can identify with or at least affirm the equal human rights and dignity of their 'opponents' (Hahn, 2018: para. 2). In other words, we must be able to humanize (or re-humanize) those with whom we are in conflict, actions ever more paramount as globalization increasingly brings together ever more divergent groups. In her discussion, Hahn further stresses the hazards of 'enclave deliberation' (Sunstein, 2002) and 'group-think,' conditions that polarize and balkanize groups, who in turn may shut down alternative perspectives and lose the ability to identify with individuals *not* in their group. Communication and intercultural communication scholars, writes Hahn, must work to make plain the multiplicity of viewpoints around conflict, advocate for equity during conflict, attend to journalistic practices and work to sensitize representations of conflict in the media, and push for intercultural communication opportunities and competence measures from early education onward. Concomitantly, Hahn (2018: para 13) proclaims that communication for peace necessitates 'the participation of ordinary citizens', or efforts will be for naught and conflict will continue.

Hahn's (2018) emphasis here on 'ordinary citizens' underscores our emphasis on *person to person* peacebuilding in our research: her general summary, moreover, equips us with a base understanding of how intercultural communication scholars might contribute to the peacebuilding endeavor. We elaborate on several of her key points in Chapter 2. We next consider, however, Remland *et al.*'s (2014: 55) textbook, *Intercultural Communication: A Peacebuilding Perspective*. These authors construct their perspective as grounded in cultural identity, with interactions always taking place in specific intercultural contexts. The authors describe intercultural communication as dialogue and frame it as a means to 'build friendships, shared identities, and peaceful communities.' They assert that their peacebuilding view of intercultural communication can happen through 'favorable impact of intercultural contact on the reduction of prejudice' (an observation reminiscent of Allport *et al.*'s [1954] 'contact hypothesis' – see also Chapter 2), and through effective and consistent dialogue used to connect and create community between disparate cultures. As with Hahn (2018), Remland *et al.*'s (2014) exploration of intercultural communication and peacebuilding relies heavily on theorists who inform our research (e.g. Galtung, 1970; Lederach, 2003) and whom we discuss in depth in Chapter 2. However, in our research approach, we first seek *evidence* and *application* of these theories as brought to light in the discourses of EAL tutors and Afghan English learners. We thus turn next to additional conceptualizations and practice of intercultural communication and peacebuilding so as to broaden understanding of their intersections, both in theory and in practice.

Peacebuilding and Intercultural Communication in Practice: The Example of International Educational Exchange Programs

As we expand on in Chapter 2, we use Galtung's (1975) term 'peacebuilding' in this book, although we draw from work based also on 'conflict resolution' (Boulding, 1962) and 'conflict transformation' (Lederach, 1995), the latter two terms used almost interchangeably in the field of peace and conflict studies (Botes, 2003). In broader research into peacebuilding and intercultural communication, we detect a burgeoning interest in bringing these constructs together (promising volumes forthcoming; publication dates quite recent; growing presence in the fugitive literature), but there remains a relative paucity of such research currently, with empirical studies and qualitative research almost non-existent.

As but one example of what does exist, a recent edited collection (Mathews-Aydinli, 2017) – *International Educational Exchanges and the Promotion of Peace and Intercultural Understanding* – begins to consider the possibilities that lie at the interface between peacebuilding and intercultural communication by focusing on international educational exchange programs, although only three out of the ten chapters explicitly use the word 'peace' in their titles. Mathews-Aydinli (2017) does lay the groundwork for understanding how intercultural communication and international educational exchange can be conceived of as forms of 'public diplomacy' and 'soft power,' crucial terms that help us assert that peacebuilding can happen, person to person, through intercultural communication. She starts from the supposition that if people from diverse cultural groups have opportunities to interact with one another and can, as a result, develop intercultural understanding, then conflict between these groups may well diminish. Given the great 'social potential' of conflict reduction in this way, she continues, it is not surprising that government decision makers have added international educational exchange to 'the menu of public diplomacy tools' (Mathews-Aydinli, 2017: 3). Indeed, it is in the realm of 'public diplomacy' and 'soft power' that Mathews-Aydinli (2017) situates the peacebuilding potential of international educational exchange. Whereas traditional diplomacy happens between government representatives at the state level, 'public diplomacy' comes about 'with the help of everyday people or civil society groups' (Mathews-Aydinli, 2017: 3) establishing relationships locally, far removed from military might or market forces. Still, Mathews-Aydinli (2017: 4) is cautious, warning that international educational exchange – with its seemingly laudable and beneficent goals of education at the center – may only appear independent from sponsoring governments with more implicit, 'propagandistic' intentions, which she puts into barbed terms: 'the doublespeak and secretive negotiating' of typical state-level diplomacy. Nonetheless, in her view, 'citizen diplomats' participating in international educational exchange harbor at least the potential to build relationships based on prolonged, thoughtful, two-way exchange and evolving intercultural awareness and mutual understanding. In short, despite the threat that this potential may involve witting or unwitting propagation of a particular government's ideologies, the possibilities of public diplomacy are, in Mathews-Aydinli's (2017: 4) vision, 'tremendous.'

Deardorff (2017) picks up where Mathews-Aydinli (2017) leaves off by reiterating the importance of 'mutuality' to international educational exchange. She ticks off a list of such opportunities (such as the International Baccalaureate Organization, the US Peace Corps, Chevening Scholarships, various Fulbright programs) to illustrate how 'peace and understanding [are] not just the purview of nation-states' but could be advanced by means of 'soft power' and person to person interaction (Deardorff, 2017: 12) (in our terms, 'person to person peacebuilding'). From the same edited collection, Wilson (2017: 31) rues the dearth of research into whether person to person peacebuilding such as that promoted by educational exchange actually contributes to 'world peace'; while he remains dubious about individual impacts on peacebuilding, he does admit that (1) clear communication is core to reconciling tensions; and (2) clear communication requires cultural competence in some form. In the end, Wilson places his hopes for peacebuilding in those individuals who, after and as a part of international educational exchange, become official diplomats and top-level decision makers themselves and therefore potentially able to enact positive change at the structural level.

Peacebuilding and Intercultural Communication: Theory and Empirical Research

In another study – one that leads us to our use of the term 'virtual intercultural borderlands' – Brantmeier (2007) talks about a peacebuilding enterprise related to developing a multi- and intercultural peace curriculum for a midwestern secondary school located in the US. While his research aims to compile and interpret participants' understandings of the terms 'peace' and 'non-peace,' for our work, we found most helpful his construct of 'intercultural borderlands.' Quoting Alred et al. (2003: 4), Brantmeier begins by describing 'being intercultural' in this way:

> The locus of interaction is not in the centripetal reinforcement of the identity of one group and its members by contrast with others, but rather in the centrifugal action of each which creates a new centre of interaction on the borders and frontiers which join rather than divide them. (Alred et al., 2003: 4, as cited in Brantmeier, 2007)

In other words, writes Brantmeier (2007: 133), 'it is in the shared space in-between, on the borders and frontiers, that the "intercultural" emerges,' a dynamic and mutable conception of 'intercultural being' which manifests in the liminal interstices – the transitional spaces – between disparate groups and individuals who are interacting. While our research is *not* about developing a peace curriculum necessarily (see also earlier discussion of peacebuilding and language teaching), we like – and adapt – the conceptualization of 'intercultural borderlands' Brantmeier arrives at, even more so in that the concept of 'liminal' is oft-used in scholarly discussion of digital spaces, which are the spaces where *our* research participants met and interacted (see also Firchow et al., 2017). Thus, for us, the 'virtual intercultural borderlands' becomes a descriptor for the site of the work we see happening online through videoconferencing between Afghan students and US-based tutors of English, a term we expand on in Chapter 3. Also salient from Brantmeier's work (2007: 134): he reminds us that while intercultural communication in the service of peacebuilding typically spotlights what is 'shared' between interactants, 'it does not [should not] neglect difference'. To this end he cites Bennett (1998: 96):

> Unless we can accept that other groups of people are truly different – that is, they are operating successfully according to different values and principles of reality – then we cannot exhibit the sensitivity nor accord the respect to those differences that will make intercultural communication and understanding possible.

This reminder of 'difference' carries special weight for us as we consider the discourses of participants and our search within them for discursive evidence of peacebuilding. That is, in addition to looking for evidence of peacebuilding at the personal, relational and structural levels, so too must we consider places where there is clear confrontation of difference and resistance in those voices, and the role of such difference and resistance finally in discursive constructions of peacebuilding.

Heleta and Deardorff (2017) take up the theoretical relationship between peacebuilding and intercultural competence by looking specifically at the context of higher education in conflict and post-conflict societies. Elaborating on a 2015 report by the Brookings Institute Doha, the authors describe the devastation to universities wrought by war:

> In most post-war societies, educational institutions lie in ruins once the relative peace and stability return. Universities suffer infrastructural damage, loss of academics, administrators, and students due to displacement, injury or death as well as the erosion of quality of teaching, learning, and research. (Heleta & Deardorff, 2017: 82)

What Heleta and Deardorff portray here, many of our Afghan participants have experienced first hand; it is just such conditions which drive the project we explore and the research conducted for this book. Heleta and Deardorff (2017: 83–86) assert that institutions of higher education can play a critical role in peacebuilding by intentionally promoting intercultural competencies among university students, along with tolerance, new norms of collaboration across divergent groups, critical thinking and equal opportunities. They then stress that it is at the *individual* (versus macro) level where the work of developing intercultural competence must flourish.

To this end, Heleta and Deardorff (2017) offer five suggestions for universities to ponder which are drawn from an array of intercultural competence frameworks:

(1) Move beyond individual qualities to real-world engagement and relationship-building (including in the local community).
(2) Move beyond knowledge to intentionally addressing skills and attitudes, including conflict-management skills and face negotiation skills.
(3) Move beyond seeing individuals as one identity, especially if that identity is 'enemy.'
(4) Move beyond results to process, given that peace-building in itself takes great time.
(5) Contextualise intercultural competence within the history and realities of the society. (Heleta & Deardorff, 2017: 87)

The authors go on to suggest bolstering intercultural competence as a peacebuilding approach by also promoting 'conflict competencies' – defined briefly as 'the ability to navigate through conflict' – and 'reconciliation competencies,' which they situate in the purview of peace education (Heleta & Deardorff, 2017: 87–88). They further promote the importance of intercultural and interreligious dialogue and recommend strategies for developing intercultural competence for higher education leadership in post-conflict settings.

Other empirical studies that list 'peacebuilding' and 'intercultural communication' as key words can be found in the fugitive literature – another indication, we argue, of the growing recognition of and urgency around peacebuilding and its relationship to intercultural communication. Karn (2016: 51), for instance, chronicles the design, piloting and assessment of a peacebuilding leadership curriculum implemented with American, Israeli and Palestinian adolescents: units included intercultural communication and nonviolent communication (based on Rosenberg, 2003); findings evidenced 'ways of thinking about leadership based primarily on national and religious identity.' Alias (2015: 32) explores the possibilities of re-imagining the role of youth from different religious backgrounds in post-conflict Nigeria: she describes the case of the group 'Naija Girls Unite,' members of which 'transformed from being the most invisible group in their communities to the forefront as leaders of peacebuilding.' Personal narrative is used by Robana (2005), who also interviews eight members from the Muslim and Jewish community of Djerbian in Tunisia, a community whose members have co-existed peacefully for hundreds of years. Akin to Gomes de Mato (2014), she discovers, compellingly, that storytelling and narrative are more than method: they are part of the means the community has relied on to live together in harmony.

Finally, we return to Oxford (2013, 2014; Oxford *et al.*, 2021) to examine how she conceives of 'intercultural understanding' in the context of peacebuilding and language education. First, she positions 'intercultural understanding' as one of six dimensions of peace (Oxford, 2013: 13) as well as a competency necessary for peacebuilding (Oxford, 2013: 278). From her edited 2020 collection, one chapter (Wei & Zhou, 2020: 216–236) in particular harks back to Mathews-Aydinli's (2017) examination of how international educational exchanges relate to the promotion of peace and intercultural understanding. Specifically, Wei and Zhou (2020: 217) recount the 'lived experiences and critical incidents' of international faculty and students at a US university, discussing the roles they played and can play in furthering peace between and across cultures and languages. From their analyses, Wei and Zhou (2020: 229–232) ultimately recommend: (1) like Kruger (2012), that students and faculty alike work to attain 'communicative peace'; (2) that international students recognize how intercultural communication is crucial 'to resolve conflicts related to racism, unjust treatment, prejudice, and misunderstanding'; (3) that international faculty should serve as role models of how to communicate for peace; (4) that *all* faculty should take part in professional development opportunities focused on intercultural communication for peacebuilding; and (5) that universities should develop regular, campus-wide programs which bring students and faculty – international and domestic – together for the purposes of mutual understanding, a vital component for peacebuilding at all levels (see also Deardorff, 2017; Mathews-Aydinli, 2017).

These diverse studies illuminate the peacebuilding prospects of intercultural communication in varied contexts with differing theoretical and analytical frameworks and an array of methodological approaches. In the next section, we explain the peacebuilding frameworks we use, discuss our methods and participants, and position participants' discourses as the site of person to person peacebuilding through intercultural communication in the virtual intercultural borderlands.

Frameworks for Peacebuilding

As introduced briefly at the start of this chapter, the peacebuilding frameworks we adopt for our study originate in the work of Lederach (2003) and are then adapted and extended by Broome and Collier (2012). The latter state unequivocally that research into intercultural communication 'intersects with peacebuilding in fundamental and meaningful ways,' and they enjoin scholars of intercultural communication to take on the work of developing peacebuilding theory and practice (Broome & Collier, 2012: 246). These are the calls we heed in our work: as we consider how participants' interactions in the virtual intercultural borderlands result in the unexpected affordance of peacebuilding; as we map just how that peacebuilding is discursively embedded in and intersects with intercultural communication; and as we imagine the force of these frameworks in future language teaching and intercultural communication settings.

Broome and Collier's (2012) definition of peacebuilding provides a useful complement to Lederach's (1998), as it helps us think about peacebuilding again at three distinct levels – the personal, relational and structural:

> [W]e view peace as much more than the absence of war, or what Galtung (1996) calls 'negative peace.' Instead, we believe that peace requires attention to *individuals'* orientations, *relationships* between individuals and groups, and *the role of institutions and social systems* that discourage violence, promote equity and offer mechanisms for dealing constructively with differences and disagreements. (Broome & Collier, 2012: 251, emphases added)

Notably, Broome and Collier locate the hope for such peacebuilding through intercultural communication in the projects and programs of civil society, such as we see in the tutoring project at the heart of this book, where actors become a part of 'public diplomacy' (Mathews-Aydinli, 2017) and a force shored up by – and then able to wield – 'soft power' (Deardorff, 2017).

To show how participants garner such power, Broome and Collier (2012) rely first upon Lederach's (2003: 23) propositions for conflict transformation (see Chapter 2 for in-depth discussion), which are in part founded upon this central question: 'What kind of [preferred] changes do we seek [in interactants]?' Lederach (2003) depicts possible changes and indicators of change at four levels – the personal, relational, structural and cultural – which he sums up as follows:

> The **personal** aspect of conflict refers to changes affected in and desired for the individual. This involves the full person, including the cognitive, emotional, perceptual, and spiritual dimensions. [...]
>
> The **relational** dimension represents changes in face-to-face relationships. Here we consider relational affectivity, power, and interdependence, and the expressive, communicative, and interactive aspects of conflict. [...]
>
> The **structural** dimension highlights the underlying causes of conflict and the patterns and changes it brings about in social, political, and economic structures. ... [I]t is about the ways people build and organize social, economic, political, and institutional relationships to meet basic human needs, provide access to resources, and make decisions that affect groups, communities, and whole societies. [...]
>
> The **cultural** dimension refers to changes produced by conflict in the broadest patterns of group life, including identity, and the ways that culture affects patterns of response and conflict. (Lederach, 2003: 23–25)

Lederach (2003) employs these dimensions to create a framework for analyzing, understanding and then intervening in conflict, with positive interventions intended to lead to transformations which meet desired change goals for social actors. For instance, at the personal level, we must recognize and work to curtail the toll conflict can take on us personally and strive as far as we can for holistic well-being and growth. At the relational level, we should work toward understanding one another, including each other's hopes and fears, all with the aim of recognizing and strengthening our *inter*dependence. At the structural level, we need to identify the sources of conflict, advocate for peaceful means to reduce violence, and foster the development of institutions and structures that value human rights, meet basic human needs and include all peoples in decision making. Finally, in the cultural dimension, Lederach (2003) asks us to root out and recognize sources of conflict embedded in culture, and then reinforce and invigorate cultural resources so as to reshape and constructively respond to conflict. Here we add one quick but important addendum: Lederach *et al.* (2007: 23) emphasize that cultural change is embedded in the other three dimensions and can be challenging to distinguish separately. Broome and Collier (2012), too, see culture and communication as the means of *linking* the first three dimensions and do not address culture as a separate dimension. Hence, in our work, we likewise examine participants' discourses for evidence of cultural change as embedded in the personal, relational and structural levels of peacebuilding and not as a separate level in and of itself.

While Lederach's (2003) framework originates in the discipline of peace and conflict studies, Broome and Collier (2012) seize upon and extend its possibilities for scholars of intercultural communication, showing in the process its applications to topics they see as fundamental to peacebuilding, including community engagement, intercultural dialogue and intercultural alliance building. Most germane to our research focus, Broome and Collier show how Lederach's framework brings to life intersecting peacebuilding and communicative processes which are best understood as arising through intercultural communication as it happens at Lederach's levels of peacebuilding. In their frameworks, the authors both add detail to and draw generalizations from Lederach's original peacebuilding dimensions, which they adapt as follows:

> **The personal dimension** includes the cognitive, emotional, perceptual, and spiritual aspects of individuals' orientations in conflict situations. ... The focus is on maximizing potential for individual changes in self-perceptions, narratives, and perceptions of the other, reducing enemy images while increasing open-mindedness and willingness to engage with the other through dialogue and other forms of constructive conflict transformation.
>
> **The relational dimension** includes the communicative and interactive aspects of conflict. ... The focus is on promoting patterns of communication and community engagement that contribute to conflict transformation, relationships that are equitable, inclusive, and enhance justice, and the work of intercultural alliances.
>
> **The structural dimension** includes ways in which societal discourses, organizational policies, and institutional practices create and enable differential access to resources and status, levels of individual agency and equity, levels of inclusion and decision making, and societal norms. ... The focus is on what needs to be changed in institutional policies and practices, creating the means to enable broader inclusion of diverse voices, and creating conditions and relations that contribute to social justice and peace. (Broome & Collier, 2012: 251–252, bold added)

The specific peacebuilding and communicative processes that Broome and Collier (2012) and Lederach (2003) enumerate become, then, the discursive evidence or indicators of person to person peacebuilding we sought in participants' voices across peacebuilding levels. As we discuss in the next section, by seeking out specific discursive indicators of peacebuilding as identified in these frameworks, we begin to map the discursive terrain and potential of person to person peacebuilding as it intersects with and is embedded in intercultural communication.

Table 1.1 breaks down the specific discursive indicators we identify in our peacebuilding frameworks and which we sought and listened for in participants' voices.

Table 1.1 Dimensions of peacebuilding: General overview

At the PERSONAL level of peacebuilding, positive change in the following:		At the RELATIONAL level of peacebuilding, positive change in the following:		At the STRUCTURAL level of peacebuilding, positive change in the following:	
Lederach (2003)	Broome and Collier (2012)	Lederach (2003)	Broome and Collier (2012)	Lederach (2003)	Broome and Collier (2012)
Cognition	Self-Perception	Perceptions of, Desires for, Goals for, & Structures of Relationships	Perceptions of Hierarchies & Status Positioning of Group Members	Understanding the Causes of Conflict	Recognizing how Societal Discourses, Organizational Policies, and Institutional Practices Create and Enable Differential Access to Resources and Status, Levels of Individual Agency & Equity, & Societal Norms
Emotion	Perceptions of the Other (Reducing Enemy Images)	Desires for Closeness or Distance	Willingness to Work for Relationships that are Equitable, Inclusive, & Social-Justice Oriented	Work to Minimize & Eliminate Violence	
Spirituality		How We Use, Build, & Share Power			
Perception	Increased Open-Mindedness	Sharing Our Hopes & Fears for Relationships	Work for Intercultural Alliances	Work to Foster Social, Economic, & Institutional Relationships to Meet Basic Human Needs & Provide Access to Resources and Decision-Making	Work for Broader Inclusion of Diverse Voices
Physical well-being		Minimizing Poorly Functioning Communication			
Emotional stability	Increased Willingness to Engage in Dialogue				Create Conditions & Relations that Contribute to Social Justice and Peace
Self-esteem		Maximizing Mutual Understanding			

In Chapters 4, 5 and 6, we elaborate on and share evidence of discursive indicators for each level of peacebuilding from participants' voices – the personal, the relational and the structural. In Chapter 7 we share how what we have learned from participants' voices can help us, as language teachers and teacher educators, more deliberately foster person to person peacebuilding in classrooms and in the virtual intercultural borderlands.

Methods, Projects, Participants

As we have seen above, the peacebuilding frameworks we use in this book provide us with discursive indicators of peacebuilding organized around three levels: the personal, the relational and the structural. We came to these frameworks after encountering consistent and numerous references to the emergent themes of peace and conflict in our analysis of the reflective journals of EAL tutors working with Afghan learners of English. Intrigued by the richness of these data, we also recognized a void that needed to be filled; if we were to begin to understand the transformation(s) participants underwent in the virtual intercultural borderlands, we needed Afghan voices too. As a result, we decided to expand our data through interviews with both Afghan students and US-based tutors to hear their perspectives on the tutoring project and its peacebuilding possibilities. We also dove more deeply into the literature of intercultural communication and peacebuilding, only to discover: (1) how limited that research is in relation to projects such as ours; and (2) Broome and Collier's (2012) call for intercultural communication scholars to take up work in the research and practice of peacebuilding.

Deductive Content and Critical Discourse Analysis

Again, in this book, we follow that call, drawing on theoretical peacebuilding frameworks (Broome & Collier, 2012; Lederach, 2003) to analyze participants' discourses as captured in their reflective writing and interview transcripts. By using these a priori frameworks, we engaged in deductive content analysis, an approach particularly conducive to researchers seeking to substantiate theory/ies and/or to apply them to completely new contexts (Elo & Kyngäs, 2008; Kibiswa, 2019): in our case, applying peacebuilding frameworks to the discourses of intercultural interactants, at least half of whom live in a conflict state. To reiterate: deductive content analysis begins with pre-existing theory and categories (Kyngäs & Kaakinen, 2020) or a 'coding agenda' (Mayring, 2000). Hence, in our analysis, we organized our findings according to categories derived from the three-level peacebuilding frameworks of Lederach (2003) and Broome and Collier (2012), such as identifying discursive evidence of cognitive change (personal level), discursive evidence of a willingness to maximize mutual understanding (relational level), and discursive evidence of work to meet basic human needs (structural level).

In addition to using deductive content analysis, we further conducted critical discourse analysis (CDA) of identified discursive indicators of peacebuilding, in order to determine how our interpretations of findings held up when considered from another perspective, and to understand in more detail just how participants' discourses were linguistically instantiating person to person peacebuilding between interactants (Wodak, 2004: 104). Of the many approaches to discourse analysis, we felt that CDA would be most illuminating, which we explain with the help of Fairclough (2013). He defines the purpose of CDA as follows:

> To systematically explore often opaque relationships of causality and determination between (a) discursive practices, events and texts, and (b) wider social and cultural structures, relations and processes; to investigate how such practices, events and texts arise out of and are ideologically shaped by relations of power and struggles over power. (Fairclough, 2013: 93)

Plainly, the relationships between English language tutoring, intercultural communication and person to person peacebuilding may initially seem 'opaque' and, plainly, we are arguing for an outcome (the unexpected affordance of peacebuilding) which is contingent upon 'relationships of causality and determination': that peacebuilding can emerge through sustained intercultural communication between interactants; and that peacebuilding person to person through intercultural communication profoundly impacts 'wider social and cultural structures, relations and processes' (Fairclough, 2013: 93). By the same token, by investigating relations of power and the ideologies which shape – and are shaped by – relations of power, particularly within educational contexts, we can better understand how our participants perceived the constraints of structural forces (e.g. conflict, education, economics, language) on their actions and interactions and the ways in which they exerted their individual agency in response to such constraints (see, for example, Giddens, 1984). In other words, participants' talk (interview transcripts) and their written texts (reflective journals) are forms of social practice which – through the accumulation and constellation of specific discursive indicators within that talk and text – lead to the affordance of person to person peacebuilding through online intercultural communication. Our argument here bolsters a central claim of Fairclough's (1989, 1992, 2013): that discourse not only reproduces, but also transforms, societies.

In our use of CDA, we followed the suggestions of Rogers *et al.* (2005: 365), namely, that CDA 'studies should pull from a hybrid set of approaches that can help to bring fresh insights to educational questions' (see also van Dijk, 2000). Our use of CDA thus embraces, quite intentionally, Weiss and Wodak's (2003) view of methodological eclecticism in CDA as a positive force. It brings diverse theories and disciplinary perspectives into dialogue with one another and with a shared goal: to theorize the mediation between the social and linguistic, between texts and institutions and between discourse and society. From Fairclough's (1989, 1992, 2013) methods of text analysis, informed both by systemic functional linguistics (SFL) and theories of semiotics, we attended to micro-linguistic features of grammar and vocabulary (e.g. nominalization, overwording): at the text dimension, which helped us also understand the discourse practice dimension (analysis of text production and interpretation), for instance, US-based tutors' discursive constructions of media representations of Afghanistan; and at the social practice dimension (explanation of how participants' discourses constitute, reproduce, challenge and/or restructure knowledge and beliefs), for instance, how Afghan participants discursively construct the need for English in order for Afghanistan to become a 'developed' country. From Wodak et al. (2009), we were guided to identify and analyze specific contents or themes (for instance, discursive constructions of gender and its relation to power), linguistic strategies (constructions of identities, in-groups and out-groups), and means of realization (such as uses of metonymy and synecdoche to personify 'Afghanistan,' instead of individuating reference to specific Afghans). Our analysis further benefits from van Leeuwen's (2008) framework of discourse as the recontextualization of social practice, which he illustrates through linguistic analysis of social actors, action, time, space and purpose. We show, for instance, how human agency can be realized through possessive pronouns or diminished through objectivation, and how discursively the instrumentalization of English comes to stand in for the human speaker thereof, in the process creating asymmetries of power. Finally, Blackledge (2005), inspired by Bakhtin (1984), helped us recognize the perpetuation of or breaks in participants' discourse chains, such as how they discursively constructed – and repeated, or adapted, or transformed – their views on building peace.

From each and all of these approaches to CDA, it should be evident how our decision to use CDA to analyze participants' discourses is founded upon post-structuralist assumptions which conceptualize discourse as a third terrain located between 'reality' and the 'imaginary,' a terrain both impelled by and brought into existence because of language. In this way, language becomes the vehicle for the social construction of reality (Berger & Luckmann, 1966; Cruikshank, 2012; Fairclough, 1989, 2001; Foucault, 1984; Gee, 2004; Laclau & Mouffe, 1985; van Dijk, 2000; Wodak, 2004). We do not mean to say here that 'reality' does not exist in the form of rock, tree, love, hate, war, peace. Rather, we are left with understandings and experience of these and all terms as always mediated through the language we use to 'construct' their (and our) mental representations, a symbolic undertaking we undergo daily in order to ascribe meaning to – and hence make – society (Cruikshank, 2012).

So, too, are 'peacebuilding' and 'conflict' constructed and mediated by language, and so too can critical discourse analysis of their uses elucidate 'the *role* discourses *play* or are *made to play*' by those who interpret them (Mitra, 2015: 4, italics in original). Chiluwa (2019), investigating the discourses of Boko Haram in Nigeria, for instance, shows in depth the role discourse is 'made to play' in the formation, negotiation and maintenance of identities and relationships as Boko Haram endeavored through Twitter to advertise its ideology and mobilize followers. The work of Karlberg (2005: 1) explores the power behind *alternative* discourses which can help us rethink constructs such as power. He points out, for example, how scholars in the West typically construct power as 'conflictual or adversarial,' and then cites, as contrast, Giddens' (1984: 15 – notably, also a Western scholar) alternative construct of 'power' as 'transformative capacity': in other words, 'power *to*' versus 'power *over*' or 'power *of*' (and which we see allied closely with K. Boulding's [1990] 'integrative power,' discussed in Chapter 2). More generally, Suurmond (2005) relates how the field of conflict studies has come to embrace discourse analysis for its manifold dividends: as a means to shed light on issues of identity and social relations; as a means to explore how power is shared (or not) and legitimized (or not) through language; and as a means to uncover how the force of discourse both constrains and enables the possibilities of its users.

We join these conversations around discourse and conflict as we show in this book how peacebuilding discursively intersects with and is embedded in intercultural communication between our participants, and how peacebuilding emerges as an unexpected communicative affordance of intercultural interaction in the virtual intercultural borderlands of online exchange. The force of discourse to constrain and enable all possibilities, including possibilities for peacebuilding – personally, relationally, structurally – is echoed within Broome and Collier's (2012) definition of intercultural communication:

> [T]he set of processes through which cultural systems emerge and are contested, reinforced and modified, as well as the processes through which personal views, group identifications, inter-group relationships, group representations, relationships within and across groups, institutional policies, public and organizational discourses, social practices and norms are formed. (Broome & Collier, 2012: 253)

The processes Broome and Collier describe are *discursive* processes: they come into existence through language, the mediating force that allows interlocutors to represent, for instance, individuals or groups of others through words. In order to understand and illuminate these processes – with our particular focus on participants' intercultural discourses as the site where peacebuilding happens – we thus analyzed participants' discourses for instances of change, resistance or stasis as they talked (or wrote) about perceptions and prejudices within themselves, their evolving relationships with their intercultural counterparts, and how their sense of their worlds and societies changed (or stayed the same, or struggled between change or stasis).

An Online Project with Afghan English Learners: Participants

In this last section, we turn from the concepts and theory that inform our work to the collaboration that inspired it. Here we provide background to (1) the community partner who helped launch the tutoring initiative, (2) project participants and (3) and the data we collected. We conclude the chapter with an overview of the book's structure and the central focus of each chapter.

The tutoring project that made this book possible was an initiative of a US-based 'people-to-people peacebuilding' program, a 501(c)(3) non-profit organization. The organization describes itself as made up of a network of global volunteers with the mission of contributing to a more peaceful world. It was founded in October 2007; in 2009, the organization began peacebuilding through education, starting with the English language tutoring program, an initiative founded upon the belief that in the processes of teaching and learning English, tutors and their Afghan counterparts can participate in mutually enriching international exchange through friendly engagement. Since then, as its primary means to achieve the organization's goal of building peace through education, the community partner has provided one-on-one online English language tutoring for more than 500 students in Afghanistan. Tutors from around the world – although mostly from various universities in the US – meet their students in Afghanistan via videoconferencing to tutor English, work which, following the views of Mathews-Aydinli (2017) and Deardorff (2017), can be framed as mutually transformative 'public diplomacy' and 'soft power.'

The collaboration we explore in this book drew upon the existing tutoring initiative, described above, to create opportunities for future EAL teachers, graduate students in a TESOL course, to gain practical experience as part of their coursework. The TESOL course instructor, the US-based director of coordination for the tutoring program and local volunteers based in Afghanistan worked together to pair graduate student tutors with adult Afghan learners of English. The pairs then met synchronously over the course of a semester for weekly 90-minute tutoring sessions through videoconferencing. As part of their coursework, the graduate students submitted six written journal entries in which they reflected on their tutoring experiences.

It was from this project that we gathered data for our study. The 72 tutors whose experiences we share ranged in age from 22 to 58 years and had varying levels of teaching experience. Approximately two-thirds of the tutors were born in the US, spoke English at home, and planned to teach in elementary schools, high schools and/or universities in the US. The remaining third of the participants included tutors who described themselves as 'native speakers' of Arabic, Mandarin Chinese, Korean, Mongolian, Tibetan and Ukrainian. Some had lived or were living outside of what they considered to be their home countries, and many planned to return to their countries of origin from the US when they completed their degrees. None of the tutors had lived in or traveled to Afghanistan.

The Afghan participants ranged in age from 18 to 40 years. Their reasons for participating in the tutoring project varied, as did their long-term goals. Some hoped to continue their education outside Afghanistan and saw English as a means not only to gain admittance to a university but also possibly to qualify for a scholarship which would help defray the cost of their studies. Others were English teachers or employees of various NGOs and humanitarian aid organizations who sought to strengthen their linguistic proficiency to better serve their students or organizations and/or qualify for promotions. Still others were university students eager to supplement their classroom study of English. In communications with their tutors, Afghan students used a number of terms to describe their 'first' or 'mother' language: some said they spoke Dari, others Farsi; some said they spoke Persian, and others, Dari Farsi.

The data for our study come from two sources. Critical, structured reflection was a key element of the project. As a result, part of our data consists of journal entries tutors composed over the course of a semester as they shared what they were experiencing in their weekly tutoring sessions and, for the final journal, as they reflected on if or how their understandings and perceptions of themselves, their tutoring partners and/or their worlds had changed. We collected tutors' reflective journals over two years and six iterations of the course and tutoring project; as each tutor completed six reflections, we gathered 300 entries in all.

We wanted to learn more about how participants perceived the intercultural communication and peacebuilding prospects of the project, so in 2018 we began to recruit participants to interview, both US-based tutors who were pre-service teachers of EAL and adult Afghan students of English. Our data thus also include transcripts of interviews with nine Afghan project participants and 15 tutors. All participants chose or were assigned pseudonyms, and we have made every effort to eliminate identifying references to the community partner and specific sites in Afghanistan so as to protect our Afghan participants. All participants were contacted, recruited and interviewed after the course was over and after participant tutors had been graded. Interviews with tutors were held through Skype and Zoom. For interviews in Afghanistan especially, as one means to better ensure participant safety and confidentiality, we asked participants to download the free Tor browser to use for all of our communications, which we also used. Macrina (2015) articulates reasons not only to use, but also to champion, Tor:

> The Tor Browser was built from an 'onion routing' project of the U.S. Navy, which was designed to protect military communications, and was turned into an independent (non-military) project by developers Roger Dingledine and Nick Mathewson in 2002. Onion routing bounces traffic from the original user across a network of three relays, providing three layers of encryption (like the layers of an onion, hence 'onion routing,' and the Tor onion logo) and masking the original IP address from the user's computer. Today, it's used by about four million people worldwide to evade censorship and surveillance, allowing users to access blocked websites in Internet-restrictive countries like Iran and China (because typically websites rely on IP location information to restrict access), keeping journalistic sources safe, and masking the identity of whistleblowers. Reporters Without Borders recommends that journalists reporting from dangerous places use Tor to protect themselves. (Macrina, 2015)

Many of the Afghan participants we contacted already used the Tor browser and were familiar with the protections it provides, so downloading and using this additional browser proved to be no barrier to the research.

Participants' reflective journals and interview transcripts from Afghans and tutors alike were then analyzed in two ways: first, using deductive content analysis according to the peacebuilding frameworks proposed by Lederach (2003) and Broome and Collier (2012) (see Table 1.1), which provide us with discursive indicators of peacebuilding at the personal, relational and structural levels of peacebuilding (e.g. discursive evidence of cognitive change, alliance-building between tutor and student, or work to minimize violence and conflict structurally); second, using CDA (Blackledge, 2005; Cruikshank, 2012; Fairclough, 1989, 2013; van Leeuwen, 2008; Wodak et al., 2009). Employing these frameworks, we examined participants' perceptions of their intercultural communications for discursive evidence of peacebuilding at the personal, relational and structural levels. As we coded the data, we also paid attention to other 'emergent' instances not covered in either framework and which we believe evidenced peacebuilding; we further paid heed to instances that suggested resistance to peacebuilding: that is, moments where participants discursively resisted opportunities for change or demonstrated no change at all, at any dimension. We present our analyses of data in Chapters 4, 5 and 6 of this book, with each chapter corresponding to one of the three peacebuilding levels from our frameworks: personal, relational, structural. In Chapter 7, we return to some of the most salient lessons we learned from participants, as we share suggestions for more deliberately leveraging the affordance of peacebuilding when teaching language and intercultural communication, in person and online.

Overview of Chapters

Our book is divided into seven chapters. This first chapter serves as an introduction to the project and participants that inspired this book along with our central purpose and aims: to show how person to person peacebuilding intersects with and is embedded in intercultural communication; and to show how person to person peacebuilding emerged as an unexpected affordance of the virtual intercultural borderlands of online exchange. The next chapter further defines peacebuilding as we use it in this book and the theoretical frameworks for peacebuilding that guide our overall analysis. It overviews existing literature that operationalizes peacebuilding, intercultural communication and language teaching in various combinations so as to highlight how our study is both informed by – and can richly complement – work that has come before; it also explains the data collection and methods of analysis, including how we worked to ensure participant confidentiality and how we analyzed participants' discourses in two ways: through deductive content and critical discourse analysis.

As this book is intended for educators – including teachers and teacher educators of language and intercultural communication – who are interested in creating intercultural communication and peacebuilding partnerships between interactants from different countries, particularly conflict countries, in Chapter 2 we take the time to explore the pivotal constructs of peacebuilding and intercultural communication in greater depth. This chapter examines Galtung's (1964) foundational work on positive peace, Boulding's (1957, 1977, 1990) work on conflict resolution, and Lederach's (2003, 2006) framing of conflict transformation. We look at how peacebuilding has been operationalized by the UN and how Lederach (2003) creates space for peacebuilding before, during and after conflict, and at three specific dimensions: the personal, relational and structural. We emphasize, too, how Lederach's vision of peacebuilding invites ordinary citizens as well as state-level diplomats into the processes that comprise peacebuilding. We further examine models of intercultural communication competence (Byram, 1997; Deardorff, 2004, 2006a, 2006b; Goodman, 2013; Gudykunst & Kim, 1984) in order to identify convergences between indicators of intercultural competence and discursive indicators of peacebuilding at the personal, relational and structural levels (Broome & Collier, 2012; Lederach, 2003).

In Chapter 3, we examine the contexts of our study, first by complicating and expanding the construct of 'context.' We bring together understandings of context(s): as spatial sites (Afghanistan, US-based graduate TESOL programs, tutors' home countries); as points of convergence between disparate actors and interests (Gould, 2008); as cultural spaces free from conventional associations with geography or ethnicity (Johnson & Callahan, 2013); and also as the diverse conditions that shape and are shaped by peacebuilding, including histories, memories, environment, climate, organizations, institutions – indeed, context as 'a constitutive force' in and of itself, 'both temporal and spatial, incorporating past, present and future' (Broome & Collier, 2012: 253). In addition, we consider in some detail theories that illuminate the possibilities of what we call the virtual intercultural borderlands of online exchange, a term adapted from Brantmeier (2007) and then enriched by Anzaldúa's (1987) 'borderlands,' Pratt's (1991) 'contact zones,' Lo Bianco *et al.*'s (1999) conception of a 'Third Place,' and Bhabha's (2006) theorization of a 'Third Space' and the liminality thereof.

In Chapters 4, 5 and 6, we turn to the voices of the pre-service EAL teachers and the adult Afghan learners of English who inspired this book. Chapter 4 offers an analysis of how tutors and students talk about and discursively construct indicators of peacebuilding (Broome & Collier, 2012; Lederach, 2003) which contribute to the personal dimension of peacebuilding. We focus first on changes in participants' beliefs about themselves: initial fears, evidence of increasing self-confidence and an example of resistance to change. Next, we share examples of changes in beliefs and attitudes about others, exploring how participants' reconfigurations of perceptions lead to the creation of new in-groups and out-groups. Finally, we trace shifts in participants' discursive constructions of Afghanistan and of their own places in the world.

Chapter 5 examines discursive indicators of peacebuilding associated with the relational dimension of peacebuilding as they intersect with and are embedded in participants' intercultural communications. We analyze how participants talk about shared social relationships and identities, including those of tutor, teacher and learner, as users of technology and speakers of English, and as family members and national citizens. We examine how they talk about structuring their relationships with each other, including similarities and differences as the catalysts of their relationships, feeling empathy toward the other, and increased awareness of social hierarchies and status within and among groups to which participants belong. In this chapter, too, we examine participants' discursive constructions of community engagement and their visions for the intercultural alliances they are building (and are hoping to build) with their tutoring counterparts.

Chapter 6 focuses on the structural level of peacebuilding as it intersects with and is embedded in intercultural communication. In this chapter, we analyze participants' discourses related to the causes and effects of conflict, including the ways in which society, organizations and institutions constrain and/or enable access to resources, status and decision making. We further consider how participants talk about individual agency and equity, levels of inclusion, the constraints of societal 'norms,' and their understandings of the structural forces of laws, policies and media discourses. Finally, we share participants' constructions of large-scale changes needed for greater social inclusivity, peace and social justice, including ways in which participants rescript and reimagine their worlds.

We conclude with Chapter 7, in which we return to some of the most compelling lessons from participants' voices. In this chapter, we share insights from and potential applications of our work, focusing on ways in which teachers and teacher educators might more deliberately leverage the affordances of peacebuilding present in the virtual intercultural borderlands of online exchange.

Notes

(1) We use the term 'English as an additional language' (EAL) in our work, which is comparable to English as a second language (ESL) or English for speakers of other languages (ESOL), terms more frequently heard in the US. Some pre-service teachers in this study plan to teach English as a foreign language (EFL), English as an international language (EIL) and/or English for academic purposes (EAP). We use EAL as it seems to account for most contexts. For an overview of terms, see 'Common Acronyms in the TESOL Profession' (2018) from the TESOL International Association, http://www.tesol.org/enhance-your-career/career-development/beginning-your-career/a-guide-to-common-acronyms-in-the-tesol-profession.

(2) As Lederach *et al.* (2007) observe, 'Culture is embedded in all three of the other dimensions, and may be more difficult to isolate for evaluation purposes.' We therefore focus on Lederach's personal, relational and structural levels of peacebuilding, noting evidence of 'deeper, and often less conscious, patterns related to conflict and peace' – or the cultural dimension of peacebuilding – only as it emerges from analysis.

2 Understandings of Peacebuilding and Intercultural Communication

Introduction

Throughout this book, we explore how intercultural interactants work as peacebuilders. More specifically, we listen to and analyze the voices of pre-service teachers of English as an additional language based in the US and tutoring online through videoconferencing, and their adult Afghan counterparts who are learning English. Ultimately, we argue that the peacebuilding discussed in this book both intersects with and is embedded in intercultural communication, and that it emerges as an unexpected communicative affordance from the virtual intercultural borderlands of online exchange, an affordance comprised of the accumulation and constellation of discursive indicators of peacebuilding which we find in and gather from the voices of tutoring project participants.

As we write this book primarily for educators interested in working at the intersections of peacebuilding and intercultural communication, in this chapter we examine in depth these two constructs and processes so central to our work. First, we trace the modern and recent history of peacebuilding as articulated in the literature of peace and conflict studies and as described by the United Nations (UN), an organization which originated from the ruins of World War II and whose first purpose as stated in its charter was and is to maintain international peace and security (UN, 1945). From this history emerge understandings of peacebuilding which inform our analysis of participants' discourses at and across three peacebuilding levels: the personal, relational and structural. Second, we investigate understandings of intercultural communication by drawing from specific frameworks of intercultural communication competence, paying particular attention to how individual elements in frameworks (e.g. the ability to relativize self and value others, skills of interpreting and relating, developing 'critical language awareness'; Byram, 1997) intersect with the three dimensions of peacebuilding we discuss. This overview and investigation lay the groundwork for our subsequent chapters in which we analyze participants' voices.

We begin with understandings of peacebuilding as articulated by scholars and practitioners and as operationalized in the language and practices of the UN.

Understandings of Peacebuilding

Research perspectives

Oft cited as the founder and father of peace studies, Johan Galtung provides essential concepts for understanding peace and peacebuilding in the very first issue of the *Journal of Peace Research*, published in 1964. In that editorial, Galtung makes an important distinction between 'negative peace' – what exists when there is no *direct* violence or war between or within states (as in a ceasefire or armistice) – and 'positive peace,' most broadly defined as 'the integration of human society' through the discernable presence of collaboration, unity, empathy, and a systemic approach to meeting conflict and change without violence (Galtung, 1964: 2). To attain positive peace, Galtung articulates conditions whereby actors seek a lasting end to both direct violence (killing, war, genocide) and structural violence: poverty, racism, conditions he describes as the 'slow, massive suffering caused by economic and political structures of exploitation and repression' (Galtung, 2010). To this framework Galtung eventually adds the need to end 'cultural violence,' that is to say, any aspect of a culture which sanctions direct and/or structural violence, including religion, ideology, art, language, even science, and the symbols thereof (Galtung, 2011).

These constructs – positive and negative peace, cultural and structural violence – are now considered cornerstones of peace research (Johansen & Jones, 2010). Galtung contributes further to the thinking and lexicon related to peace research with his differentiation between 'peacekeeping,' 'peacemaking' and 'peacebuilding' (Galtung, 1969), terms arising in response to violent conflicts from World War II onward and now commonplace in discussions of conflict, global and local. The actions of peacekeeping – typically initiated by third parties such as the UN – strive to scale down direct violence between actors through military intervention and troop presence, if possible restoring order, while the next step of peacemaking works to establish mutually acceptable agreements between warring parties.[1] Peacebuilding, Galtung's (1969) word, involves actions intended to cut off the root causes of conflict and violence, structural and cultural: from efforts to end racism and nationalism to rehabilitating and educating child soldiers. Cutting off such causes is not the end game, however: Galtung (1975) further envisions positive peace as the presence of far-reaching change and change activities within and throughout existing social structures, from the free flow of information to developing good relationships with neighbors.

Just a few steps ahead of Galtung – and then alongside – were wife and husband team Elise and Kenneth Boulding, who both critique and complement Galtung's works and enrich our own understandings of peacebuilding. Kenneth Boulding was part of the early movement of conflict resolution research in the US in the 1950s, a movement inspired first by work from the 1920s conducted by British mathematician and physicist Lewis Richardson. Among other achievements, Richardson sought to quantify historical data on war and the race to build weaponry, an approach that energized K. Boulding and other scholars to explore conflict resolution from a multitude of interdisciplinary perspectives. In 1957, at a time when the Cold War was growing colder and US school children practiced duck and cover drills in the event of nuclear attack, K. Boulding and other pacifist scholars founded the *Journal of Conflict Resolution*. In his editorial in the first issue, K. Boulding stated the journal's goal: to 'devise an intellectual engine of sufficient power to move the greatest problem of our time – the prevention of war' (K. Boulding, 1957: 2). With this mission, we see the first important contrast between K. Boulding and Galtung, as K. Boulding focuses on the prevention of war, Galtung on creating conditions for the presence of positive peace. We also see the beginnings of global conversations around peacebuilding and conflict resolution, with K. Boulding in the US and Galtung in Norway.

Later in these conversations, in what he described as 'friendly quarrels,' K. Boulding (1977: 83–84) takes to task Galtung's understandings of peace as 'static' and structuralist; instead, K. Boulding disentangles poverty from violence, acknowledging only remote (and not equal) relationships between structural oppression and literal, physical violence. K. Boulding (1977) further challenges Galtung's conceptualization of positive peace as essentially meaningless, dependent upon one man's (Galtung's) interpretation of peace work and whether or not that work achieved 'high marks on his scale of goodness' (K. Boulding, 1977: 78). In lieu of this structuralist view, K. Boulding advances a picture of peace which is relational and evolutionary, in which 'the dominant mode of relationship is *interaction* not "struggle"' (K. Boulding, 1977: 76, emphasis added). The implication of interaction to peace research grows clearer in K. Boulding's *Three Faces of Power* (1990), in which he defines power as the potential for change, and in which he demarcates personal power into three types: as destructive, economic or integrative. A testament to his Quaker roots, K. Boulding's 'integrative' power is proffered as most productive and salient, the highest form of power, encompassing community, identity, relationships and, in its most basic form, love, with '[t]he capacity to build organizations, [...] to inspire loyalty, to bind people together, to develop legitimacy' (K. Boulding, 1990: 25).

K. Boulding's (1990) vision of relational interaction and integrative power aligns forcefully with the paradigms of intercultural competence we deploy in our research in order to explore how Afghan learners of English and their tutors in the US build peace, person to person – and in order to explore the potential integrative power of future projects. While we address these paradigms in detail in the next section, a closer look at K. Boulding's (1990) integrative power is in order here. First, it depends on trust between actors, which can only be created through interaction and exchange (K. Boulding, 1990: 27) and which, in varying forms, is posited as crucial to many forms of successful intercultural interaction (Chua *et al.*, 2012; Hofstede, 2009; Vulpe *et al.*, 2001). With integrative power, moreover, we begin to see K. Boulding and Galtung come together, as we recall Galtung's definition of positive peace: 'the integration of human society' through the discernable presence of collaboration, unity, empathy, and a systemic approach to meeting conflict and change without violence (Galtung, 1964: 2). We can also see how K. Boulding's vision of integrative power informs our study of the peacebuilders in this book, tutors and their tutoring counterparts, whose collaborations develop and depend on regular interaction and mutual trust.

Perspectives from practice

Kenneth Boulding's contributions to conflict resolution are accompanied by those of scholar and activist Elise Boulding, his wife and Nobel Peace Prize nominee. Among her accomplishments, E. Boulding ran for Congress as the Peace Party candidate during the Vietnam War and served as Chair of the Women's International League for Peace and Freedom. Her writings and practice are frequently cited as part of the feminist critique of Galtung's theories on violence, which pushes for the inclusion of gender as a social construct that embodies power relations, that posits binary categories as gendered and central in engendering violence at all levels, that asserts that language creates both violence and peace, and that argues that violence creates and defines gender identities, just as gender identities create and define violence (Confortini, 2006: 333; 2012). Through scholarship and practice, E. Boulding in her own right took on issues related to gender and peace in concert with her husband's work and beyond, decrying the absence of women at decision-making tables at the highest levels along with their general invisibility throughout history. She writes of links between patriarchy and militarism (E. Boulding, 1990: 46); and she endeavors to make visible women's peace work, 'as guerillas, freedom fighters and revolutionaries' as well as 'scientists, artists and philosophers' (E. Boulding, 1990: 63).

Throughout her work and service, moreover, E. Boulding underscores the indispensable role of the education sector in peace work, which she chronicles in her 1990 treatise, *Building a Global Civic Culture*. In that book, in addition to a fiercely negative assessment of Western education practice, E. Boulding explores and celebrates peace work undertaken by civil society such as that discussed in the introduction to this chapter: international and national non-governmental organizations, religious societies, people's associations and community groups – peacebuilding, that is, undertaken *at all levels*, a decision well in keeping with her lifelong efforts to make the invisible visible and to provide the voiceless a voice (Brock-Utne, 2012). E. Boulding's focus on the multidimensional components of peacebuilding – along with the importance she places on bringing in the voices of the voiceless – underscores our own aims in this book: to learn from our participants – both Afghan learners of English and pre-service teachers – as they describe how, through intercultural interaction, they availed themselves of the unexpected affordance of peacebuilding.

In a 1990 interview, Elise Boulding stated: 'My goal has been to initiate a dialogue between the action and research perspectives .... [M]y mediation role has been between researchers and activists, each of whom thinks the other is failing to address the real needs of our time' (cited in Adams, 1991: 1). The weight E. Boulding places here on the dialogue between research and action emphatically affirms the central purpose of this book, which locates person to person peacebuilding in the voices and discourses of participants in an English language tutoring project. It further leads us to another pioneer of peace research and practice whose work, as we explain in Chapter 1, provides the theoretical underpinnings of this book: John Paul Lederach.

Lederach (1998) elaborates extensively on the work of Galtung and, in so doing, provides a definition of peacebuilding widely embraced by scholars and practitioners (Paffenholz, 2014) and which we embrace as well. We cited this definition in Chapter 1, and we repeat it here:

> [Peacebuilding is] a comprehensive concept that encompasses, generates, and sustains the full array of processes, approaches, and stages needed to transform conflict toward more sustainable, peaceful relationships. The term thus involves a wide range of activities that both precede and follow formal peace accords. Metaphorically, peace is seen not merely as a stage in time or a condition. It is a dynamic social construct. (Lederach, 1998: 20)

Lederach's (1998) vision aligns with Galtung's (1964, 1969, 1975, 1990, 2011) and K. Boulding's (1990) in his argument that peacebuilding mechanisms and their subsequent activities be integrated into social structure and infrastructure. As a practitioner, though, Lederach goes further, encouraging peacebuilders to look beyond top-down traditional diplomacy, which is too often reactive rather than proactive, with short-term outcomes addressing the crisis moment.[2] In contrast, Lederach's long-term, holistic view of the peacebuilding process encompasses people and activities at all levels, from grassroots to grasstops, with particular emphasis on working with mid-level actors and groups inside conflict zones who can in turn mobilize local peacebuilding initiatives at macro and micro levels. Ultimately, for Lederach, peacebuilding takes place through multiple paths and over time: it is transformative, instantiating social change; it welcomes a multiplicity of peacebuilders with a multiplicity of creative approaches to peacebuilding; and its aim, always, is to create the conditions for just and sustainable peace (Lederach, 1998; Lederach & Appleby, 2010).

Lederach has worked on peace and conciliation projects in over 25 countries across the globe. What is perhaps most germane from his work – at least given *our* purposes in this book – are the clear dimensions he delineates at which conflict transformation practitioners[3] might work to build peace. As discussed in Chapter 1, Lederach (2003) relates the potential for peace work with how the force of conflict exerts change – including positive, preferred change – at four dimensions: the personal, relational, structural and cultural. Changes at the personal dimension, Lederach writes, are comprised of shifts in 'the cognitive, emotional, perceptual, and spiritual aspects' of a person experiencing conflict and striving for peace: we thus (all) need to attend to the ways in which conflict is destructive within us and work to maximize positive and desired change (growth) resulting from that conflict. At the relational dimension, Lederach avers, we need to seek changes in our ongoing interactions[4] with others in order to amplify potential for mutual understanding based on the distance (or lack thereof) between us, our willingness to share power, and our acknowledgment of our interdependence. At the structural dimension, writes Lederach, we must attend to 'the ways people build and organize social, economic, and institutional relationships to meet basic human needs and provide access to resources and decision-making' (Lederach, 2003: 24–25). Unmet human needs, unequal access to resources and top-down decision making often lie at the root of conflict: as peacebuilders we must therefore work to revamp institutions and systems through non-violent means, in the process ensuring that institutions and systems serve all more equally and justly. Lastly, Lederach addresses the cultural dimension of peacebuilding, asking us to uncover and transform cultural patterns that contribute to violence, while simultaneously augmenting cultural resources that support peaceful means for confronting conflict.[5]

In our research, we draw from these understandings of peacebuilding as put forward: in the work of Galtung (1964, 1969, 1975, 1985, 2011) – particularly his emphasis on positive peace; in Kenneth Boulding's (1990) construct of integrative power as harboring the potential for the most positive of changes within interactants; in Elise Boulding's feminist vision of peace education at all levels and in profuse forms (1990); and primarily from Lederach's (1998, 2003; Lederach & Appleby, 2010; Lederach *et al.*, 2007) multidimensional framework for peacebuilding. The visions and constructs of these preeminent researchers and practitioners have likewise shaped the vision and agenda of international peacebuilding agencies, including the UN, an agency born from the atrocities of World War II.

Peacebuilding in Practice: The UN Example

As we turn next to discuss understandings of peacebuilding as codified in the language of the UN, we start with a caveat. The world's most recognized peace, security and human rights organization, with 193 member states, the UN has taken substantial fire itself throughout its history: for prioritizing the national interests of its permanent members – the Russian Federation, China, Britain, the US and France – over actual *people*; for its disinclination to expand permanent membership to include Germany, Japan or India, despite the 75+ years since the end of World War II; and for the limits of its powers despite its global platform, most visible perhaps in its failures to keep peace or save more lives in Rwanda, Bosnia, the Congo, Sudan or Yemen (Sengupta, 2018). At the same time, a quote by the former Executive Director of Amnesty International, Margaret Huang, may sum up its symbolic power: 'The UN is like your conscience. It can't make you do the right thing, but it can help you make the right decision' (Huang, as cited in Sengupta, 2018). We hence turn next to the language of the UN to understand how peacebuilding is codified within it – to understand, that is, how peacebuilding is constructed by the foremost global peace and security organization which, at the very least, may serve as a global 'conscience.'

'Peacebuilding' as a term first appears in the UN lexicon with former UN Secretary-General Boutros Boutros-Ghali's (1992) *An Agenda for Peace* (Reychler, 2010, 2017). In that report, peacebuilding is posited as actions taken *post*-conflict 'to identify and support structures which will tend to strengthen and solidify peace in order to avoid a relapse into conflict' (Boutros-Ghali, 1992: para. 21). Shortly thereafter, genocide broke out in Rwanda and Bosnia, and the UN's failure to keep, much less build, peace was devastating. In 2000, the UN published *The Brahimi Report*, which still constructed peacebuilding as reactive rather than proactive, made up of activities 'undertaken on the *far side of conflict* to reassemble the foundations of peace and provide the tools for building on those foundations something that is more than just the absence of war' (Brahimi Report, 2000: para. 13, emphasis added). The desire for 'more than just the absence of war' – a direct reference to Galtung – led the UN General Assembly and Security Council to establish the Peacebuilding Commission in 2005, which in turn led to a more comprehensive definition in a 2007 report: 'Peacebuilding aims to reduce the risk of *lapsing or relapsing* into conflict by strengthening national capacities at all levels for conflict management, and to lay the foundation for sustainable peace and development' (cited in UN, 2010). With this definition, we see peacebuilding become codified as peace-oriented actions taken before, during and after conflict, and as actions taken at all levels, understandings of peacebuilding now in line with Lederach's (2003) and E. Boulding's (1990) multidimensional visions. A 2012 UN report adds to that definition by including the following language, which even more closely calibrates with Lederach and E. Boulding's language about peacebuilding: '[S]uccessful peacebuilding processes must be transformative, creating space *for a wider set of actors* – including women, youth, marginalized groups, civil society, and the private sector – to participate in national post-conflict decision-making' (UN Secretary-General, 2012, emphasis added). While this language still emphasizes 'national' and 'post'-conflict decision making, the inclusion of actors from civil society (separate from government and business) creates space for the multiplicity and greater visibility of the peacebuilders that Lederach (2003) and E. Boulding (1990) invite to the table. We see that space as ample enough to include the voices of our project participants as well, voices that evince peacebuilding as intersecting with and embedded in intercultural communication as participants express profound personal change, share how they form relationships with each other, and together re-envision their societies and worlds.

Understandings of Intercultural Communication Competence

Already in this chapter we have seen places where peacebuilding and intercultural communication overlap and converge in meaningful ways, such as the compelling alignment of Boulding's (1990) vision of relational interaction and integrative power with paradigms of intercultural communication hinging on trust (Chua *et al.*, 2012; Hofstede, 2009; Vulpe *et al.*, 2001). In order to better understand how person to person peacebuilding intersects with and is embedded in intercultural communication, in our next section we share various understandings of intercultural competence, with close attention paid to components in specific intercultural competence frameworks which intersect with the personal, relational and structural dimensions of peacebuilding as theorized by Lederach (2003) and Broome and Collier (2012).

As background, we start with Hall's *The Silent Language* (1959), which has been described as the first work published in the field of intercultural communication, emerging as it did – like the literature of peacebuilding – right after and in response to World War II. Hall's book is essentially derived from a decade-long training program he conducted with diplomats and staff at the Foreign Service Institute of the US Department of State (Leeds-Hurwitz, 1990: 262). In his work, Hall examined with diplomats how to communicate with members of multiple different cultures. During this process and in part at his trainees' behest, Hall's training moved away from generalizations of culture (religion, history, food), concentrating instead on what Leeds-Hurwitz (1990: 263) describes as 'specific small moments of interaction.' While eventually Hall became best known for his work with proxemics, 'high' and 'low' cultures and the 'iceberg' analogy for understanding culture (Hall, 1976; Hall & Hall, 1990), his decade of working with Foreign Service initiates led to training practices that are influential today, including: the use of authentic materials from specific countries for training; his advocacy of participants interacting with foreign nationals during the training period; and his expectation that it was up to participants to continue their learning once they were established in their new countries (Leeds-Hurwitz, 1990: 264). These practices remain in wide use in intercultural communication and other forms of training globally, although, as Baldwin (2017) points out, it is important that we keep in mind the origins of intercultural communication as a discipline. In the same way as 'liberalized peacebuilding' has too often reinforced Western dominance globally, so too did intercultural communication begin as 'a means of control' through diplomacy as the US sought (and seeks) to exert influence over the policies and populations of other nations, including its own Indigenous First Nations (Baldwin, 2017).

In the years following the publication of Hall's *The Silent Language* (1959), the field of intercultural communication itself was relatively silent up until the founding of two journals, *The International and Intercultural Communication Annual* in 1974 and *The International Journal of Intercultural Relations* in 1977, which, as Gudykunst (2003) observes, began to publish a number of intercultural communication articles. In Gudykunst's (2003) foreword to his book *Cross-Cultural and Intercultural Communication*, he spells out how understandings of the terms 'cross' and 'inter' differ, with the former being focused on comparing communication across cultures, the latter describing communication between actors from different cultural groups (Gudykunst, 2003: 2). Significantly, Gudykunst's distinction between 'cross-' and 'inter-'cultural understandings of communication does not yet lend that much clarity: as recently as 2011, researchers have lamented the elusive nature of the concept, with over 300,000 definitions to be found on the internet (Witte & Harden, 2011: 1). For our purposes in this book, we avail ourselves of models and understandings of intercultural communication competence (ICC), the components of which dovetail with the three levels of peacebuilding we explore: the personal, relational and structural.

Intercultural Communication Competence across Peacebuilding Levels

We start by acknowledging the complexity of the two concepts, peacebuilding and intercultural competence, which are central to our work. This complexity contributes to various definitions and frameworks in the fields of both peacebuilding and intercultural competence. In addition, many components *within* various peacebuilding and intercultural competence frameworks overlap and influence each other, providing us with ways to measure 'positive' or preferred change in interactants (Lederach, 2003). Given these overlaps and convergences, it may be no surprise then that Broome and Collier (2012: 246) state the following: first, that 'the study of intercultural communication intersects with peacebuilding in fundamental and meaningful ways'; and second, that 'intercultural communication scholars can play an important role in advancing the study and practice of peacebuilding.'

As examples of overlaps and convergences, consider: 'attitudes' (one component of intercultural communication) are informed and based on the previous 'knowledge' (another component) each person has about the other. This attitude might change as new knowledge (or 'awareness') is acquired through listening, observing or analyzing interactions with others, which are categorized as 'skills' (yet another component). This action of acquiring knowledge can in turn contribute to the change of attitudes in a positive or negative way. The change of attitudes as a result of acquiring knowledge through different skills creates a change in behavior and communication, and if this change is 'effective' and 'appropriate,' it can indicate intercultural competence (Deardorff, 2006b, 2015; Spitzberg, 1989; Spitzberg & Changnon, 2009). In the same way, such changes may be seen as the kind of positive, 'preferred changes' (movement toward 'the horizon of preferred future') we seek in and between individuals engaged in peacebuilding (Lederach, 2003: 35).

With the anchors of 'effective' and 'appropriate' communication (Deardorff, 2006a, 2015; Spitzberg, 1989; Spitzberg & Changnon, 2009) stabilizing the construct of 'intercultural competence' we use as our guide, we next examine well-known intercultural competence frameworks in order to identify specific elements that accord with the levels of peacebuilding defined by Lederach (2003) and Broome and Collier (2012). The discursive indicators of peacebuilding we examine often criss-cross peacebuilding levels. For example, a realization at the personal level (let's say, positive intellectual growth due to new knowledge) may concurrently impact relational and structural levels of peacebuilding (e.g. sudden understanding of an interlocutor's expressed fears, which leads to new understandings of a root cause of conflict). The same holds true as we turn to intercultural communicative competence (ICC): we organize ICC levels around personal, relational and structural levels, but with the understanding that this tripartite division is mostly a contrived heuristic intended to clarify understanding. With ICC, too, indicators at these levels criss-cross and overlap.

The Personal Dimension of Peacebuilding and Intercultural Communicative Competence

The personal dimension of the peacebuilding frameworks we use involves 'the cognitive, emotional, perceptual, and spiritual aspects of individuals' orientations in conflict situations' (Lederach, 2003: 23). In other words, the personal dimension is based on how someone thinks of, feels about and/or perceives themselves and others. Language describing this dimension by Lederach (2003) and Broome and Collier (2012) corresponds with components at the personal level of many intercultural competence frameworks, such as: attitudes and knowledge (Byram, 1997; Deardorff, 2004); curiosity, withholding judgments (Deardorff, 2004); mindfulness (Ting-Toomey & Kurogi, 1998); feelings such as uncertainty and anxiety (Gudykunst & Hammer, 1988); and understanding and valuing others (Goodman, 2013). Indeed, individual characteristics we look for at the personal level of peacebuilding unsurprisingly occur in most if not all intercultural competence frameworks. For our purposes in this book, we explain this dimension in more detail with Byram's (1997) intercultural communicative competence framework and Deardorff's (2004) process and pyramid models of intercultural competence.

Byram's early (1997) framework focuses on intercultural communicative competence in foreign language education. Byram explores how to assess students of foreign language teaching and their development as intercultural 'sojourners,' travelers (not tourists) who engage with and use the languages of other worlds – other people – to communicate, in the process leading all involved to confront their actions, their beliefs and their thinking, sojourner and 'other' alike (Byram, 1997: 1). We concur with this definition of sojourner, even as we extend it to include 'digital sojourners,' intercultural interactants like those in our study who meet online synchronously during language tutoring for semester-long forays into what we call the virtual intercultural borderlands.

In his framework of intercultural communicative competence, Byram (1997: 34) examines four facets of interaction involving such individuals in contact and two sets of an individual's skills: (1) individuals' 'knowledge of self and other'; (2) individuals' 'attitudes' which allow for 'relativizing self' while 'valuing others'; (3) an individual's skills of 'interpreting and relating'; and (4) of 'discovery and interaction.' He arranges these facets or *savoirs* (dimensions) into a schema, with 'education' – defined as 'political education' and 'learners' critical cultural awareness' – in the center. While Byram's (1997: 7) model addresses assessment and teaching of students of foreign languages, he is careful to conjointly attend to the forces of context in the shaping of this model of intercultural communicative competence, in turn, underlining the importance of adjusting models of ICC to the contexts in which interlocutors (and teachers of interlocutors) find themselves.

Just as pertinent to our work in this book are the details Byram (1997) elaborates on for each *savoir* or dimension (not to be confused with Lederach's [2003] 'dimensions' or levels of peacebuilding), allowing us to articulate further the abilities of the *individual* intercultural speaker and to seek positive change in the discourses of our participants. Byram discusses, for instance, how two of his five *savoirs*, 'attitudes' and 'knowledge,' are both preconditions of – and reshaped by – intercultural communication. For 'successful' intercultural interaction, Byram (1997: 34) describes the need for personal 'attitudes of curiosity and openness, of readiness to suspend disbelief and judgement with respect to others' meanings, beliefs and behaviours,' attitudes, that is to say, that can lead individuals to 'decenter' and shift their perspectives, and even take apart what they have believed to be their 'subjective reality' and build it again in consonance with new structures of realities and norms.

'Knowledge,' Byram continues, has impact across levels: knowledge is 'brought to an interaction by an interlocutor from another country' and hence it is relational; at the same time, it should include an individual's personal 'knowledge about social groups and their cultures in one's own country,' along with, eventually, 'similar knowledge of the interlocutor's country' and 'knowledge of the processes of interaction at individual and societal levels' (Byram, 1997: 34–35). Byram goes on to explain how individual/personal knowledge comes about first from our 'primary' socialization within our families and other social groups to which we belong and with whom we have contact; this knowledge may be conscious or unconscious and may include a sense of national culture or identity in addition to religious, ethnic, socioeconomic or other identities, all of which develop from informal and formal socialization (such as schooling). Byram's discussion here helps alert us to: evidence in participants' discourses that indicates attitudes open (or not, or partially open) to intercultural others; evidence that indicates stasis or change in knowledge according to personal, relational and structural forces; evidence of knowledge participants have learned from primary socialization; and what (and how) knowledge becomes restructured upon contact with their intercultural others.

Equally relevant to the personal dimension of intercultural competence, Deardorff's (2006b) frameworks emerge from a Delphi study which sought to identify consensus among prominent intercultural communication experts (including Byram, 1997) and their understandings of intercultural competence (Deardorff, 2006a: 242). Her resulting frameworks (visualized as both process and pyramid) join models that describe primarily personal/individual attributes of interculturally competent interactants. Deardorff (2006b) identifies 15 attributes (or indicators) of intercultural competence, organized under five broad categories: (1) attitudes; (2) knowledge and comprehension; (3) skills; (4) internal outcomes; and (5) external outcomes. Deardorff then elaborates on each of these categories, providing us, as did Byram, with specific details to seek in the discourses of participants as evidence of peacebuilding intersecting with and embedded in intercultural communication. Of attitudes she lists, for instance, 'respect, openness, curiosity, and discovery'; knowledge ranges from cultural self-awareness to sociolinguist awareness; skills are comprised of 'observation, listening, evaluating, analyzing, interpreting, and relating'; internal outcomes lead to 'ethnorelative perspectives and empathy'; and the summation of these competencies culminates in the definition of intercultural competence widely agreed upon by intercultural scholars: 'the effective and appropriate behavior and communication in intercultural situations' (Deardorff, 2006b, 2015; Spitzberg, 1989; Spitzberg & Changnon, 2009).

In reviewing definitions of communication competence in addition to intercultural competence, Deardorff (2004) synthesizes many scholars' perspectives about the appropriateness and effectiveness of communication as an indicator/outcome of intercultural competence (Chen & Starosta, 1996; Fantini *et al.*, 2001; Lustig & Koester, 2010; Spitzberg & Cupach, 1984; Wiseman, 2001). Also from her Delphi study, the definition worded as the 'ability to communicate effectively and appropriately in intercultural situations based on one's intercultural knowledge, skills, and attitudes' was the top-rated definition, receiving '100% consensus from administrators and 95% acceptance from the experts' (Deardorff, 2004: 171). As in Broome and Collier's (2012) peacebuilding framework, all the components are interrelated in Deardorff's (2004) framework and one component is not enough to ensure intercultural competence, now defined as 'effective' and 'appropriate' intercultural communication. Deardorff maintains that intercultural competence typically begins with pre-existing internal attitudes which, when developed, support and lead to external outcomes; meanwhile, the extent of one's intercultural competence is coupled with the acquisition of various new attitudes, knowledge and skills, as discussed above. Deardorff notes that intercultural interactants can 'enter' her pyramid model of intercultural competence at any level; however, the more attributes one has acquired from the pyramid's base levels (e.g. openness, respect, curiosity), the stronger the likelihood for attributes in the upper levels to be correspondingly strengthened (such as adaptability or flexibility; Deardorff, 2006a: 255). Furthermore, Deardorff (2006a: 257) emphasizes the 'ongoing' process of intercultural competence, saying 'one may never achieve ultimate intercultural competence,' an observation which is similar to Lederach *et al.*'s (2007) argument indicating that peacebuilding has no 'end-state.' Deardorff's framework, drawn from her extensive research among intercultural communication experts and administrators, provides yet more indicators we may look for in participants' discourses as we seek evidence of intersections between peacebuilding and intercultural competence at the personal dimension, and as we seek evidence of person to person peacebuilding in participants' discourses.

The Relational Dimension of Peacebuilding and Intercultural Communicative Competence

The relational dimension of the peacebuilding frameworks focuses on the communicative, interactive, and social and inter-group relationships that build equitable and inclusive dialogue and which lead to individual and group transformation (Broome & Collier, 2012; Lederach, 2003). This dimension, while related to the personal, steers away from simply describing individual attitudes, perceptions and judgments, and steers more toward the behaviors participants engage in during communication and interaction as a result of their attitudes, perceptions and judgments. Lederach shares critical questions to ask at this dimension, as follows:

> How close or distant do people wish to be in their relationships?
> How will they use, build, and share power?
> How do they perceive themselves, each other, and their expectations?
> What are their hopes and fears for their lives and relationships, their patterns of communication and interaction? (Lederach, 2003: 24)

In the main, for Lederach, peacebuilding at the relational dimension is about interactants finding ways to diminish problematic communication and improve understanding to the highest degree possible. Similarly, in their culture, communication and peacebuilding framework, Broome and Collier (2012: 251) encourage 'scholar/practitioners of culture and communication working at this level [to] examine social relationships, intergroup relationships, the nature of hierarchies and status positioning of group members' in order to find evidence (in our case, discursive evidence) of peacebuilding at this dimension.

For deeper understanding of the relational dimension of intercultural competence, we first go back to Allport *et al.*'s (1954) contact hypothesis, which remains the benchmark for research focusing on the relationships between different groups. Although 'intercultural competence' as a term is not directly mentioned in Allport's hypothesis, he does claim that prejudice between the members of different ethnic groups or majority/minority groups can diminish through interpersonal contact, and communication between these same groups can lead to increased appreciation and understanding of the other, outcomes which support peacebuilding and intercultural competence at the relational dimension. However, says Allport, certain conditions must exist: groups must perceive their status as equal; groups must share common goals; groups must be cooperating and not competing; and contacts between groups must be supported by social and institutional structures. Put another way, as Elosúa (2015: 75), building on Allport *et al.* (1954), writes, 'Mere contact is not sufficient to develop intercultural competence.'

Gudykunst and Kim (1984: 14) shed further light on the relational dimension of intercultural competence and peacebuilding when they define intercultural competence as 'a transactional, symbolic process involving the attribution of meaning between people from different cultures.' This definition, with its emphasis on the 'transactional,' invites us to attend to processes and change through exchange and relations between intercultural interactants. Byram (1997: 17) draws on Gudykunst (1994) to discuss how the new 'shared world' of intercultural interactants by definition creates a social group among its members: both world and group are created by prolonged interaction and socialization, including continual negotiation around 'details' of understandings which may lead to dramatic changes in 'beliefs, behaviors and meanings.' These changes, in turn, through interaction, can transform interactants' worldviews. Also noteworthy at this dimension, particularly given Lederach's (2003) discussion of relational power, Byram points out how, despite possible power differentials, this interactionist perspective has the potential to value and accommodate multiple forms of cultural capital (Bourdieu, 1989), a potential that impacts as well on peacebuilding at the relational level. In other words, in our analysis we need to keep in mind: forms of cultural capital from dominant societies and those from non-dominant ones; the cultural capital of those who speak a lingua franca and of those who do not; and the cultural capital of those who represent a national culture and identity along with the cultural capital of those who represent *intra-national* ethnic and other differences (Byram, 1997: 17–20).

Key to this balance in cultural capital and negotiated understandings of behavior, meanings and beliefs, according to Byram (1997), are the interactants' abilities to effectively analyze their interactions with others. Indeed, as language teachers – and Byram (2009: 409) stresses that the 1997 model was designed with 'the pedagogical purposes of foreign language teaching in obligatory education' in mind – our work becomes about 'equipping learners with the means of accessing and analysing any cultural practices and meanings they encounter, whatever their status in a society' and 'whatever social world their interlocutors inhabit' (Byram, 2009: 19–20). For peacebuilding at this relational level, and in the context of our study, the access and analysis of 'cultural meanings and practices' participants encounter should further involve implications of that analysis, such as the resulting distance or closeness of their relationships with interlocutors, participants' willingness to build and share power together, and/or their willingness to share their hopes and fears – for the project, for their lives – with one another. As Broome and Collier (2012: 252) put it, analysis is not the end game but should extend to the point where participants collaborate to work for 'communication and community engagement that contribute to conflict transformation, relationships that are equitable, inclusive, and enhance justice, and the work of intercultural alliances'.

Such work joins other indicators of how peacebuilding intersects with intercultural communication at the relational level. Previously we glimpsed how Byram's (1997) framework contains components which can be understood as both personal and relational: his construct of 'knowledge,' for instance, is relational, in that it is 'brought to an interaction by an interlocutor from another country' (Byram, 1997: 35), personal in how it is held and evolves in individuals. Other of his *savoirs* (like the skill of analysis) has implications for both the personal and relational levels of peacebuilding. He writes:

> *Skills* of interpreting and relating, of using existing knowledge to understand a specific document or behaviour for example, and to relate these to comparable but different documents or behaviours in their own social group;
>
> *Skills* of discovery and interaction ... the means of augmenting and refining knowledge about the [intercultural] other and knowing how to respond to specific features of interaction with a particular individual. (Byram, 1997: 36–37)

The details Byram shares here allow us to look at when and how participants interpret and relate information and behaviors from interactions with intercultural others, and allow us to consider places where knowledge between interactants becomes more developed, more nuanced, such that their individual responses to each other and back and forth become 'more effective,' 'more appropriate,' and contribute, in the final analysis, to the positive, 'preferred' change in individuals, relationships and even structures that Lederach (2003) discusses. Such change, in turn, becomes a marker of intercultural interaction, person to person peacebuilding and the intersections thereof.

The Structural Dimension of Peacebuilding and Intercultural Communicative Competence

In Broome and Collier's (2012) exploration of the intersections between peacebuilding and intercultural communication, they encourage scholars to look into the structural dimension as well as the personal and relational. In their words: 'The structural dimension includes ways in which societal discourses, organizational policies, and institutional practices create and enable differential access to resources and status, levels of individual agency and equity, levels of inclusion and decision making, and societal norms' (Broome & Collier, 2012: 257). As a reminder, they develop their framework according to the work of Lederach (2003), who adds to our understanding of how intercultural communication can intersect with peacebuilding at the structural level. More precisely, Lederach (2003) charges peacebuilders at the structural level to work to acknowledge and tackle underlying causes of conflict and violence, to engage with the tools of nonviolence (or Galtung's 'positive peace') to weaken conflict to the point where violence ends, and finally to strengthen structures that serve our basic needs and include all participants in decision-making processes. Positive, preferred change at this dimension is change in the service of justice and peacebuilding: thus, in our study of the intersections between peacebuilding and intercultural interaction, we seek evidence of change in participants' discourses related to their perceptions of and commitments to working explicitly for peace and justice with their intercultural other, from creating equal access to resources, to equal partnership in decision making, to working to eliminate underlying causes of social injustice and conflict.

As we look to intercultural competence frameworks which inform this structural dimension of peacebuilding, we turn again first to Byram (1997: 33). We have already discussed how four of his *savoirs* illuminate the intersections between peacebuilding and intercultural competence at the personal and relational levels. At the structural level, we turn to his fifth *savoir*, which calls for infusing the teaching of intercultural competence with a 'philosophy of political education' and the 'development of learners' critical cultural awareness' – facets that are plainly necessary for change to happen at structural levels. Byram (2009: 323) compares this *savoir* to the '*politische Bildung* in the (West) German educational tradition,' which advocates that learners 'reflect critically on the values, beliefs, and behaviours of their own society,' to which we add, 'the values, beliefs, and behaviors' of their interlocutors' societies. This *savoir* is well in keeping with Byram's more current work in education for intercultural citizenship (Byram, 2009; Byram *et al.*, 2017), and it is also paramount to the project of change (positive, preferred) at the structural level (Lederach, 2003). In much the same way, the culture, communication and peacebuilding framework Broome and Collier (2012: 253) propose 'is heavily influenced by critical, practical, and justice-oriented sensibilities.'

Focusing on a range of educational contexts, Goodman (2013: 2) not only integrates but also fronts social justice in the development of cultural competence, which she defines as follows: 'Cultural competence for social justice is the ability to live and work effectively in culturally diverse environments and enact a commitment to social justice.' We find Goodman's work most useful to our exploration of intercultural communication and peacebuilding at the structural level: we just rephrase her model as '*intercultural competency for social justice*.' What Goodman describes here we see as closely akin to Galtung's positive peace, 'the integration of human society' (Galtung, 1964: 2), by actors working to diminish violence in all forms and by actors working for social justice. Goodman's words also recall K. Boulding's 'integrative' power which is proffered as most productive and salient, the highest form of power, encompassing community, identity, relationships and, in its most basic form, love, with '[t]he capacity to build organizations, [...] to inspire loyalty, to bind people together, to develop legitimacy' (K. Boulding, 1990: 25).

Goodman's framework also intersects with and extends that of Deardorff (2009). Goodman, too, highlights the importance of 'self-awareness' and having the 'skills to interact effectively with a diversity of people in different contexts,' but she adds the explicit responsibilities of not just being empathetic to, but valuing and appreciating 'ways of being, doing, and thinking other than our own,' in language evocative of Byram (1997: 34) and his *savoir* of attitudes, 'relativizing self' while 'valuing others.' By the same token, Goodman's framework makes essential the 'knowledge of social inequities' (forms of the cultural and structural violence explained by Galtung, 1985), and how 'they affect people's experiences, opportunities, and access to social power' (Goodman, 2013). Here her words forcefully conjure up what Broome and Collier (2012: 252) describe as essential to the structural level of peacebuilding: participants' understandings of the relationships between peacebuilding and 'differential access to resources and status, levels of individual agency and equity, levels of inclusion and decision making, and societal norms.' Goodman (2013) also promotes action and the 'skills to foster diversity and inclusion' with actors working for social and societal change, which, as Galtung (1985) puts it, is work for 'positive peace.' In our exploration of participants' voices and views, then, we will examine how and whether participants interpret and enact 'the mutual exchange of ideas and cultural norms' Goodman describes, along with other relevant characteristics of her model for cultural (intercultural) competence for social justice. Concurrently, we consider how person to person peacebuilding may be manifest in participants' discourses related to the 'mutual exchange of ideas and cultural norms,' discursive evidence of which illuminates how peacebuilding at the structural level may come to life in the voices of our participants.

Conclusion

In this chapter, we provided a closer look into understandings of peacebuilding and intercultural competence which guide our thinking throughout this book. For our understanding of peacebuilding, we draw on Galtung's (1975) concept of 'positive peace' and Lederach's (1998) conception of peacebuilding: as taking place through multiple paths and over time; as transformative and instantiating social change; as welcoming a multiplicity of peacebuilders with a multiplicity of creative approaches to peacebuilding; and as seeking to create the conditions for just and sustainable peace (Lederach, 1998; Lederach & Appleby, 2010). For our understanding of intercultural communicative competence and intersections with peacebuilding, at the personal level, we recognize the impact of attitudes, skills, knowledge and comprehension on internal and external outcomes (Byram, 1997; Deardorff, 2006b). At the relational level, we believe that both intercultural competence and peacebuilding are transactional (Byram, 1997; Lederach, 2003), and changes in attitudes, behaviors and indeed worldviews can be shaped by and through interaction and engagement with 'the other.' At the structural level, we see peacebuilding and intercultural competence as being shaped by – and having the power to forcefully shape – change in societies and worlds (Byram, 1997; Goodman, 2013). It is these understandings that inform our exploration of how peacebuilding intersects with and is embedded in intercultural communications.

Before we turn to our analyses of how peacebuilding is embedded in and intersects with intercultural communication – and how participants build peace discursively – at the personal, relational and structural levels, we must first say more about the rather complicated context(s) of our research, including Afghanistan, US TESOL graduate programs and the virtual intercultural borderlands. To this task we turn next.

Notes

(1) For access to a database containing over 800 peace agreements, see the UN Peacemaker site: https://peacemaker.un.org/document-search.
(2) Paris (1997) describes this type of traditional diplomacy or 'liberal peacebuilding' as 'transplanting Western models of social, political, and economic organisation into war-shattered states in order to control civil conflict: in other words, pacification through political and economic liberalisation' (Paris, 1997: 56).
(3) Paffenholz (2014) notes how the term 'conflict transformation' in the literature has shifted into the term 'peacebuilding,' although both fundamentally share the same meaning. We rely on the term 'peacebuilding' (specifically, 'person to person peacebuilding') in our work.
(4) Lederach (2003) describes these changes as 'face-to-face,' which we update to 'online' and 'virtual' as well as 'face-to-face.'
(5) It is important to add here that Lederach *et al.* (2007: 23) emphasize that cultural change is embedded in the other three dimensions and can be challenging to distinguish separately: hence in our work we likewise look for evidence of cultural change embedded in the personal, relational and structural levels of participant discourses.

3 Context(s)

In this chapter we take on the construct of 'context,' no easy task. As Dervin (1997) puts it, in research, '[T]here is no term that is more often used, less often defined, and when defined defined so variously as "context"' (Dervin, 1997: 13–14). Indeed, the term and meanings of 'context' in research have come to embody a multiplicity of elements that frustrate its analysis, despite the fact that at the very core of research design lie the critical abilities to determine, define, demarcate and theorize our research contexts (Gould, 2008: 56). We have found the task of explaining our research context(s) equally challenging with this project, as we consider the complex geopolitical and institutional locales and histories of our participants (Afghanistan; US university graduate TESOL programs; the home countries of international graduate students) along with 'the virtual intercultural borderlands,' the 'sites' where participants (and we as authors) met *online* through videoconferencing and from which emerged the unexpected affordance of peacebuilding.

Context(s) and Our Research

By necessity, then, as we set out to explain the contexts of our research, we draw from a range of disciplines. First, writing from the field of development studies, in his discussion of 'aidnography' Gould (2008) draws attention to research 'sites' of 'developing' countries: 'the spatially diffuse "field" … [which] comprises a totality of localities linked together by the process/flows of the relationship' (Gould, 2008: 60), such as the international office of a donor organization in London or Tokyo or Budapest, and the local offices of aid recipients in Nairobi, Myanmar or Karachi. Gould goes on to observe that 'localities' do not have to be strictly geographic or spatial, but rather can be 'points of convergence of various actors and interests as well as of the contexts in which they are embedded' (Gould, 2008: 60). Certainly, our project involves 'spatially diffuse' sites, as participants at the time of tutoring were located throughout Afghanistan and at various universities in the northeast and midwest of the US. In our analysis of participants' discourses, too, we encountered 'a totality of localities linked together by the process/flows of the relationship' (Gould, 2008: 60), meaning that Afghans and their tutors met online, brought together by the tutoring relationship (initially) and hence (initially) through converging interests: to teach/tutor – and learn/practice – English, while simultaneously developing their intercultural relationships in a virtual context, that of online videoconferencing. Moreover, we as authors and researchers likewise met in a virtual context, online, from distant geographic points (Massachusetts, New Hampshire, Turkey, Missouri, San Francisco), with the converging interests of analyzing and understanding data as well as considering implications for future language teaching/tutoring, intercultural communication and – eventually – peacebuilding projects.

In terms of *cross*-cultural research, we take the descriptions of Im *et al.* (2004) of context in such research as equally helpful to our own research into *inter*cultural communication and what emerges from it in the virtual intercultural borderlands. They aver that discussion of 'context' should include 'sensitivity to structural conditions that contribute to participants' responses and to the interpretations of situations informed by experiences, by validation of perceptions, and by a careful review of existing knowledge' (Im *et al.*, 2004: 895). We are confident in our review of existing literature: of language teaching, intercultural communication, and the peacebuilding that intercultural communication intersects with and is embedded in. Perhaps most importantly, we not only recognize the structural conditions that inform both participants' responses and our own interpretations thereof, but we further devote an entire chapter to analysis of those structural forces and how they constrain and enable the agency of our participants, a decision informed by the peacebuilding frameworks we use in our analyses and by the obvious presence of those forces in participants' discourses.

Croucher *et al.* (2015) introduce another important element of context which they couch in the process of identity expression in both in-person and online contexts. They discuss how expressions of identity vary based on what interlocutors perceive as cues from context, and they share in part the assumption of McEwan and Sobre-Denton (2011): that 'virtual spaces can allow individuals to open and renew the scope of available identity categorizations.' The authors share, too, a claim made by Johnson and Callahan (2013), that globalization and its many intertwined processes have created 'cultural spaces [and therefore *contexts*] independent of traditional geographical or ethnic identifications' (Johnson & Callahan, 2013: 319, cited in Croucher *et al.*, 2015).

While we do not believe that, in the case of our research, the 'cultural' spaces created by our intercultural participants are wholly 'independent' of geography, we do believe that the online space (the virtual intercultural borderlands) where our participants met and interacted over the course of a semester should be considered separately and as made up of the elements we have described so far in this chapter: participants are spatially diffuse even as they are virtually together and connected through the processes and flows of their relationship building (Gould, 2008); they shape and are shaped by structural forces (Im et al., 2004); and the virtual intercultural borderlands are not just a 'cultural space' but an *inter*cultural space created in part by intertwining processes of globalization, including opportunities for 'face-to-face' *virtual* connections made possible through videoconferencing. As we prepare to discuss our contexts for research, then, we do so through a series of discrete descriptions while acknowledging that these elements converge continually through participant interaction: we describe both the diffuse spatial contexts our participants live and interact in along with the structural forces exerting pressures in those spaces; we further examine the virtual intercultural borderlands in which participants interacted by first overviewing the very brief history of virtual exchange, and then by considering 'virtual intercultural borderlands' in light of 'borderlands' as conceptualized through the work of Anzaldúa (1987), Pratt's (1991) 'contact zones,' Bhabha's (2006) 'third space' and Lo Bianco et al.'s (1999) 'third place' of 'intercultural language learning.'

First, however, we provide one last description of 'context' important to our research and which is derived from Broome and Collier's (2012) 'reflexive, multidimensional, contextual framework' for peacebuilding. Their definition of 'context' is both concise and expansive, and we find within it iterations of critical contextual elements along with additional contextual elements relevant to our study:

> Context refers to material and environmental conditions which drive, and can be changed by, peacebuilding. Context includes such factors as histories and collective memory, climate and ecological conditions, food, housing, transportation, war/violence/safety conditions, organizations and services related to governmental, legal, and educational institutions, technologies in use, and resources. The context is more than the 'scene' of peacebuilding; it is a constitutive force and set of dynamic and material conditions. Contexts are both temporal and spatial, incorporating past, present and future. (Broome & Collier, 2012: 253)

What we find most striking from this definition is how the authors construct 'contexts' as themselves a structural, 'constitutive' force, one that can both bear down on participants and (we add) be transformed by the same. They remind us, too, that context is temporal as well as spatial, which brings into play participants' histories and their imagined futures as equally influential to our analyses as their present, which of course is present for one moment only, then gone. Broome and Collier (2012) help us see our contexts as, indeed, the 'scenes' of peacebuilding as well as the conditions thereof, and the dynamism and constant flux of those conditions will be at work throughout our analysis of participants' voices and discourses within the research contexts of this project.

Context 1: Afghanistan, history and the lives of our Afghan participants

In providing an overview of Afghanistan, we have chosen to start at a point in history still in the living memories of Afghans, at least in the memories of our Afghan participants' parents and grandparents. These memories and histories help us understand the spatial 'site' of the Afghan context along with structural forces that still shape the daily Afghan experience, markedly, one of conflict, part of the 'scene' of the lives of half our participants. To understand the voices of our participants, we must understand the contexts in which they and their families have been living.

It is important to know, for instance, that in the time period between the 1950s and the 1970s, Afghanistan was a relatively progressive country. This was a time referred to as 'Afghanistan's golden age,' when Kabul was 'the Paris of Central Asia,' women were free to wear miniskirts and attend university, and hippies were frequent among the travelers to the region (Bumiller, 2009). During this time, under the reign of Afghanistan's last king, Mohammad Zahir Shah, Afghanistan was (albeit, slowly) 'modernized': infrastructure developed as major highways and airports were built, and a constitutional monarchy was established, with women serving in parliament. Under this monarchy, the government was able to implement basic state functions, such as keeping the peace and maintaining order within its borders, although importantly, basic needs such as education and healthcare were mostly available in urban areas only, and mostly for the country's 'elite' (Byrd, 2012).

Several prominent features stand out from this time period: Afghanistan *has* experienced peace; there persisted unsurprising tensions over the competing forces of US and Soviet interests in the region, tensions that persist to this day; and the worlds and cultures of urban and rural Afghans were in stark contrast to one another. This was the Afghanistan of our Afghan participants' grandparents and parents. According to Jackson (2017), it was only after King Zahir was deposed in 1973 (in a bloodless coup by his cousin, Daoud Khan) that 'Afghanistan entered into the spiral of governmental instability, insurgency, outright civil war and foreign interventions that has plagued it to the present day.' With Khan's takeover – backed by Soviet rubles and military training – the existing political system fell apart: before it could be righted or formalized, the communist People's Democratic Party of Afghanistan (PDPA) overthrew and killed Khan, in 1978, after which internal conflict and civil unrest intensified. This was the point when the Soviets moved from exerting profound political influence (courting Afghan ministers, providing free education and medical treatment to Afghans in the Soviet Union, sustaining the country economically with vast amounts of aid) to a full-scale invasion by Christmas 1979 (Jackson, 2017), in large part due to pleas from the PDPA (Gandomi, 2008). By then, too, the US Central Intelligence

Agency (CIA) – with support from its Pakistani counterpart, the Inter-Services Intelligence directorate (ISI) – had already launched Operation Cyclone, a campaign to fund, arm and train the Afghan resistance to the Soviet Union, the Mujahideen (Jackson, 2017) or 'holy warriors.'

Over the next decade of occupation, more than a million Soviet soldiers fought in Afghanistan, razing whole villages with fierce force, chemical weapons and little to no regard for civilian life, as they sought out and battled Mujahideen insurgents (Gandomi, 2008). During this decade, as is tragically typical of war, more civilians died than either Soviet forces or those of the Mujahideen, approximately 1 million, with roughly 90,000 deaths among Mujahideen fighters, 18,000 Afghan troops and 14,500 Soviet soldiers (Taylor, 2014). The human and financial costs eventually became untenable for the Soviet Union, which found it impossible to defeat the Mujahideen in order to continue supporting communist leadership in Afghanistan. The last soldiers exited the country in February 1989.

While much of the war in the 1980s took place in rural Afghanistan, Dorronsoro (2007) describes how in the time period afterwards, specifically 1992–1996, Kabul became the primary political and military objective for actors continuing to fight. Significantly, the collapse of the Soviet Union in 1991 promptly ended economic aid from both the US and the USSR, and assorted actors and interests were left jockeying for power, including: the holdover Afghan communist regime who had been allied with the Soviets, some of whom switched allegiances and allied themselves with the Mujahideen; the Mujahideen, who broke apart into various ethnic factions including Pashtuns, Tajiks, Hazaras and Uzbeks (Lawrence, 2010), former allies now fighting each other; and there was even a failed attempt by the UN with the last vestiges of Soviet support to return the popular King Zahir to power (Dorronsoro, 2007). The civil war that ensued was devastating.

This was the 'context' from which emerged the Taliban under the leadership of Mullah Omar, a group initially well received as it arrived pledging to bring stability and order to the violent disorder left in the wake of the Soviet occupation and withdrawal. By 1996 they had seized Kabul and declared Afghanistan an Islamic Emirate, with Mullah Omar 'the commander of the faithful'; by 1998 they controlled over 90% of the country (Maizland & Laub, 2020). Once in charge, the Taliban ruled by implementing the most extreme interpretations and misinterpretations of Sharia Law, rendering Afghanistan into one of the most oppressed societies in the world, one that violated human rights and especially those of women: girls over 10 were attacked if they went to school, often by having acid thrown in their faces (Torgan, 2016); men were forced to wear beards, while women were forced to wear burqas and were not allowed outside the home unless in company of a close male relative. Girls were forced into child marriage. Punishments became a public spectacle of hangings, shootings, stonings, floggings, amputations. Cinemas, music and television were banned. By this time, most of our Afghan research participants and all of our US-based participants had been born.

After the terror attacks of September 11, 2001, US and NATO coalition forces invaded Afghanistan, initially due to the Taliban's unwillingness to give up the location of Osama bin Laden. By 2003, the Taliban were described as 'toppled' (Chughtai & Qazi, 2020). But over the length of the longest US war, the Taliban slowly reorganized into decentralized pockets of insurgents who launched ever stronger, ever more deadly attacks, increasingly with the help of al-Qaeda and other insurgent militias. By 2010, coalition forces were at their highest number, with around 150,000 troops, two-thirds of which were US soldiers. In 2011, both the US and NATO forces began the process of drawing down troops as NATO declared the end of their combat mission in Afghanistan. Correspondingly, the Taliban stepped up their terror attacks and spread throughout Afghanistan again, and high numbers of civilians continued (and continue) to die, due in part also to continued US air attacks in response to Taliban bombings (Chughtai & Qazi, 2020). In addition to al Qaeda, by 2015 the Islamic State of Iraq and the Levant (ISIS) had established itself in Afghanistan: they began a fierce campaign against the Taliban, always with civilians caught in the middle and continuing to die (Quraishi, 2015).

With the new threats of ISIS and other insurgent groups gaining power in Afghanistan, in late 2018, under President Donald Trump, US officials met with Taliban representatives in Qatar in the first tentative movements toward peace. The initial discussions came to a halt with the death of a US soldier in Afghanistan, but by 2020 the Trump administration had made a deal with the Taliban: to withdraw the remaining troops in exchange for a reduction in violence and the release of Taliban prisoners. According to Boot (2020), and unsurprisingly, 'Many of the released Taliban fighters have returned to the battlefield, and violence continues unabated.' This is the context Trump left for his successor, President Biden – what Coll (2021) describes as 'no good choices.' In September 2021, Biden plans to withdraw all troops, proclaiming:

> We cannot continue the cycle of extending or expanding our military presence in Afghanistan, hoping to create ideal conditions for the withdrawal, and expecting a different result. I'm now the fourth United States President to preside over American troop presence in Afghanistan: two Republicans, two Democrats. I will not pass this responsibility on to a fifth. (Biden, 2021)

Ultimately, Coll (2021) insists, with Biden ending the US troop presence, we are left to reflect on 'the tragic cost of hubris,' with more than 2000 US troops and 100,000 civilians dead in Afghanistan, a threat of the return to Taliban control for those who have survived 'America's longest war,' or possibly, probably, civil war, with no cessation of violence.

Educational contexts of Afghanistan

The Soviet invasion, decades of civil war, and the Taliban brought tremendous harm to all aspects of Afghanistan, and education was no exception. Ignorance or neglect of local education pressures and the inefficient use of limited aid funding had a long-term calamitous impact on education in Afghanistan. Among all the humanitarian actions taken to provide stability in the country, education has proved one of the most problematic, as religious and secular pressures vie for power in the educational arena, demonstrating how 'the continued neglect of education's humanitarian role may prolong or intensify conflict in ways that have not been anticipated by the aid community' (Burde, 2014: 29). This neglect of education was also reflected in financial support: among the humanitarian funding provided for Afghanistan, education had the smallest portion, only 1% of the overall funding (Burde, 2014: 35). Moreover, according to Khan (2015), citing an investigation of schools built by aid money, 'at least a tenth of the schools BuzzFeed News visited no longer exist, are not operating, or were never built in the first place,' leading to 'ghost teachers', 'ghost students' and 'ghost schools.'

After UNESCO's 'Education for All' movement, many countries gave priority to expanding primary and secondary education to make education accessible to larger populations, and Afghanistan was one of the countries included in and affected by this movement, such that: by 2010, secondary school graduation rates increased by 36%; by 2011, by 25%; and by 2012, by 29% (Hayward, 2015: 2). However, there were not enough higher education institutions to accommodate the numbers of graduates in Afghanistan. Lack of security, funding and ongoing conflict were among the barriers to the expansion and development of higher education. This fact is particularly poignant considering Afghanistan once had the reputation of having the best higher education in the region and was preferred by Asian and Middle Eastern students (Hayward, 2015).

Limited access to opportunities to pursue higher education may help explain part of the strong interest among students in Afghanistan – at least among the Afghan participants whose experiences we explore in this book – in English language tutoring after high school, along with a distinct tendency for participants to want to pursue higher education in the US, India or the UK. Nazari *et al*. (2021) furnish us with the most current look into the Afghan educational context as it relates to language education by focusing on the professional identities of Afghan 'second language' (English) teachers. Based on interviews with teachers, the authors sum up specific challenges Afghan English teachers face:

> The cultural conundrum of pulling the strings to reach one's goals, low economic status of families, the long-standing negative impact of war on individuals' mindset, lack of coeducational classes, low engagement of parents, and biased and discriminatory perceptions about teachers were

seen [by their participants] as barriers to effective investment in education more broadly and in English teaching and learning in particular. (Nazari et al., 2021)

The authors then focus on two themes readily apparent in our data, including 'the negative impacts of war' (which we view as a structural force constraining participants; see also Chapter 6) and 'the dominance of native-speaker ideologies and prestige even in the eyes of educational participants.' One of their research participants, 'T7,' shares an example of the dominance of these ideologies: having studied at a 'Western university,' with classmates or professors who were 'native speakers,' he is accorded greater credibility as an English teacher:

> War can influence the students' mindset, and they transfer it to the classroom and the predispositions about teaching English. Teacher's educational background influences students' and my colleagues' attitudes toward me as a teacher. If I come with a Western university degree, they do not question my teaching credibility; they even trust my teaching skills without hesitation. (T7, as quoted in Nazari et al., 2021)

These particular themes – war and the myths of 'native speaker' and uniquely 'Western' credibility and privilege – correlate and converge with our next section in this chapter.

Context 2: US-based graduate TESOL programs and our participants

The other half of our research participants lead us to the second 'context' of our research, US-based graduate TESOL programs in which were enrolled the 72 US-based tutors whose written reflections inspired our research and provided the beginning data for our analysis. Some familiarity with the background of these students helps us continue to explain the contexts of our research.

Among these tutors, 15 agreed to be interviewed; transcripts from these topic-oriented interviews added to and enhanced our understanding of participants' interactions with one another. As we noted in Chapter 1, the tutors were all pursuing graduate degrees in teaching English to speakers of other languages (TESOL); while we describe these tutors as 'future' or 'pre-service' 'EAL teachers,' some were or already had been teachers when they participated in this project. Their experiences included working with young multilingual students who were born in or who had immigrated to the US, or in language programs designed to prepare students for higher education in countries where English was the medium of instruction, and teaching English composition courses in US universities. Some tutors were just beginning their graduate degrees and some were in their final semesters. Some planned to work with immigrant or refugee students in elementary and secondary schools; some hoped to teach EAL in universities or private language schools. Others were preparing to work as teachers and administrators internationally, in their home countries or in countries around the world.

The tutoring project was embedded in a course on the teaching of English grammar, and the data we share come from graduate students who completed this course. Throughout the project, the course instructor collaborated with representatives of the community partner, in the US and in Afghanistan, to pair these future EAL teachers with Afghan learners for weekly synchronous online tutoring sessions. When the graduate students took part in this tutoring project, they were all living in the US. These tutors brought to their interactions with their Afghan students varying levels of formal training, teaching experience and language learning. Approximately two-thirds of the tutors were born in the US. These participants had grown up speaking English in their homes, in school and in their daily lives. Most described themselves as having limited levels of linguistic proficiency in languages other than English. While most of these participants had traveled outside of the US on at least one occasion, and several had lived outside of the US for periods of up to one year, many were living and hoped to work in the geographic area in which they were born and raised. These communities included: a city where the university was located, which has a significant population of residents from the Dominican Republic; a neighboring city which is home to immigrants from Haiti and Central America; and another nearby city which has a significant Brazilian population. In addition, these communities house immigrants and refugees from countries in North and Sub-Saharan Africa including Eritrea, Liberia and Sudan.

Approximately one-third of the tutors described English as their second or sometimes third language. Most of these non-US born participants were 'international students,' a term used in higher education for students who pursue their education in the US with the expectation of returning to their home countries upon completion of their degrees. These participants described their first languages as Arabic, Chinese, Korean, Mongolian, Tibetan and Ukrainian. Throughout the project, tutors drew on their experiences to find areas of common ground with their Afghan students. For example, some shared their tips for taking the TOEFL exam and others offered suggestions for applying to study abroad. Others found connections to the contexts of students which were personal and historical. Snippets of their voices provided below suggest the intricacies and variations of contexts our participants worked in.

For instance, after learning that her Afghan student might speak Dari, one tutor whose first language is Mongolian made the following connection in her first reflection:

> My name ... is a Mongolian word ... borrowed from Persian language because there are no Coconut tree growing in the Mongolian grassland,

when Mongols took over the territory in the middle East in 13th Century, they borrowed some words from Persian language.

Like the Afghan participants, some of the future EAL teachers came from countries experiencing overt conflict. One tutor was an immigrant from Iraq, where she had lived during the time of the US occupation. Another participant, a recent immigrant to the US from Syria, shared her own context as she reflected on her interactions with her Afghan student:

> I belonged to one of these countries where accessing the education is considered to be a privileged before the war. Nowadays it is impossible to study in Syria because the destruction of the school facility due to the constant bombardments by the ISIS.

In addition to participants from conflict countries occupied by the US and NATO and besieged by ISIS, tutors included a number of students from Ukraine whose lives were shaken up by the Russian occupation of Crimea. A participant from South Korea had spent much of her life in Seoul, close to the Demilitarized Zone (DMZ) that divides north from south. Her words, too, illumine the complexity of the 'context(s)' our project participants hailed from and worked in:

> I kind of never thought ... too much about peace even though I grew up in a country where a lot of people see ... second dangerous country in the world, which is North Korea and South Korea, always in a kind of tense situation, but I never felt in danger, in terms of what they call a war or, I never thought about it those kinds of terminology before, until I actually came to the United States, I came to United States about a month, two months before 9/11.

As our analysis in subsequent chapters will show, the diverse backgrounds and experiences of the tutors and their Afghan counterparts alike diverged and converged throughout their interactions. As one last complication of context, it is significant that the graduate student participants from China included speakers of Mongolian and Tibetan and a Mandarin speaker who was a devout Muslim: each of these participants had the status of 'minority' in their home country and were thus a part of what Kumaravadivelu (2014: 70) describes as the 'marginality of the majority.'

As we close this section, we note that any description of the context in which this tutoring took place would be incomplete without acknowledging the power and presence of a mythical being too often present in the minds of participants, tutors and students alike: the idealized 'native speaker of English.' Here we acknowledge that any extensive exploration of 'native speakerism' in our project (see, for example, Holliday, 2015) goes beyond the scope of this book, the focus of which is on person to person peacebuilding. However, we cannot ignore the hopes many Afghan students shared of interacting with and learning from a 'native speaker,' or the Afghan teacher in Nazari *et al.*'s (2021) study who observed, 'If I come with a Western university degree, they do not question my teaching credibility.' Nor can we ignore the fact that tutors who grew up outside of the US frequently referred to themselves as '*non*-native speakers' and shared reservations regarding their own levels of linguistic proficiency in English. Therefore, in Chapters 4 and 6, by necessity we touch upon some issues related to 'native speakerism' as they arise from our participants, and in our conclusion (Chapter 7), we encourage others to return to this issue and to explore projects such as ours transpiring in languages other than English. We note in closing this section: these first few voices we submit illustrate some of the particular complexities of our contexts; they will speak again in subsequent chapters of analysis.

Context 3: The virtual intercultural borderlands of online exchange

As we define what we mean by the '*virtual* intercultural borderlands,' we adapt a term from Brantmeier (2008: 69), who describes '*intercultural* borderlands' (emphasis added) as 'fluid, liminal spaces of intercultural opportunity that, when opened, potentially bridge cultural differences and foster positive relationships.' When people or groups from differing cultures meet and interact in these spaces, he writes, the dynamism and fluidity of 'being intercultural' invite possibilities for cultural transformation and the creation of new communities (Brantmeier, 2008: 69). While Brantmeier looks to these borderlands as affording the action possibilities of 'transformation' and 'forging new communities,' it is our aim to show how these borderlands afforded both the expected action possibilities of 'transformation' and 'forging new communities' along with the unexpected affordance of person to person peacebuilding.

To better understand the virtual intercultural borderlands in which participants interacted, we first offer an overview of existing models for online education collaboration. Next, we examine the concept of affordances, which is key to our analysis of participant voices. We conclude by overviewing 'borderland' and related theories (Anzaldúa, 1987; Bhabha, 2006; Crozet *et al.*, 1999; Pratt, 1991) which illuminate the context of these virtual spaces where our participants met and interacted.

Virtual exchange and existing models

Since the emergence of the internet, educators have leveraged online technologies to bring participants in different parts of the world together. O'Dowd (2018) offers a comprehensive overview of the history of such collaborations, exploring models of implementing online exchange in different educational contexts and academic fields. Most of the earliest online educational projects, generally referred to as e-tandem, took the form of exchange between two 'native speakers' of different languages; such projects were intended to provide participants with authentic input and opportunities to practice the language they were studying (O'Rourke, 2007). In the 1990s, a second model, often referred to as 'telecollaboration,' emerged within the field of foreign language education. This model placed a focus on intercultural learning and communication (Warschauer, 1996) and offered an 'institutionalised, electronically-mediated intercultural communication under the guidance of a "languacultural" expert (i.e. a teacher) for the purposes of foreign language learning and the development of intercultural competence' (Belz, 2003: 2).

With time and technological developments, collaborations began to incorporate both asynchronous (email, written documents, video or voice recordings) and synchronous exchange. Synchronous interactions in which participants could both see and hear one another were recognized as offering unique learning opportunities. As O'Dowd explains:

> [V]ideo conferencing was seen as developing students' abilities to interact with members of the target culture under the constraints of real-time communication and to also elicit, through face-to-face dialogue, the concepts and values which underlie their partners' behaviour and their opinions. (O'Dowd, 2018: 11)

Noting the frequent lack of formal structures or articulated learning objectives, Thorne (2010: 144) described this model of telecollaboration as 'intercultural communication in the wild.' As such, Thorne suggested, one-on-one collaborations between participants from different parts of the world 'present interesting, and perhaps even compelling, opportunities for intercultural exchange, agentive action, and meaning making' (Thorne, 2010: 144).

Current virtual exchange projects in higher education settings span a variety of academic fields and are often integral parts of syllabi. Together, university instructors design course modules that engage students in different parts of the world in communication and collaboration (O'Dowd, 2018). Often the outcomes of such interactions are projects or products tied to course objectives; a dominant model for this approach is the Collaborative Online International Learning (COIL) Institute for Globally Networked Learning in the Humanities (COIL, n.d.). In such exchanges, the emphasis is on both collaboration and examining different cultural and national experiences or interpretations of subject content (O'Dowd, 2018).

While virtual exchange projects are often designed by individual instructors, they can also follow what is known as a 'service provider' model. Independent organizations design curricula and online environments in which university students and others can collaborate. For example, Soliya, a non-profit founded after and in large part in response to the aftermath of the attacks in the US on 9/11, collaborates with university and youth organizations in Europe, the US and Southern Mediterranean countries on virtual exchange programs intended to facilitate 'dialogue exchange opportunities that bring together a diverse group of young people to explore an urgent theme affecting the global landscape today' (Soliya, 2020). The non-profit iEARN, which works primarily with secondary school students, has collaborated with more than 30,000 schools in 140 countries on a variety of projects which seek to provide 'a safe and structured environment in which young people can communicate; an opportunity to apply knowledge in service-learning projects; a community of educators and learners making a difference as part of the educational process' (iEARN, n.d.). The reach of virtual exchange continues to grow, including initiatives such as 'The Experiment Digital,' a two-month summer virtual exchange implemented by World Learning, which 'helps high school-aged youth become more civically engaged by empowering them to plan and execute a community service project'; in 2020, participants in this program included high school-aged Syrian refugees in Jordan and Lebanon (Stevens Initiative, 2020).

The past six years have seen increased interest in and support and funding for Virtual Exchange, accelerated by the pandemic. O'Dowd (2021) asks: '2020: the year virtual exchange finally came of age?' He goes on to introduce newer initiatives: the Stevens Initiative, with projects in the US and MENA region, was launched in 2015. UNICollaboration was established in 2016. In 2017 and 2018, the European Commission funded two projects providing training for university faculty, making possible large-scale research on impacts of virtual exchange (O'Dowd, 2021). Then came the era of COVID-19, in which classroom buildings were closed and traditional study abroad programs were put on hold. As faculty and staff collaborated to move classes and projects online, organizations and universities explored how virtual exchange can be integrated into strategies for what has been termed 'internationalization at home' (Nilsson, 2003) and into curricula (Cossey & Fischer, 2021; O'Dowd, 2021). A study of US community colleges found that many institutions built on or developed new virtual exchange programs in response to restrictions that made international travel, and therefore education abroad opportunities, impossible (Cossey & Fischer, 2021). The 'Digital Education Action Plan' (European Commission, 2020) offers an example of ongoing commitment to broadening virtual exchange opportunities. In the European Community Action Scheme for the Mobility of University Students, or Erasmus, 'blended mobility will be "mainstreamed" (i.e. integrated) … by introducing a "virtual learning" component to Erasmus' (European Commission, 2020: 38). Moreover, O'Dowd (2021) and Cossey and Fischer (2021) offer numerous examples of newly implemented academic and co-curricular online opportunities in US and European university contexts. Referring to one such co-curricular program, a US community college staff member shared, 'All over campus we have people that had never left the US. They didn't get this international thing. … The virtual world tours … are certainly bringing internationalization at home at almost no cost' (Cossey & Fischer, 2021: 4); it is important to note that a 'virtual world tour' in which participants may play a passive role is distinct from virtual exchange, which as the name suggests is predicated on participant interaction.

Despite differences in institutional settings, models and individual course goals, virtual exchange initiatives, including the one we explore in this book, share a commitment to experiential learning, collaborative critical inquiry and cross-curricular learning (Cummins & Sayers, 1995). Anticipated outcomes of online collaboration include the development of digital literacies and intercultural awareness (Guth & Helm, 2010); as such, these outcomes represent expected affordances of interactions in the virtual intercultural borderlands. This book attends, however, to the unexpected affordances of these borderlands – the action possibilities of person to person peacebuilding.

Understanding affordances and constraints

The constructs of 'affordances' and its opposite, 'constraints,' are now oft-used terms in language teaching and intercultural communication research – with various understandings and recontextualizations. The terms originate with psychologist Gibson's (1979) work in visual perception. Drawing from ecology, he described the interdependent relationship between organism and environment: what the environment 'offers the animal, what it provides or furnishes, either for good or ill,' and how different animals in turn see and use various aspects of that environment for various purposes (Gibson, 1979: 127). In other words, for Gibson, the world we perceive is more than the objects and organizations of space in our environment – it is also our *perceptions* of that environment and its objects and space, and how we perceive potential uses (or 'action possibilities') of the same. Hence, the chairs we sit on afford us the outcome of sitting, but they could just as easily be propped against a door to bar strangers from coming in (one affordance), or they could be broken down into kindling and used to light a fire on a winter night (yet another action possibility). Regardless of circumstance, at least three elements are needed for an affordance to emerge: an environment, an actor, and the action possibilities the actor perceives from what is available in the environment.

Gibson's definition and theory of 'affordances' has been taken up and adapted in varying contexts: from describing the affordances of new tools and technologies in the language classroom (Haines, 2015), to Harjanne and Tella's (2007: 202) construction of 'affordances' as 'the linguistic and social potential that the world and our environment "affords" to us or puts at our disposal.' Conole and Dyke (2016) begin a taxonomy of the affordances of communication technologies, which includes the potentials of immediate access to an astonishing amount of information, simulation experiences, discussion board platforms and recordability. Darhower

(2008: 50), in examining 'telecollaborative chat,' defines *linguistic* affordances in this way: 'any discursive move ... that intends or appears to activate a learner's awareness of specific language structures and/or lexical meaning,' such as learners asking directly about the meaning of words or teachers reformulating a learner's question. Van Lier (2000: 246), a key figure in adapting Gibson's affordances to the fields of sociolinguistics and language learning, explains his use of linguistic affordances thus: 'From an ecological perspective, the learner is immersed in an environment full of potential meanings. These meanings are available gradually as the learner *acts within and with* the environment' (emphasis added). Emphasizing learner action as he does, van Lier (2000) further underscores the centrality of learner agency as it relates to affordances and constraints, observing that only through participation and use can learners capitalize upon learning opportunities, with constraints on participation and use constituting barriers to the same.

In the context of foreign language teacher development, Harjanne and Tella (2007) envision affordances yet more broadly, writing that *'all* the conceptions of language, language proficiency, language teaching, studying and learning associated with it' may be considered affordances; in turn, language and teacher educators will avail themselves of different affordances or action possibilities, *'depending on what they regard as relevant'* (Harjanne & Tella, 2007, emphases added). Here we see emphasis fall on *teacher* agency: teachers must likewise use affordances to capitalize upon teaching opportunities for learners and for themselves. Tella (2005), importantly, makes a further distinction between 'dominant' and 'dormant' affordances, a distinction that sheds light on our understanding of what might be happening in the virtual intercultural borderlands of online exchange and how we might more purposefully engage with certain 'dormant' affordances. He explains that in the context of language teaching, 'dominant affordances' are what teachers *consciously* perceive and engage with in their work (for instance, peer collaboration and review as forms of authentic interaction). 'Dormant' affordances, conversely, are action possibilities teachers might not yet see or know about or with which they might refuse to engage (we use as an example – *again* – peer collaboration and review, albeit in *teacher*-centered contexts and classrooms). Another way to think of dormant affordances is that, while dormant affordances exist, uncertainty circulates around whether such affordances will be actualized (Sarathy & Scheutz, 2016). In other words, teachers must be able and willing to perceive affordances in the first place – and then use such affordances deliberately in their teaching (Feng Tang, 2019).

Returning to the environs of the virtual intercultural borderlands and to the voices of our participants, with Tella's (2005) help, we readily found evidence of how tutoring pairs availed themselves of the dominant or expected affordances. Tutors availed themselves of affordances to practice 'teaching,' to reflect on their experiences and to gain confidence before the start of their classroom practica the following semester. Afghan participants, similar to participants in Darhower's (2008) study, availed themselves of the opportunity to develop fluency and confidence while using English with their tutors. Throughout the project, tutors and Afghans alike clearly availed themselves of the affordance of evolving their intercultural communication competence (Byram, 1997; Deardorff, 2004; Ekici, 2018; Goodman, 2013). As we read through tutors' reflective writing and listened to the voices of participants captured in interview transcripts after their tutoring course had ended, however, we discovered another, unexpected outcome from the communicative affordances in the virtual intercultural borderlands. Not only was this an outcome we did not anticipate as emerging from the data, it was an outcome we believe is greater than the sum of its parts (English language teaching and intercultural communication). Briefly stated, as we coded and organized our data, what we discovered from participants' voices – in their reflections on and retellings of their experiences – was that the communicative affordances of the virtual intercultural borderlands led them also to discursively build peace, person to person, as participants' voices consistently brought to life the elements of peacebuilding articulated by Lederach (2003) and then adapted by Broome and Collier (2012).

As we ourselves, as authors, have worked in a similar virtual space in order to write this book – meeting online through videoconferencing from sites as distant as Izmir, Turkey; Tampico, Mexico; and from across the US including Arizona, California, Massachusetts, Missouri, New Hampshire and New York – we find it necessary to close this chapter on 'context' by taking time to consider how spaces such as our 'virtual intercultural borderlands' have been conceptualized, to what ends, and how those 'ends' might enrich our understanding of the same.

Conceptualizing the virtual intercultural borderlands

Naples and Méndez (2014: 2) provide us with a foothold into this discussion by reminding us that implications from any form of 'border' study apply to both geographic and imagined borders, to which we add *virtual* borders, 'territorial dividing lines as well as sociocultural boundaries' and likewise digital boundaries. What are at stake on and at these borders, however, are the same: identities and how we make meaning; questions of inclusion and exclusion; and how divisions between self and other can be erased, crossed or more deeply entrenched, in *this* study, through interaction on those borders and in the borderlands between interlocutors from different cultures. While theoretical trends conceptualized as 'border politics' make their primary concern how to understand contestations and confrontations at literal and figural borders, we find it equally compelling to consider how the virtual intercultural borderlands we write of have afforded our participants the action possibility of peacebuilding. They are thus in line with Brantmeier's (2008: 69) words, whose term we adapt for this book, as he describes '*intercultural* borderlands' (emphasis added) as 'fluid, liminal spaces of intercultural opportunity that, when opened, potentially bridge cultural differences and foster positive relationships.' These are opportunities we have discovered in the virtual intercultural borderlands as well.

Anzaldúa's (1987) landmark book, *Borderlands/La Frontera: The New Mestiza*, helps us further understand the concept of a liminal state, the state we use or are in when we move from one phase of our 'self'/our identity to the next. For Anzaldúa, a self-described 'Chicana' born in the US, 'liminal' was a permanent state, as she constantly experienced being perceived by others as neither 'Chicana' nor 'American,' but 'other,' always, and in that otherness, living a life both fraught and enriched by hybridity, instability, a state of in-betweenness. Ultimately she conceptualized 'borderlands' as 'paradoxical, contested spaces of everyday life,' 'a third country' which she brings to life for us through one vivid example:

> The US-Mexican border *es una herida abierta* [an open wound] where the Third World grates against the first and bleeds. And before a scab forms, it haemorrhages again, the lifeblood of two worlds merging to form a third country – a border culture. (Anzaldúa, 1987: 25)

Such spaces – as described so strikingly by Anzaldúa and as argued in the work of Naples and Méndez (2014) – are places of 'resistance and continual reconstruction where new identities are formed and "radical political subjectivities" are forged' (Naples & Méndez, 2014: 4). While again, the 'context' of our *virtual* intercultural borderlands may be different from the liminal spaces that made up Anzaldúa's 'third country,' the features she conceptualizes in *Borderlands/La Frontera* allow us to offer 'person to person peacebuilding' and commitment thereto as – at the very least – part of the formation of the new 'radical political subjectivities' (Nayak & Suchland, 2006) our participants evolved during their interactions in the virtual intercultural borderlands.

Another important way of understanding the borderlands we explore in this book is through Pratt's (1991: 37) construct of 'contact zones' and their various arts: 'autoethnography, transculturation, critique, collaboration, bilingualism, mediation, parody, denunciation, imaginary dialogue, vernacular expression – these are some of the literate arts of the contact zone.' Pratt (1991) conceptualizes these arts and the contact zones in which they occur by considering the implications of a letter written in 1613 by an Andean in Cuzco, Peru, whose name was Felipe Guaman Poma de Ayala. Guaman Poma's letter – written in a mix of Quechua and 'ungrammatical, expressive Spanish' – was addressed to King Phillip III of Spain (Pratt, 1991: 34). The letter, Pratt narrates, was 1200 pages long and titled *The First New Chronicle and Good Government*. It was discovered in an archive in Copenhagen, Denmark, in 1908, although no-one knew how it had got to said archive or even how to read it, since Andeans were not thought to be literate and Quechua was not known as a written language. Peruvianists and Americanists alike were confused, Pratt writes, and it was not until the 1970s that 'Western scholars found ways of reading Guaman Poma's *New Chronicle and Good Government* as the extraordinary intercultural tour de force that it was. The letter got there, only 350 years too late, a miracle and a terrible tragedy' (Pratt, 1991: 34).

Most important for our purposes here, Pratt (1991) situates the letter (along with its readings and misreadings) as part of the 'arts' of 'contact zones,' spaces that shed further light on the virtual intercultural borderlands we examine. Pratt (1991) situates writing and literacy as follows:

> Writing and literacy in what I like to call the contact zones. I use this term to refer to social spaces where cultures meet, clash, and grapple with each other, often in contexts of highly asymmetrical relations of power, such as colonialism, slavery, or their aftermaths as they are lived out in many parts of the world today. (Pratt, 1991: 34)

As with Anzaldúa's 'borderlands,' we view Pratt's definition of 'contact zones' as important for thinking about virtual intercultural borderlands. Specifically, the social structural force of the English language is what brought participants together in the borderlands that we explore, and while we rarely saw participants openly 'clash' or 'grapple with each other,' we do see how relationships could be construed as 'highly asymmetrical relations of power,' and we know of course that tutors and students alike live in societies in which power *is* highly asymmetrical and in which there are clashes, grapplings and (even terrible) divisions. In the virtual intercultural borderlands that came to life in our project, however, we found in many participants' voices an openness and even eagerness to share power: we found Afghan students giving their tutors homework; we found tutors of EAL equally intimidated by the social structural force of 'standard' English as they imagined their students would be. Despite 'highly asymmetrical relations of power,' we frequently read and heard about how participants sought to balance those relationships, acknowledge power, and humble themselves in the faces thereof.

We also hear and will share how participants engaged in the 'arts of the contact zone' (Pratt, 1991: 37) in the virtual intercultural borderlands. They took part, for instance, in 'autoethnography' as they reflected by putting themselves in the center of their 'cultural analysis,' just as Byram (1997) calls for the importance of 'critical cultural awareness' as a dimension of intercultural communication competence. Together, participants explored the impacts of 'transculturation' as they encountered over the course of a semester the tensions, merging and converging of cultures (Ortiz, 1947). They engaged in 'critique' (of structures), 'collaboration' (to learn English), 'bilingualism' (and multilingualism), 'mediation' and negotiation as they worked to understand each other. They took part in 'parody' ('playing' teacher, mimicking 'Americans') and 'denunciation' (of the Taliban, of the US); they took pleasure in teaching each other 'vernacular expressions' in multiple languages. So, very much like Pratt's (1991) 'contact zones,' participants deployed the arts of the same as they worked together in the virtual intercultural borderlands.

We read in participants' voices and texts an understanding of the virtual intercultural borderlands which is supported also by descriptions of Bhabha's (2006) 'Third Space.' Bhabha describes this space as follows:

> It is that Third Space, although unrepresentable in itself, which constitutes the discursive conditions of enunciation that ensure that the meaning and symbols of culture have no primordial unity or fixity; that even the same signs can be appropriated, translated, rehistoricized and read anew.... it is the 'inter' – the cutting edge of translation and negotiation, the inbetween space – that carries the burden of the meaning of culture. ... And by exploring this Third Space, we may elude the politics of polarity and emerge as the others of ourselves. (Bhabha, 2006: 55)

From Bhabha's (2006) description, we find his emphasis on the 'discursive conditions of enunciation' integral to our analyses of participants' voices (in reflective journals and interview transcripts) according to discursive indicators of peacebuilding and to our own critical discourse analysis thereof. His mention of the 'inter' and the 'in-between space' of transition and transformation is actualized in the virtual liminal space of videoconferencing in which our participants from dramatically different cultures met and occupied – a new, 'Third Space' we find beautifully summed up by Motha (2014: 47):

> For Bhabha, liminal spaces are spaces of hope and possibility because they can serve as sites of transition and ambiguity, sites in which individuals are permitted to be neither wholly one category or culture nor the other, sites in which hybridity is allowed and can therefore be formed and imagined, become visible and maybe even be explored. (Motha, 2014: 47)

It is the great possibilities for change and movement toward Lederach's (2003: 35) 'horizon of preferred future' within these liminal spaces that allow us to share in the 'hope and possibility' that Motha (2014) and others[1] offer as emerging from sites such as borderlands, contact zones, Third Spaces – what we find encompassed in the 'the virtual intercultural borderlands' of online exchange.

Our understandings of the virtual intercultural borderlands are further informed by the work of Crozet *et al.* (1999: 11), who envision the possibility of a liminal space they describe as a 'third place' – a 'meeting place' in which interactants from different cultural and linguistic backgrounds 'meet and communicate successfully.' In their edited volume, *Striving for the Third Place: Intercultural Competence through Language Teaching*, Lo Bianco *et al.* (1999) advocate for a paradigm shift away from a conceptualization of language learning as a process of assimilation in which language proficiency is measured in relation to users of the target language. They describe and critique paradigms for the teaching of culture in the language classroom, focusing first on a 'high culture' or literary studies approach; then on the 'culture studies' paradigm in which learners learn about but remain 'external' to a country and culture; and finally on the 'culture as practice' model, in which culture is perceived as relatively static, leading – the authors argue – to the likelihood of stereotyping (Crozet *et al.*, 1999: 17–19). They describe instead 'intercultural language teaching' as a process of discovery which takes place in and leads to the development of a hybrid space, or 'third place.' Using language is a cultural act, they argue (see also Kramsch, 1993), which simultaneously emerges from and creates the third place:

> a meeting place where the understanding of how different worldviews operate (in one's own linguaculture and foreign linguacultures) frees the mind to explore and at the same time to create interculturality. (Crozet *et al.*, 1999: 23)

In this dynamic space of 'interaction, hybridity, and exploration,' participants are not observers but experiencers of difference (Crozet *et al.*, 1999: 15). The third place is not a place of accommodation but one of negotiation in which participants become aware of their own as well as other cultures and worldviews. Acknowledging the complexity of cross-cultural interactions, the authors cite De Sousa (1999: 2), who describes possible reactions to such experiences as ranging from 'a form of seduction or confrontation, discovery or recovery, desire or loathing, wonder or disillusionment, peace or war.' While the process is neither predictable nor simple, through their dialogic encounters (Bakhtin, 1981) with others in the third place, learners can become aware of their own experiences and beliefs and cease to be 'servant[s]' to their own cultural boundaries. Of particular relevance to our understanding of the virtual intercultural borderlands as a potential site for peacebuilding is the notion that successful navigation of this third place requires not only linguistic and cultural knowledge but 'choosing harmony/peace over conflict/war orientation' (Crozet *et al.*, 1999: 15). 'It is in the intercultural space,' the authors write, 'that unity and diversity can be reconciled' (Crozet *et al.*, 1999: 13).

In the analysis that follows, we begin to share how participants choose 'harmony/peace' over 'conflict/war' orientations, as their voices and discourses change through their work together in the virtual intercultural borderlands, which ultimately afforded participants the unexpected action possibilities of person to person peacebuilding. In Chapter 4, we look at how participants' interactions in these borderlands led them to build peace personally; in Chapter 5, relationally; in Chapter 6, structurally. In this chapter, by providing a greater understanding of the complex contexts of our research – including Afghanistan, US graduate TESOL programs, the astonishingly diverse home countries of participants, and the virtual intercultural borderlands of online exchange – we have sought to both complicate and enrich the construct of 'context,' as our participants' contexts have both complicated and enriched the analyses we turn to in the next three chapters.

Note

(1) For more on the importance of hope, and especially 'critical hope,' see Duncan-Andrade (2009) and Zembylas (2014).

4 Person to Person Peacebuilding at the Personal Level

This is the first of three chapters in which we turn our focus to the participants' voices at the heart of this book to examine discursive constructions of what Lederach (2003: 35) describes as 'preferred,' positive changes which evidence peacebuilding: in this chapter, at the personal level of peacebuilding. At the same time, here and throughout the book, we are guided by the perspective put forth by Broome and Collier (2012: 254): that 'peacebuilding scholarship/praxis that focuses on a single dimension – personal, relational, or structural – in isolation offers an overly narrow view of peacebuilding.' Personal change is deeply entwined with change at the relational level and can be caused by or result in structural inequities (or greater structural equity). Our decision to focus on only one peacebuilding dimension per chapter is thus a heuristic decision intended to help us delineate and analyze in greater and clearer depth the individual discursive indicators of peacebuilding at each level. Ultimately, however, we argue that it is the accumulation and constellation of these discursive indicators at all three levels which evidence the unexpected affordance of peacebuilding that emerged from participants' discourses in the virtual intercultural borderlands.

We begin by outlining the personal dimension of peacebuilding as discussed in the works of Lederach (2003) and Broome and Collier (2012). Then we turn to analysis of participant voices, gathered in the form of: (1) written reflections submitted by the EAL teachers as part of their graduate coursework; and (2) transcripts of topic-oriented interviews conducted with both graduate students and Afghan participants after the project had been completed.

The Personal Dimension of Peacebuilding

Like many intercultural communication scholars (e.g. Deardorff, 2004; Ting-Toomey & Kurogi, 1998), Lederach (2003: 36) frames change in relation to conflict transformation as a never-ending process, a journey toward a more peaceful horizon which is always there but can never be touched. Our focus in this chapter is on what Lederach (2003: 23) describes as 'changes affected in and desired for the individual.' At the personal level of peacebuilding, Lederach guides us to seek evidence of positive change in an individual's:

- physical well-being
- self-esteem
- emotional stability
- capacity to perceive accurately
- spiritual integrity. (Lederach, 2003: 24–25)

Building on Lederach's (2003) framework, Broome and Collier (2012: 251) propose that change at the personal level can be observed in individuals' preferences and self-descriptions in relation to conflict, greater open-mindedness, a newfound or increased willingness to engage with the other and/or engagement in efforts to minimize destructive effects of conflict. As we can see, there are significant intersections between the two frameworks (Table 4.1). Shifts in self-descriptions can result in changes in attitudes toward and an increased willingness to engage with the other (Broome & Collier, 2012: 251): as an EAL future teacher gains confidence in her own linguistic abilities, for example, she leverages her experiences as a language learner to find common ground with her Afghan counterpart. New ways of perceiving, thinking about and reacting in and toward a situation lead to changes in group identification (Broome & Collier, 2012) and, sometimes, to increased self-esteem or greater emotional stability (Lederach, 2003: 23): for instance, as they share their own experiences in countries undergoing conflict, US-based tutors overcome fears of self-disclosure and form powerful bonds with their Afghan students.

Table 4.1 Dimensions of peacebuilding: Positive change at the personal level of peacebuilding

At the PERSONAL level of peacebuilding, positive change in the following:	
Lederach (2003)	Broome and Collier (2012)
Cognition	Self-perception
Emotion	Perceptions of the other (reducing enemy images)
Spirituality	Increased open-mindedness
Perception	Increased willingness to engage in dialogue
Physical well-being	
Emotional stability	
Self-esteem	

The frameworks of Broome and Collier (2012) and Lederach (2003) offer us, then, valuable discursive indicators of person to person peacebuilding to help structure our analysis. Nonetheless, we recognize the limitations of frameworks to capture the complexity of human emotion and experience. We note, too, that within any one excerpt, we may find multiple discursive indicators of peacebuilding and at multiple levels. Finally, we acknowledge the challenge of choosing, from the many powerful interactions participants wrote and spoke about, a limited number of examples to analyze and share: we thus share quotes that stood out to us as the most compelling and most representative discursive evidence of peacebuilding – and change in the direction of peacebuilding, or Lederach's (2003: 35) 'horizon of preferred future' – from among our participants' voices.

Broome and Collier (2012) explain in greater depth change work at the personal level of peacebuilding which intersects with and is fundamental to intercultural communication:

> The focus is on maximizing potential for individual changes in self-perceptions, narratives, and perceptions of the other, reducing enemy images while increasing open-mindedness and willingness to engage with the other through dialogue and other forms of constructive conflict transformation. (Broome & Collier, 2012: 251)

The participants whose voices we share do not negotiate treaties or lay down weapons. They are not enemy combatants and do not view their tutoring counterparts as 'enemies' with whom they have to make peace. These intercultural collaborators are, however, from vastly different backgrounds, and almost one-third of the participants come from countries experiencing ongoing conflict, including Afghanistan, Iraq, Syria and Ukraine. In the words and voices we examine throughout the book, in US-based tutors' reflective writing and in transcripts of topic-oriented interviews with tutors and Afghans alike, we find evidence that these participants are social actors who avail themselves of the communicative affordances of the virtual intercultural borderlands to build peace, person to person, through their discourses.

This chapter is divided into sections and subsections focused on particular discursive indicators of the personal dimension of peacebuilding. We look first at how participants talk about themselves. Next, we explore what they write and say about others. We conclude with their 'beliefs and attitudes' about 'the world.' In each section, we discuss implications of the changes we observe, acknowledge overlaps across discursive indicators of peacebuilding, and explore intersections between intercultural communication and peacebuilding, intersections which can help us more deliberately leverage the affordances of peacebuilding available in the virtual intercultural borderlands of online exchange. Implications for teaching are explored in Chapter 7.

Changes in Participants' Beliefs and Attitudes about Themselves: Resistance, Fear, Self-Confidence

We begin our exploration of change at the personal level of peacebuilding with evidence of shift in participants' beliefs and attitudes about themselves (Broome & Collier, 2012). Lederach (2003: 39) suggests that the ways in which people see themselves are reflected in narratives of 'who they are, where they have come from, and what they fear they will become or lose.' Moreover, as the construction of the other can simultaneously serve to reinforce and protect the self (Abu-Lughod, 1991), shifts in self-descriptions can be linked to changes in ways of thinking about and reacting toward the other.

In the words and experience of Tayba, a US-based tutor, we find powerful evidence of how emotional change (Lederach, 2003: 24) can lead to an increased capacity to 'perceive accurately' and an increased willingness to engage with the other (Broome & Collier, 2012), both of which are critical indicators of peacebuilding. In the process, she overcomes dramatic resistance.

Like all of the US-based participants, Tayba composed six written reflections over the course of the project. In her fifth reflection, as she recalls her initial attitudes about the tutoring project, Tayba discursively constructs her collaborator as 'other,' describing him as 'the student' and 'someone from Afghanistan.' Her emotions are powerful and indicate her initial *unwillingness* to openly engage with her counterpart:

> I had fears with working with someone from Afghanistan. It was not about the student personally, but rather the culture. I was unsure how accepted he would be working with an American student. He began asking me questions about where I lived and what college I attended. I was fearful to answer these questions and did not give him specifics. (Tayba)

Tayba was born and spent most of her childhood in Iraq. She has lived in a country in conflict and her fear is palpable as she describes her resistance to engaging with the other (Broome & Collier, 2012), her Afghan counterpart. As we note her initial unwillingness to share information about herself, we also find it significant that she attributes her 'fears' to the 'culture' of Afghanistan but doesn't say more about the culture: rather, she states next her uncertainty around whether 'someone from Afghanistan' would be accepting of 'working with an *American* student' (emphasis added). Here we see Tayba discursively foreground national identity as significant (Afghan/American) as she describes their collaboration: she pushes to the fore national identity, as one key difference (Wodak *et al.*, 2009), rather than what they might have in common. This difference drives her fear, even to the point where she perceives potential threat in what might be normal 'getting-to-know-you' questions, 'specific' answers to which she was reluctant to disclose.

An 'unwillingness' to engage with an 'other' suggests an initial resistance to what it takes to build peace at the personal level. We find this same element of peacebuilding intersecting with and embedded in 'self-disclosure,' which plays an important role in intercultural communication (Croucher et al., 2010, 2012; Maier et al., 2013; Schug et al., 2010). In intercultural competence frameworks (Byram, 1997; Deardorff, 2004), self-disclosure may be referred to as 'openness.' Research on self-disclosure has found that norms regarding the sharing of personal information vary from the practices of one culture to another (Croucher et al., 2010). Willingness to engage in self-disclosure has been linked, too, to the nature of the relationships between interlocutors in studies examining friendship and intimacy (Collins & Miller, 1994; Wong & Bond, 1999).

With time, people may become more open to self-disclosure as they become closer to their interlocutors (Lustig & Koester, 2010). Tayba's reflections do not reveal how much she shared about herself over the course of her interactions with her Afghan counterpart. They do offer evidence, however, that information her student shared about himself led to a critical shift in her perspective, a shift that indicates peacebuilding at the personal level. In Tayba's discourse, her ways of perceiving, thinking about and reacting toward her student become shaped by her knowledge of his experiences with conflict:

> In my last session, I learned that his life was in danger for being able to speak English and having previous experience with the U.S. Army. He said he lived in a safe city that was far away from political wars we hear on the TV. I was upset that I had judged him and learned that he is just like me, a human! (Tayba)

Here we note a change in what Lederach (2003) terms 'emotional stability.' Despite or perhaps because of her initial fear, Tayba's words offer evidence of profound change in her feelings, beliefs and attitudes. As the focus of her reflection moves from her own emotions to her narrative regarding her student, she shares a distinctive shift in perspective, discursively evincing the unexpected affordance of peacebuilding through intercultural communication and online English language tutoring. Through their exchanges in the virtual intercultural borderlands, Tayba has gained vital knowledge about her Afghan counterpart. No longer the representative of a country or a culture, Tayba's student is an individual whose 'life was in danger for being able to speak English and having previous experience with the U.S. Army,' information that complicates her earlier perceptions and assumptions: the fact that her student's life was in danger for speaking English and working with the military lends new, profound nuance to this 'other,' perhaps even nuance she especially understands, given her childhood in Iraq. Integral to Tayba's shift in her perception of the other is also a profound acknowledgment of her initial framing of her tutoring partner as someone to be feared. Now she questions her own ways of perceiving and reacting toward a situation (Broome & Collier, 2012): 'I was upset that I had judged him.' Tayba discursively constructs her partner and herself now in ways that transcend national identity and cut across national difference; in the process, she acknowledges their likeness, not only demonstrating a willingness to engage with the other but declaring a powerful commonality: 'he's just like me, a human!'

As we see in Tayba's experience, bringing together international participants for synchronous online interactions created space for 'maximiz[ing] potential for individual changes in self-perceptions' (Broome & Collier, 2012: 251). Participants' engagement in virtual interaction, intercultural communication and language teaching and learning can lead to 'preferred change' at the personal level (Lederach, 2003), as evidenced in increased development of tutor and student self-esteem and self-confidence, an outcome that supports both teacher development and peacebuilding at the personal level.

Unlike Tayba who exhibited initial resistance, from the very outset of the project Sangmu, a future EAL teacher, frames her interactions with her student, and even her concerns, as an opportunity for growth. 'We might get improvement from the uncertainty and fears,' she writes before the project begins. As she faces and overcomes these fears and uncertainties, we see a powerful change in Sangmu's self-perception over the course of her interactions with her Afghan counterpart. Unlike most of the tutors who grew up speaking English at home or had studied English since middle school, Sangmu began studying English only as an undergraduate student. Born in the Tibetan autonomous region of China, she completed her education in schools where Tibetan was the medium of instruction; Mandarin was taught as a second or 'foreign' language.

When asked to reflect on the question, 'What fears or concerns do you have about teaching English grammar, about tutoring, about teaching online, or about working with your tutee?'[1] before meeting her Afghan student, Sangmu wrote the following:

> I am fear about this project since I don't have any idea about the tutees's field of knowledge, his/her English ability. I am worry that if we could not understand each other because of the accent. (Sangmu)

In this first reflection, Sangmu is concerned that she will not be able to communicate effectively with her collaborator. Notably, she discursively constructs her partner through metonymy by representing her student through 'field of knowledge' and 'his/her English ability.' More specifically, she defines her student through 'instrumentalization,' objectivating her partner through 'the instrument with which she [and they] can carry out an action [communication]' – which is English (van Leeuwen, 2008: 46). In turn, Sangmu backgrounds the identity of her as yet unknown partner behind the instrument of 'English' (and ability, and accent) which become, in turn, foregrounded. Van Leeuwen (2008: 47) observes an important implication with this use of metonymy through instrumentalization: that 'it can lend impersonal authority or force to an action or quality of a social actor,' an authority supported here by Sangmu's 'fear.' Although Sangmu uses a plural with 'we could not understand each other,' which includes her student, her words combined with her use of instrumentalization emphasize her lack of confidence in her own linguistic proficiency in English, as she expresses 'worry' that 'the accent' might block their abilities to understand each other.

Still, Sangmu seeks to identify commonalities on which to build her relationship with her student. In another reflection, Sangmu shares what she has learned about how English is generally taught in Afghanistan:

> [I]t is taught through the tradition translation method, there is very few native English teachers, and even the English teachers teach English by their mother tongue. First of all, the teaching and learning situation is quite similar with my own experience back in-home country. It is an advantage that we could exchange the ideas of study. (Sangmu)

Sangmu's use of the word 'similar' highlights the commonalities she sees between her experiences and those of her student. Both are learners of English, both have been taught using the '[grammar] translation method,' and both had limited opportunities to use English outside the classroom. With her use of the verb 'exchange' in 'we could exchange the ideas of study,' Sangmu frames herself as a collaborator with her student; the two are learning with and from one another, and she has moved past 'instrumentalizing' her partner through English, instead, with 'we,' forming an 'in group' with him built on mutual exchange.

As we see in her final reflection, interactions with her student have led to powerful change in Sangmu's beliefs and attitudes about herself. She writes:

> I had mentioned in my first journal I had expressed that it is difficult to change my role from being a long-time student to an instructor. I had lots of anxieties about me if I could instruct her well? How am I going to work on this project well? If I could make this project successful? I felt more nervous when I knew that she had an even longer experience of English than me and her English is genuinely advanced. However, anxieties and worries can be overcome with a willing of hard working with confidence. I found that teaching and learning situation of my tutee is quite similar to my own experience back in-home country. That produced many common views about English study between us. (Sangmu)

While Sangmu still fronts 'anxieties and worries' through her use of the passive voice, they can nevertheless 'be overcome.' Sangmu focuses here on her own strengths as she explicitly points to the role of 'hard work' and of 'confidence' in the process of overcoming. By constructing their shared 'common view,' she no longer objectivates herself or her partner through the instrumentalization of English (van Leeuwen, 2008: 46). Instead, acknowledging and building on the commonalities she and her student share, Sangmu has leveraged her own experience as a learner of English as an asset, as she makes the self-described transition from 'long-time student' to 'instructor.'

Sangmu's initial uncertainty about her English proficiency and her ability to successfully take on the role of 'instructor' was not unique. Many multilingual tutors shared feelings of vulnerability based on their own language backgrounds. For example, Jiang, a US-based Mandarin speaker from China, expresses concern about how his English – and how *he* – might be perceived in an interview following the completion of the project:

> Actually, to be honest with you, I was very intimidated. Very intimidated. Because, my English was, not very fluent at that time, and I was afraid the student would want a native USA speaker, not just a Chinese English speaker, and I was afraid that I might be, got, I was discriminate? ... Because, I have to turn on the camera, and I have, not, an American face. I just imagine that the student may be disappointed. (Jiang)

Jiang's repetition ('very intimidated. Very intimidated') in his discourse re-enacts the strength of the stress he felt at the outset of the project (Wodak *et al.*, 2009: 93). In the words 'afraid,' 'concern' and 'disappointed,' we hear Jiang discursively construct both his own emotions and the imagined attitude of the other, his future student, who he fears will discriminate against him for not having 'an American face.' In Jiang's experience, we also see the perpetuation of the ideology and 'myth of the native speaker' (see, for instance, Chow, 2014; Davies, 2003; Hackert, 2013; Kumaravadivelu, 2014; Medgyes, 2012; Swan *et al.*, 2015), a global ideology which constructs 'native' speakers as somehow uniquely qualified to be language teachers, and much more so than 'non-native' speakers. Here we note that confronting this ideology in depth and detail remains essential for equity in the field of TESOL (see Swan *et al.*, 2015, for a thorough overview), but is also beyond the scope of our work in this book. For Jiang (and other tutors), however, the ramifications of this myth are deeply personal and are tied to his beliefs about himself as an English teacher/tutor and the attitudes he imagines others will take toward him. Hence we provide a brief outline of this ideology and myth below.

Within the field of English language teaching, 'native-speakerism' has been thought to mirror narratives such as Orientalism (Said, 1978) and colonialist myths like those of Robinson Crusoe 'civilizing' Man Friday (Pennycook, 1998), leading to the construction of 'an imagined, problematic *generalized Other*' (italics in original) and its counterpart, 'the unproblematic Self of the "native speaker"' (Pennycook, 1998: 386). As an embodiment of English language and 'Western culture' (Braine, 1999; Canagarajah, 1999; Holliday, 2005; Kubota, 2002; Kumaravadivelu, 2014; Pennycook, 1994; Swan *et al.*, 2015), the mythical 'native speaker' of

English serves to reinforce discourses of systemic racism, colonialism (Kubota, 2002; Motha, 2014), linguistic imperialism and capitalism (see Canagarajah, 1999; Phillipson, 1992, 2009; Swan *et al.*, 2015). Motha (2014: 16) argues that 'associations between English ... and Whiteness, prestige, and power ... work together to exclude racial minorities ... from ownership of and even access to the English language.' While the NNEST (non-native English speaking teachers) movement in TESOL has offered an organized critique of the term 'non-native,' advocating for increased professional recognition of individuals with a wide range of accents and linguistic experiences (Braine, 1999; Moussu & Llurda, 2008), as we see here, 'the native speaker myth' continues to reinforce social, racial and economic structures that define or limit access to what for many is seen as a valuable resource, English (see also, Chapter 6). As for the state of the TESOL profession now, we agree with Kumaravadivelu's (2014) characterization of the field as 'schizophrenic': that is, despite the impressive and growing knowledge production contributed by so-called 'non-native speakers' in TESOL (including one author in *this* book), 'the deafening discourse on the marginality of the majority has not changed the ground reality much. If anything, the forces of domination seem to be getting even more entrenched' (Kumaravadivelu, 2014).

In the case of Jiang, we clearly see how he is experiencing feelings related to the 'marginality of the majority.' As Jiang recalls his emotions at the start of the project, he describes his English as 'not very fluent at the time,' suggesting that the intimidation he felt came from a lack of confidence in his linguistic proficiency. However, he then ties his fear directly to his national or cultural identity and, by extension, to his appearance: 'I was afraid the student would want a native USA speaker, not just a Chinese English speaker.' His self-perception as other exemplifies the associations Motha points to between Whiteness, or in Jiang's case an absence of Whiteness, and English; he fears blatant discrimination: 'I have, not, an American face.'

Despite the initial fears he describes, when asked if he was discriminated against, Jiang is happy to elaborate:

> As soon as we talked, that kind of feeling, that sense, just disappeared. ... I think she learned from me like, I am an international student in the USA, and Asian students could also be English tutor, to Afghanistan students, like, that's very global ... and I think she learned that we, as second, we as non-native English speakers, we both have insights, but we both want, wish, we both eager to speak like a native speaker, in the way we express our ideas, not through, like, simple sentence, but more like sentences in which we can express our insights, like complete, complex, all native and complex, like that. (Jiang)

As with Sangmu, Jiang's increased willingness to engage with the other (Broome & Collier, 2012) accompanies an increase in self-confidence and self-esteem (Lederach, 2003). Of his student he concludes, 'I think she learned from me.' Rather than rejecting his identity as 'an international student,' an act of self-othering, he affirms that his knowledge and experience are valuable assets and calls into question the very native speaker myth underlying his initial fears. 'Asian students could also be English tutor,' he asserts, claiming for himself and for others the right to serve as teachers of English; moreover, both Jiang and Zahra (his Afghan student) are 'Asian,' as he acknowledges elsewhere in his interview. Jiang and Zahra have become a 'we,' an in-group, with 'ideas' and 'insights' to be shared. At the same time, while we note a shift in Jiang's self-perception and self-confidence, we acknowledge, too, the complexity of relinquishing long-standing constructions such as that of the mythical other both Jiang and Zahra seek to resemble, evidenced in their combined insistence on wanting 'to speak like a native speaker' and their mutual desire (as Jiang constructs it) to 'express' their 'insights' and 'ideas not through, like, simple sentence,' but in ways that are 'complete, complex, all native and complex.'

Changes in participants' beliefs and attitudes about themselves were not unique to the tutors. We find discursive evidence of a shift in self-description in the words of Sadaf, an Afghan participant; like all of the Afghan students, she was interviewed after the project was complete. Reflecting on her experiences in the virtual intercultural borderlands, Sadaf makes an explicit connection between her interactions with her US-based tutor and both her self-esteem and her self-confidence. 'Now I can speak with you,' she affirms to the interviewer, offering a concrete result of her participation in the virtual exchange: 'it was really good for me.' She continues:

> I appreciated every moment spending with her and you know it was really good for me, a good experience, and I am really grateful of her, because she helped me to build my self-esteem and also my self confidence that now I can speak with you. Before that, it was hard for me. I don't even know meeting with foreigners especially Americans. (Sadaf)

Sadaf's repeated use of 'good' discursively accentuates the impact her interactions had on her beliefs and attitudes about herself, as does her emphasis on 'every moment.' Before participating in this project, Sadaf explains, she had had limited opportunities to interact with 'foreigners, especially Americans.' Sadaf ties her increased willingness to engage with the other, her self-esteem and her self-confidence (all indicators of peacebuilding at the personal level) directly to her interactions in the virtual intercultural borderlands. Of her international tutor, Sadaf affirms, 'I am really grateful of her.'

Changes in Participants' Beliefs and Attitudes about Others: Reconfiguring Perceptions, Out-Groups and In-Groups

As we continue our analysis of how change at the personal level of peacebuilding is evidenced in participants' discourses, we turn next to evidence of shifts in participants' beliefs and attitudes about others. 'Attitudes,' key elements of the peacebuilding frameworks we draw on in our analysis, are also integral parts of intercultural competence frameworks (Byram, 1997; Deardorff, 2006b; Lynch & Hanson, 1998; Okayama *et al.*, 2001). In the voices of project participants, we find evidence that the virtual intercultural borderlands became a site for the examination and (re)formation of participants' sense not only of self but also of others. We find evidence of change in participants' ways of perceiving, thinking about and reacting in and toward a situation (Broome & Collier, 2012), evidence of change in participants' preferences or personal views (Broome & Collier, 2012), and an 'increased capacity to perceive accurately' (Lederach, 2003: 24).

Relatedly, Broome and Collier (2012: 253) frame peacebuilding at the personal level as 'a process through which personal views, group identification, inter-group relationships, group representations, [and] relationships within and across groups' change. In the words of Nadiya, a US-based participant from Ukraine, we see evidence of cognitive change which leads to a shift in how she represents groups and, as we explore later in this chapter, change in her sense of group identity, which is tied to perceptions of both self and other.

From the start of the project, Nadiya articulates a desire to examine, and ultimately change, her beliefs and attitudes about others as she puts forward a desire to learn more about a country and a group of people. Before her first tutoring session, Nadiya lays out what she hopes to learn about Afghanistan and about her student:

> I want to learn more about this country and its people, about their culture and education. I want to change my stereotypes (that are in my mind) about Afghani and change my attitude toward Afghanistan. (Nadiya)

Nadiya links the acquisition of knowledge to the potential for cognitive change as she admits her preconceived 'stereotypes' and 'attitude,' which remain in her 'mind' only. The implications of her stereotypes may be interpreted in her discourse: in her first group representation, through her word choices, 'this country,' 'its people,' Nadiya discursively constructs a plural or collective other ('people') who belong to the country (as opposed to a country belonging to the people), a construction which, by the possessive pronoun 'its,' discursively backgrounds 'people' to the place they come from and whatever preconceived notions she may have about that place. Just as we saw Sangmu represent her tutoring partner through the instrumentalization of English, discursively endowing greater authority on her student, here we see something of the opposite as Nadiya refers to the people through a form of spatialization (van Leeuwen, 2008), which backgrounds the social actors ('people') to the place they come from ('Afghanistan'). In this instance, in Nadiya's view, the agency of Afghans (generally) is constrained by where they come from. As she frames this out-group as distinctly different and both literally and figuratively distant from herself, Nadiya simultaneously suggests a willingness to engage with and a barrier between herself and this plural other.

Intercultural communication scholars observe that increased knowledge can contribute to increased understanding about the differences among cultures and languages, beliefs, and increased awareness of stereotypes and assumptions (Huber & Reynolds, 2014). Nadiya does not elaborate on her attitudes and beliefs here, nor does she share the source of what she herself terms her initial 'stereotypes.' However, in her final reflection she shares that initially she worried that 'Afghani people' would be 'rude, impatient, or unable to learn anything.' In this same reflection, she reports having achieved her goal to learn more about a group she refers to as 'Afghani':

> Before the project I knew nothing about these people and I was afraid that they may be rude, or impatient, or unable to learn anything. But they are the same as we all, they are intelligent, they are pleasant, they have a strong desire to learn something new. (Nadiya)

Nadiya now describes 'these people' as 'pleasant, they have a strong desire to learn something new,' evidence of a decisive and positive change in her perception and one of a number of possible indicators of person to person peacebuilding at the personal level (Lederach, 2003). Further evidence of change in her beliefs and attitudes is the affirmation of a commonality between a plural other, 'these people,' and a plural self, 'they are the same as we all,' similar to Tayba's acknowledgment of the likeness between her counterpart and herself. Still, as Lederach (2003) reminds us, transformation at the personal level is not a linear progression, but rather an ongoing and cyclical process. As we note a shift in Nadiya's group representation, we note, too, her ongoing use of dichotomous language. Integral to the construction of the other is the establishment of an out-group (Dervin, 2008, 2010; Holliday, 2010; Virkama, 2010). Through her use of the third person plural, 'they' and 'these people,' when Nadiya speaks generally, she continues to discursively construct a plural other of which she is not a part.

As we now see in Nadiya's change of attitude toward 'these people,' the construction of the other can be one of objectification in which the complexity and subjectivity of the individual are disregarded (Abdallah-Pretceille, 2003). Alternatively, an individual can become a representative or stand-in for a group, such as when Jiang fears Zahra will judge him as he 'has not an American face.' Our data offer evidence that, through participant interactions, existing identities and divisions between in-groups and out-groups can be reconfigured. The virtual intercultural borderlands serve as a site in which attitudes toward the individualized other can also be redefined, a redefinition that can contribute strongly to peacebuilding at the personal level. Powerful evidence of the discursive construction of such an in-group is Tayba's declaration regarding her student: 'he is just like me, a human!'

Unlike Tayba, who is initially reluctant to engage with her Afghan student, from the beginning Nadiya envisions the relationship she and her collaborator might build. Although we have seen how Nadiya acknowledges 'stereotypes' regarding the plural other backgrounded to the country they come from, she also discursively constructs a singular other, 'my student,' with whom she is willing to engage (Broome & Collier, 2012). 'We will need to talk a lot,' she writes in her first reflection, 'I will have plenty of time with my student during our lessons.' Nadiya's use of the first person plural 'we' and 'our' in this first reflection anticipates the reconfiguration of roles and group identity or membership she describes at the end of the project.

In her final reflection, Nadiya offers evidence that she and her Afghan student, Hassan, have indeed 'talk[ed] a lot' during their 'lessons'; they have leveraged the communicative affordances of the virtual intercultural borderlands to form a new group identification (Broome & Collier, 2012) imperative for peacebuilding. Recalling the reticence she felt when she first met Hassan, Nadiya writes:

> Well, I was a little bit careful during the first session because I didn't want to begin the war or political topic, but my tutee started to talk about this himself. I believe that is because his major is politics, and, maybe, because of his age and place of work too. Hassan is 36 (usually, people in his age are not interested in some 'childish' topics …) and he works as a social worker (he helps families who were injured, lost something or somebody during the war). (Nadiya)

The person she describes now is not an unknown other. Instead, he is an individual about whom she shares specific details including his age, educational background, professional experience and name. Her reference to Hassan as someone who 'helps families who were injured, lost someone during the war,' serves as a reminder that peacebuilding dimensions are intertwined; working to meet basic human needs is discussed in Chapter 6, in relation to the structural level of peacebuilding. Moreover, Nadiya's use of the plural recalls her references to 'we' and 'our' at the project's beginning, as she discursively constructs a new in-group she has formed with her student:

> After our first class I understood that we can talk about various things and I don't need to be afraid to raise any topic during the conversations. We were talking about wars in our countries, about politics and government, system of education, cultures and traditions, American people and their way of living. (Nadiya)

Nadiya and Hassan have each lived in places where conflict is a palpably present structural force and these experiences bring them together. Despite Nadiya's initial reticence ('I was a little bit careful during the first session'), she discovers that war and conflict are not topics to be feared but rather, like 'politics ... government, system of education, cultures, and traditions,' to be shared. We note again the intersections of different dimensions of peacebuilding; the sharing that takes place between Nadiya and Hassan is relational.

Perhaps just as importantly, together, Nadiya and Hassan create not only an in-group based on common experiences, but an out-group (Gudykunst, 2004; Halperin, 2016; Tajfel & Turner, 2004): 'American people and their way of living.' Nadiya is studying and teaching in the US; Hassan, we presume, has observed and perhaps interacted with members of the US military or NGOs. Nadiya and Hassan's new in-group invokes implications raised by Gudykunst (2004: 74): 'The most important component ... influencing our communication with strangers is our social identities, which are based on our group membership,' and one's willingness to *change* group membership and join the group of the 'other' is a powerful indicator of peacebuilding at the personal level (Broome & Collier, 2012).

Participants, both tutors and students, acquire knowledge through and as a result of their interactions in the virtual intercultural borderlands. Across participants' voices, we find evidence of change which leads to what Lederach (2003: 24) terms the 'capacity to perceive accurately,' to new ways of thinking about and reacting in and toward a situation, and to an increased willingness to engage with the other (Broome & Collier, 2012). As we have seen in the participant experiences described in this chapter, cognitive change can intersect with emotional change, with shifts in self-perception and with changes in beliefs and attitudes about others. The words and experiences of Lisa, a US-based participant, offer further forceful examples of these intersections, beginning with how she discursively constructs her tutoring partner, and moving to how she discursively constructs their joint and disparate worlds.

From the beginning, Lisa puts forward her intention to learn more while simultaneously framing her lack of knowledge as a concern:

> I don't want to offend my tutee by being culturally insensitive by asking the wrong question or speaking in a way that my tutee finds offensive. I would feel terrible if my good intentions to learn about my student's life were somehow misconstrued and come off as intrusive. (Lisa)

Lisa's initial framing of her student presumes an undefined but inevitable difference between her and her future student. Her fear is not of what she knows but of what she does not know about the other; she perceives herself as lacking the 'deep cultural knowledge' (Deardorff, 2006a: 255) to engage in what Deardorff's model of intercultural competence describes as 'effective and appropriate communication and behavior.' Nonetheless, Lisa's initial cognitive uncertainty is underlined by her 'good intentions to learn about [her] student's life,' which demonstrates a sensitivity to the possibilities of change in her ways of perceiving, thinking about and reacting in and toward a situation (Broome & Collier, 2012). Underlying her initial concerns is a desire for positive change (Lederach, 2003) in her abilities to successfully engage with, and perhaps learn from, her Afghan student. This desire, we argue, holds promise for peacebuilding at the personal level.

Moreover, it is the force of the personal interactions that allows tutors like Lisa to explore and dismantle inaccurate or limited perceptions of their Afghan counterparts as being exclusively defined by country and conflict (recall Nadiya's discussion of the country of Afghanistan and *its* people, who become backgrounded to their country). With Lisa, we begin to see something similar, as in her first reflection she discursively constructs her future student as a representative of 'a country in constant turmoil and war.'

> At the end of this project, I hope to have a greater knowledge of one Afghani citizen. My only frame of reference of Afghanistan is that which is presented to me by the media, which presents a country in constant turmoil and war. (Lisa)

Lisa's framing of the information she has as being 'presented to [her]' by the media is noteworthy. In this linguistic construction, she has been the receiver/object rather than the pursuer, or constructor/agent, of 'knowledge,' 'the media,' the scope of which she knows is limited. As she recognizes these limits (discussed in more detail in Chapter 6), she puts forward her 'hope to have a greater knowledge of one Afghani citizen.' It is the personal level of person to person peacebuilding that allows her to shift her perceptions (Lederach, 2003) and potentially her orientations regarding conflict and peacebuilding (Broome & Collier, 2012), to more accurately perceive her student as one individual Afghan, among many.

In her final reflection, Lisa describes profound shifts in her ways of perceiving, thinking about and reacting toward (Broome & Collier, 2012) her Afghan student. Evoking her initial concerns about offending her student, Lisa shares the following about their collaboration and about him:

> The reality has been quite different, as I have told my class on many occasions, 'Mustafa is my new best friend.' I now realize that I was overthinking the whole thing. (Lisa)

Lisa's experience in the virtual intercultural borderlands reminds us again that levels of peacebuilding overlap. We see change in Lisa at the cognitive and emotional level, which is personal, and in the friendship she and Mustafa have developed, which is relational. Finally, her declaration, 'I was overthinking the whole thing,' points to what Lisa has learned not only about Mustafa but about the structures of 'turmoil and war,' as she suggests she might have been 'overthinking' and potentially overgeneralizing based on media representations. In Chapter 6, we return to the role and power of media in participants' perceptions to explore the impact of such representations in greater depth. Here we find that learning about an individual other – Mustafa – leads, too, to change in Lisa's beliefs and attitudes about Afghanistan.

Changes in Participants' Beliefs and Attitudes about the World: Discursive Constructions of Afghanistan and Beyond

In Broome and Collier's (2012) framework, shifts in beliefs and attitudes about selves, about others and about the world are all associated with the personal dimension of peacebuilding. Participants in the virtual intercultural borderlands maximize intercultural communication opportunities which lead to powerful, positive changes in their self-perceptions and their perceptions of others. We look now at how participants' discourses evidence change in their beliefs and attitudes about the world, change which is part of the accumulation and constellation of other changes in our participants that manifest finally in peacebuilding: at the personal, relational and structural levels.

Changes in beliefs and attitudes about the world can overlap with and be powerfully influenced by beliefs and attitudes about others. At the beginning of the tutoring project, Christine, a US-based participant, frames the individual she will be working with as a potential source of knowledge and insights she hopes to apply in her work with future students. Before meeting her Afghan student, Christine writes:

> I am ... hoping to learn more about what it's like to work with students from a war-torn country with limited access to education and technology. Many recent immigrants to the U.S. have similar experiences in their pasts, and I hope that this will be a valuable experience from which I can draw in my future years as an ESL teacher. (Christine)

Christine constructs her future student as a representative, the embodiment of the experiences of 'students from a war-torn country.' Her choice of the plural 'students' indicates Christine's understanding of Afghan students through 'oneness,' as in 'one and the same thing' (Ricœur, 1992: 116, quoted in Wodak *et al.*, 2009), defined metonymically by 'a war-torn country with limited access to education and technology' (Wodak *et al.*, 2009: 38). In much the same way, her comparison with 'many recent immigrants in the U.S.' pushes the potential uniqueness of her student, and of some immigrants to the US, to the background, foregrounding a presumptive similarity which discursively levels potential (important) differences through comparison (Wodak *et al.*, 2009: 36), creating an out-group.

The very existence of this out-group supposes a commonality of experiences across individuals and across countries experiencing conflict. Christine is not alone in her discursive construction of Afghanistan as 'war-torn.' This term appears across participants' reflections: in a decidedly unscientific search of the words 'Afghanistan' and 'war-torn,' the Google search engine yielded approximately 7,210,000 results in 0.56 seconds, a repetition that essentializes the country and empties the word of its force. Nor is Christine unique in associating conflict with limited access to education and technology. As we see in Chapter 6, numerous US-based participants share a similar vision of Afghanistan. Although such a perception is not entirely inaccurate, we note that it is complicated by the fact that the very interactions that allowed participants to learn more about each other's world were made possible by a virtual exchange project.

Despite this othering through sameness/discursive leveling of difference, we observe in Christine's words also the potential for cognitive change (Lederach, 2003). 'I am … hoping to learn more,' she writes in her initial reflection, suggesting a willingness to examine and perhaps change her beliefs and attitudes about others and about the world. In her final reflection, we find her hope substantiated as we see evidence of knowledge Christine has gained over the course of the project. For instance, as a result of her interactions with her student, she has learned about the languages of Afghanistan:

> I learned that my student's first language is Persian, not Arabic, which was a surprise to me. I researched at the beginning of the course which languages are spoken in Afghanistan and was surprised to learn that Arabic was not commonly spoken. (Christine)

Christine's experience mirrors that of a number of tutors who assumed their students would use Arabic in their daily interactions; we learn from US-based tutors and Afghans alike that students spoke Pashto and/or Dari (which both US and Afghan participants also referred to as 'Persian' and 'Farsi').

The following quote is representative of another (mis)perception we encountered in tutors' reflections related to geopolitical understandings of region. Ellen writes:

> I hope to gain understanding of another culture that I do not often interact with. As an ESL teacher I have almost no experience teaching students from the middle east. (Ellen)

Ellen was not alone; several tutors described Afghanistan not as a country in Central Asia but as part of the 'Middle East,' a mistake which highlights how vast and vastly different regions can be assimilated into one uncertain entity (Wodak *et al.*, 2009). In the following quote, Soyoung, a US-based tutor from South Korea, acknowledges her own limited knowledge about the geopolitics of the region as she conveys her eagerness to learn more about her student and her student's environs:

> I do not know too much about, especially geography of that area. So I am still learning and … because I never had interaction with people who is from like Middle East area. Sometimes like people think that Dubai and

Saudi Arabia and other like ... Afghanistan, everywhere is kind of same place. It's not like separate different area. ... So obviously, I do not know too much about it. (Laughter) (Soyoung)

Soyoung's discourse highlights what was present in several tutors' discourses: how the ramifications of countries and regions constructed as 'everywhere is kind of same place' are always leveling of difference, geography, languages, cultural practices and so on (Wodak *et al.*, 2009). It also highlights the importance, therefore, of creating opportunities for intercultural interactions: interactions within the virtual intercultural borderlands, that is, can and do complicate and nuance understandings of the world beyond.

As we discussed earlier in this chapter, transformation at the personal level is not a linear progression, but rather an ongoing and cyclical process (Lederach, 2003). In Christine's final reflection, she continues to discursively frame the person she has interacted with as other. She refers to him by the role he played in their interactions, 'student,' and by his country of origin, 'Afghanistan.' He is 'a person from a culture that was so different from mine.'

> I appreciate the opportunity to have met a student from Afghanistan. He briefly talked about his experience living in Afghanistan, and how it can be dangerous to live and work there. However, I was surprised to find that he and I had many similarities, and his way of thinking was similar to mine. I am grateful to have had the chance to meet a person from a culture that was so different from mine, and yet find common ground. (Christine)

Although we do not see the creation of an in-group here, Christine's experience still offers evidence of how intercultural communication creates a place for peacebuilding and the acquisition of knowledge that leads to shifts in perceptions. Pointing to their similarities, Christine identifies the seeds for an in-group composed of Christine and her Afghan collaborator: 'his way of thinking was similar to mine.'

Aaban, an Afghan-based participant, offers evidence of connections participants themselves envision between peacebuilding and their interactions in the virtual intercultural borderlands. Of his tutor and the project as a whole, he shares:

> In general, like, it's amazing to me to meet people around the world cuz we can share our thoughts, our feelings, our society problems, uh, and we're going to find a solution, cuz my tutor, she was was from Syria, she was from Syria, I forgot it, she was Arab____ (inaudible) and she's speaking really fluently American, she was like American, when I first met her I didn't know she was from Syria, she's Arab, then she introduced herself and I [was] amazed. (Aaban)

Aaban and his tutor engage in peacebuilding at the personal, relational and structural level. At the personal level, they leverage the communicative affordances of the virtual exchange to work toward preferred cognitive and emotional change as they share '[their] thoughts, [their] feelings.' At the relational level, the changes he hopes for will come, he is sure, through connections like the one he and his tutor have built: 'we're going to find a solution.' Finally, Aaban links communication with 'people around the world,' and with his tutor more specifically, to change at the structural level; the 'solution' he seeks is to '*our* society problems' (italics added), with his use of the possessive pronoun 'our' suggesting to whom these problems belong (to him and his tutor, or the people of Afghanistan and Syria, or to all of us).

For Aaban, then, the virtual intercultural borderlands constitute a space in which he can express his own beliefs, opinions and experiences, and where he can learn more about the world with and from others, just as we see with Soyoung. The powerful promise of the interactions that occur in this space is evident in Aaban's use of the word 'amazing.' Describing the opportunity to interact with a plural other, 'people,' Aaban discursively constructs his tutor both as the individual with whom he interacted and as an embodiment of the many perspectives and experiences he and others can learn about through their interactions and participation in the project. His use of the plural 'we' suggests, too, that he is speaking not only for himself but for an unnamed group: perhaps other participants in the project; other people in Afghanistan; and/or other people in other countries experiencing conflict around the globe.

Changes in Beliefs about Self, Others and the World

We close this chapter with Yi, a tutor whose reflections evidence shifts in beliefs and attitudes about self, others and the world, on the part both of a future EAL teacher and of her Afghan student. Yi's experiences remind us that peacebuilding levels overlap: individual changes (personal level) can be tied to relationships participants build with one another (relational level); interactions between participants can create spaces to share perspectives on topics such as the effects of conflict and on access to resources such as education (structural level).

Yi's interactions with her Afghan student are infused with her own understandings of conflict. A Han Chinese Mandarin speaker and devout Muslim, Yi completed all of her undergraduate coursework in Arabic. After her first year, conflict forced her to leave her university in Syria, and she finished her degree at a university in Jordan. Before meeting her student, Yi links her participation in the project to her own past experiences and to her future professional goals:

[T]his project looks like part of my goal, which I wish to work with refugees' students in future. I know it is a different situation, but I think this still can help me finds the connection and reach my goal. I have studied and lived in Syria for one year and a half. I understand people who have experienced war and trauma. (Yi)

Like Christine, Yi presents tutoring as a means of becoming better prepared to work with 'refugees.' Although Yi acknowledges 'it is a different situation,' she suggests that participating in the project will help her 'reach [her] goal.' In this way, like Christine, Yi frames her student as a source of knowledge and representative of a group of people. Unlike Christine, Yi points to her own experiences which, she suggests, prepare her to 'understand people who have experienced war and trauma,' as Yi frames this unknown other as someone who has lived in a country in conflict.

As Yi gets to know her student, her description of the other shifts. She frames her Afghan student as an individual with whom she is sharing personal experiences and building a relationship that goes beyond the limits of the tutoring project. In her second reflection, Yi describes how they are leveraging technology to communicate with one another: 'we are always chatting on Facebook.' Of these exchanges, Yi writes:

> She [...] asked me a lot of questions about my country, family, and study. She was surprised when she knew that I am the only child in my family. In her country that seems very weird. She said that she has three brothers and two sisters and she feels happy with a big family. (Yi)

The emotions Yi describes, 'surprised' and 'happy,' are not those of an abstract 'refugee' student but of a person she is collaborating with. Through their interactions in the virtual intercultural borderlands, Yi and her student learn not only about each other but about the world; Yi becomes a source of information for her student, answering questions about her 'country, family, and study.' In this excerpt we see how self-disclosure, discussion of the participants' family backgrounds, can lead to cognitive change. Learning about the one-child policy in China, a topic we return to in Chapter 6, challenges the student's 'perception' (Lederach, 2003) of what constitutes a family. 'She was surprised when she knew I am the only child in my family,' Yi remembers. 'In her country that seems very weird.'

Through their interactions, like her student, Yi learns not only about an individual but about the world, gaining insight into topics we return to in Chapter 6, at the structural level of peacebuilding: access to resources such as technology, education and English. In her fifth reflection, Yi writes of her student:

> She enjoyed doing her homework, and she wanted to improve her writing skills. She tried so hard and handed in her homework on time even though she does not have internet at home. She told me a great news on Friday, which the government will give 10–14 scholarships to female students from Afghanistan to study in the United States. She wants to get this opportunity and continue her education in the United States. I hope she can make her dream come true. At the end of the meeting, I encouraged her to keep going to practice the materials that I sent to her because

> English language skills are essential to someone who wants study in the country that speaks that language. (Yi)

Here, our focus is on what Yi has observed about the determination and dedication of the student she is working with: 'she tried so hard and handed in her homework on time,' an accomplishment that is particularly noteworthy as 'she does not have internet at home.' Yi's student was not unique in her lack of access to technology in her home; as we note in Chapter 1, for many Afghan students, participating in the tutoring project required traveling to an educational resource center where they could use the internet. Finally, framing the information as 'great news,' Yi shares her student's excitement that 'the government will give 10–14 scholarships to female students from Afghanistan to study in the United States'; as we examine in Chapter 6, for many participants, having access to English may lead to access to greater professional and educational opportunities. Drawing a direct connection between this 'opportunity' and 'English language skills,' Yi hopes that their tutoring sessions, and the materials they have shared, might play a role in helping her student's 'dream come true.'

Lederach (2003) and Broome and Collier (2012) maintain that the willingness to share hopes and fears and dreams between intercultural interactants is indicative of peacebuilding at the relational level, but Lederach (2003) talks also about the importance of positive change in one's individual emotions. Yi's sensitivity to her Afghan student's dreams in this last quote seems an appropriate place to close this chapter, as it creates the bridge from the personal level of peacebuilding to the relational level of peacebuilding, which we discuss next in Chapter 5.

Note

(1) Tutors were originally asked to write about their experiences with their 'tutees.' Through our analysis, we came to realize the implications of functionalizing Afghan students by the suffix '-ee,' which refers to their roles as they are being *acted upon*, with agency discursively diminished (van Leeuwen, 2008: 42).

5 The Relational Dimension of Person to Person Peacebuilding

The dynamics of relationship building take different forms and may well bring challenges to intercultural communication, but the question of how these dynamics shape and unfold through the intersectionality of peacebuilding and intercultural communication has not been sufficiently studied by scholars. As Broome and Collier (2012: 246) state, even though 'the study of intercultural communication intersects with peacebuilding in fundamental and meaningful ways,' peacebuilding has been relatively neglected in the field of intercultural communication. Our goal in this chapter is to address this neglect by bringing more attention to how intercultural communication and relationship formation contribute to the relational dimension of peacebuilding, person to person, through analysis of participants' voices engaged in online intercultural interaction. For our analysis of participants' discourses, we continue to draw on the peacebuilding frameworks of Lederach (2003) and Broome and Collier (2012), along with frameworks for critical discourse analysis (Blackledge, 2005; Cruikshank, 2012; Fairclough, 1989, 2013; van Leeuwen, 2008; Wodak et al., 2009).

Lederach (2003: 8) acknowledges that conflict is normal in human relationships and emphasizes the importance of 'building right relationships' for peace. He emphasizes the necessity of 'find[ing] ways to understand peace as a change process based on relationship building' (Lederach, 1999: 32). As teachers of language and intercultural communication who have encountered the unexpected affordance of peacebuilding in the virtual intercultural borderlands of online exchange, we – like Lederach – also believe in the necessity of exploring how relationship building contributes to peacebuilding. Hence, in this chapter, we look to themes that emerged in participants' voices as they described the processes of relationship building, including their descriptions of bumps they encountered along the way. According to Lederach (2003: 9), establishing solid relationships in global and local communities is the 'horizon toward which we journey' for transformation, and to achieve this goal we need to change 'our current way of relating.'

Our participants were looking for ways of relating to each other during their journey: some of them preferred to build bridges based on similarities, whereas others were courageous enough to start with difference. For some, empathy was a catalyst for relationship building. For others, it was safer to take guard and be cautious, taking little steps at a time which sometimes still ended in resistance. No matter which way they sought to build relationships with each other, they cleared the pathway to do so as they walked and talked, and they worked to build peace, person to person, throughout their journeys.

The relational dimension of peacebuilding focuses on communication and interaction specifically centered around 'social relationships, intergroup relationships, the nature of hierarchies and status positioning of group members' (Broome & Collier, 2012: 252). When we synthesized the features of the relational dimension from both Lederach's (2003) and Broome and Collier's (2012) frameworks, we identified discursive indicators of change and change actions which, they argue, are crucial to the processes of building solid relationships for peacebuilding (see Table 5.1). These indicators included participants' discursive constructions of closeness with or distance from each other, expectations of/from each other, how they shared their hopes and fears, how they used or shared power, and how they emphasized or enacted hierarchies and status, equitable relationships and community engagement. As we looked for discursive evidence of these elements in the voices of participants, we also examined participants' willingness to enrich their communication and develop mutual understanding in addition to their efforts to work for inclusion and social justice. The following sections present the occurrences of some of these themes in the discourses of our tutors and students while they

Table 5.1 Dimensions of peacebuilding: Positive change at the relational level of peacebuilding

At the RELATIONAL level of peacebuilding, positive change in the following:	
Lederach (2003)	Broome and Collier (2012)
Perceptions of, desires for, goals for and structures of relationships	Recognizing the nature of hierarchies and status positioning of group members
Desires for closeness or distance	Willingness to work for relationships that are equitable, inclusive and social justice-oriented
How we use, build and share power	Work for intercultural alliances
Our hopes and fears for relationships	
Minimizing poorly functioning communication	
Maximizing mutual understanding	

were developing their relationships – and building peace, person to person – in the virtual intercultural borderlands of online exchange.

The Growing Nature of Relationships through Dialogue

Dialogue contributes to each level of the peacebuilding frameworks: personal, relational and structural (Broome & Collier, 2012; Lederach, 2003). From the relational perspective, dialogue provides the land that yields all roots of relationships:

> Dialogue is needed to provide access to, a voice in, and constructive interaction with, the ways we formalize our relationships and in the ways our organizations and structures are built, respond, and behave. (Lederach, 2003: 27)

This 'constructive interaction' Lederach refers to can be explained with more details by Bohm (1996: 2) as cited in Broome and Collier (2012: 256): Bohm construes 'dialogue' as 'non-polarized discourse, an interactive process in which "people are making something in common, i.e. creating something new together".' In our study, this constructive interaction was an outcome of relationship building despite the different ways in which participants approached their interactions.

The virtual intercultural borderlands of online exchange – made possible through videoconferencing – was the only setting where the participants, who were from many different parts of the world, could meet 'face to face,' if virtually, to communicate. Yet throughout the project, participants faced technical and technological challenges. Facing these problems together brought participants closer since they were creating solutions together and brainstorming on how to remove these obstacles from their way, in the process demonstrating their mutual willingness to 'minimize poorly functioning communication' (Lederach, 2003: 24) and overcome technical difficulties as they navigated between Skype, Zoom, Google Docs and WhatsApp texts on laptops and cellphones, in order to 'maximize' communication and understanding and find ways to meet and collaborate. Research on dialogue as central to peace (Chakraverti, 2009) emphasizes its potential for improving understanding, enhancing communication and building viable relationships, providing the foundation for collaborative problem solving and action. During the tutoring project, this problem-solving practice started with some technological troubleshooting between tutors in the US and students in Afghanistan, a collaboration which set the foundation for brainstorming and collaborating on greater problems, including problems that overlapped with the structural level of peacebuilding (see Chapter 6).

Through the tutoring project, participants engaged in intercultural dialogue to get to know each other better and, as a result, to reduce the ambiguity that was caused because of not knowing much about the culture and context of one another at the beginning of their partnership. Participants, who were connected through virtual meetings, started this project without knowing anything about each other; some of them were nervous and some of them were excited as a result of these unknowns. No matter what kind of feelings they started their relationships with, they were mostly able to develop the nature of their communication through dialogue by first finding and then 'making something in common' and 'creating something new together' (Bohm, 1996: 2, cited in Broome & Collier, 2012: 256–257). This happened over time, of course. According to Lederach (2003: 21), 'Rather than seeing peace as a static "end-state," conflict transformation views peace as a continuously evolving and developing quality of relationship.' This kind of growth occurred generally in the middle or toward the end of participants' semester-long communications with each other, when they started to find similarities between each other as opposed to their anticipation of 'difference.'

Structuring Relationships: Starting from Similarities

In participants' reflections, we find examples of similarities they discovered with their tutor or student. For example, Emily's discovery of one of the greatest similarities among human beings – smiling – was the catalyst for her discursive transition from 'difference' to 'similarity' and might have been the start of structuring their positive relationship:

> I was hoping to learn how to connect with people that might be very different from me in various ways. I can certainly say that I got better at it. One of my revelations – smile is universal! :) ... I believe if my tutee and I had more time to spend together we would certainly did become good friends. (Emily)

Emily's quote explains how, at the beginning of the project, she anticipated the possibility of experiencing difference with her Afghan student, which she hoped would help her learn how to 'connect' with people who 'might' be 'different.' As she is reflecting back in this journal entry, she expresses 'a willingness to engage with others' through her desire to 'learn how to connect,' discursive moves important to peacebuilding at the personal level and promising for peacebuilding at the relational level (Broome & Collier, 2012: 260). Emily's hopes seem to have been realized as, in this same entry, we see that she believes she 'got better at' 'learn[ing] how to connect with people' who were very different from her.

In the process of 'getting better at connecting,' Emily implies that she had multiple 'revelations,' one of which leads Emily's focus to shift from differences to similarities as she realizes a common point: smiling. The change indicated by her reference to the 'smile,' reiterated through the emoji, demonstrates the type of positive 'relational affectivity' Lederach (2003: 24) encourages us to seek at the relational level of peacebuilding.

Moreover, as the following sentence demonstrates, 'smile' is not only meant as a facial expression but also as a catalyst that makes the tutor, Emily, consider potential friendship – making something new – for the future, if they had had more time. Emily's last sentence, ending on 'we *would certainly did become* good friends' (emphasis added), may also be noteworthy, given the inclusion of multiple verb tenses – 'would' + 'did become' – as the conditional 'would' competes with the certainty of past tense 'did become,' with 'certainly' between them emphasizing all the more the likelihood in Emily's mind of their becoming 'good friends.' As Hansen (2006: 21–22), drawing from Laclau and Mouffe (1985), explains: as we analyze discourse, it is important to attend to such discursive 'slips and instabilities,' places, that is, where ambiguities in language challenge or complicate how a discourse attempts to fix meaning. Moments of discursive instability and the shifting of boundaries and relations between meanings at the sentence level can indicate 'meaning' in flux – unstable, contested and undergoing transformation – and here we see Emily's sense of friendship with her tutoring partner also in flux as it oscillates between likelihood and certainty.

Yulia was another US-based participant who found similarities with her student, in her case not at the near 'universal' level (like smiling) but at the individual level. Yulia grew up and completed her undergraduate studies in Ukraine, where she planned to return after completing her graduate degree. Yulia and her tutoring counterpart found some common desires (Lederach, 2003: 24) to structure their relationship, as one was an international student in the US, and the other longed to follow the same path:

> I found out that it is very helpful to develop friendly and supportive relationships with one's students. ... For example, with Reshad we talked a lot about studying in the USA and peculiarities of being an international student so far away from home, friends and family. ... I had a lot to share with him during our presentations. So our sessions were very authentic and helpful for him. (Yulia)

This time what connected a tutor and a student was their similar pursuit. Yulia had a lot to share from her experiences as an international student, which made Reshad excited since this was something he had wanted for a very long time. In other words, their common goal to pursue their education in the US was a point of converging interest that helped them develop their relationship. We know from Lederach (2003: 24) that finding and sharing common desires is an essential component of peacebuilding at the relational level, one that intersects with and is embedded in intercultural communication, which Bennett (2018b) helps us understand: 'Intercultural communication necessitates understanding the unique experience of others as the key to coordinating meaning and action towards some common goal.' While both Yulia and Reshad were excited to 'study abroad,' and both had lived in a country in conflict, Yulia describes their 'common goal' in relation to 'the peculiarities of being an international student so far away from home, friends and family.' Hence we see how Yulia's own 'peculiarities' as an international student helped her be 'authentic and helpful' in her view – part of how they 'coordinated meaning and action' in helping Reshad achieve his goal (Bennett, 2018b), and part of how she discursively enacts peacebuilding at the relational level. From the perspective of critical discourse analysis, too, we see Yulia's discourse re-enact the evolving closeness of their relationship as she discursively moves from the general, impersonalizing 'one's students,' to the excited, 'with Reshad, we talked a lot,' naming or nominating and thus particularizing and humanizing her student, who quickly joins her in the pronoun 'we' (van Leeuwen, 2008: 17).

Reshad's dream was ambitious but not impossible (he did eventually get a scholarship). He was not the only participant whose hopes related to studying in the US (see also Chapter 6). Haroon, who was very excited about his classes with his tutor, 'dreamed' about speaking with someone from the US. When he talked about how he achieved his goal, he disclosed his excitement with these words:

> [The tutoring project] was really helpful for me, and that was great, because, this was one of my dreams, to talk with a native speaker, especially she, or he or she should be from USA. That was really for me a great dream. And I achieved my dream. (Haroon)

Here, Haroon's 'dream,' like Yulia and Reshad's shared desire to study abroad, discursively evidences important answers to questions raised by Lederach (2003) regarding the transformations needed at the relational level of peacebuilding. Lederach asks us to consider:

> How close or distant do people wish to be in their relationships? How will they use, build, and share power? How do they perceive themselves, each other, and their expectations? What are their hopes and fears for their lives and relationships, their patterns of communication and interaction? (Lederach, 2003: 24)

As Lederach (2003: 24) continues, he stresses the importance of bringing 'to the surface explicitly … the relational fears, hopes, and goals' of interactants in order to 'maximize mutual understanding.' Lederach's description – 'to bring to the surface explicitly' – becomes even more poignant when Haroon shares his struggles with relationships and communication in Afghanistan:

> It's really, the surface or the atmosphere of here is really closed. I mean, it's a closed surface. (Haroon)

In both of these examples, we see Haroon's discourse enact Lederach's (2003) push that we bring our hopes and dreams to the surfaces of our relationships. Haroon's discourse – and, more specifically, his repetition and hence overwording of both 'dreams' and 'closed' – further evidences his 'preoccupation with certain aspects of reality' (Pierce, 2008: 293; see also Fairclough, 1989, 1992), as we experienced earlier with Emily's preoccupation with difference. If we accept this interpretation of the discourse, we see Haroon almost equally preoccupied with his fervent desire to connect with someone from the US and his frustration with the 'closed' nature of relationships and communication in Afghanistan, attributable perhaps to what we know of the instability, division and mistrust of others which still haunt the context from which Haroon speaks (see also Chapter 3).

Haroon was excited to talk to his tutor, or someone from the US, as he shared in his interview. This dream also came with some expectations. Haroon expected his tutor to be very different from him, as evidenced by his surprise in the following quote. He said:

> I suddenly met her and I can share, and she's also like me, she or he was like me, we felt many common points with each other. That surprised me a lot. (Haroon)

The 'common points' Haroon 'felt' with his tutor in the open atmosphere of their exchange contrasts sharply with the 'closed atmosphere,' 'closed surface' he described in Afghanistan, where 'we can't share our own thoughts to others. ... We can't share our thoughts really, expanded, in expanded form.' Again, we note Haroon's powerful desire to share ('I can share') with someone who is 'like him,' and he suggests he can do so in 'expanded form' with his tutor, in English, despite the fact that he's sharing in another language. Indeed, he believes he has more in common with his tutor than with his Afghan friends, a powerful testament to the peacebuilding opportunities through relationship building available in the virtual intercultural borderlands.

Haroon's feelings of astonishment mixed with excitement continued when he was talking about technology and how it is possible for two people so far from each other to still be able to connect. 'She was in USA and I was in Afghanistan,' he said, and continued, 'We didn't realize that we are very far.' What we realize from Haroon's expression is that the connection they created made him forget about the geographical distance between them and focus on just the similarities or 'common points' they shared. Even though this was a new phenomenon for Haroon, relationship building for peacebuilding purposes through virtual interaction is not a new concept. As Puig-Larrauri and Kahl (2013: 1) state, 'Technology can contribute to peacebuilding processes by offering tools that foster collaboration, transform attitudes, and give a stronger voice to communities.' In Haroon's perception, technology enabled them to forget about the physical borders and distance between them and focus on their 'common points': as they developed their relationship; as they collaborated to tutor and learn English together; and as their attitudes toward each other were shaped by this collaboration and how they shared (at least in Haroon's case). Moreover, returning to Lederach's (2003: 24) questions, we see how Haroon experiences 'closeness,' not distance, with his tutor – a closeness that is likewise embedded in his attitude of 'openness,' which Deardorff (2006b) embeds as a requisite at the base of her model of intercultural communication competence.

Sometimes home languages functioned as a meeting point of similarities for the tutors and their students. Yuqing, who was originally from China, said that linguistic features of Chinese and Dari enabled her and her student to structure their relationships. It is worth pointing out here that it was the Afghan student who was enthusiastic about comparing Chinese with Dari: he even asked his tutor to memorize some expressions in Dari. This was the start of their friendly relationship:

> He even asked me how to say something in Chinese. He is also proud of his first language, when I showed him some simple Chinese and he translated to Dari and made me memorize them. On such occasion, I reminded him of inductive learning on similarities and differences between different languages. This made us establish not only a friendly relationship but also a habit of thinking linguistically and understand learner language more clearly. (Yuqing)

Yuqing did what many language teachers might do to make connections with their students: use the native language of the student. According to Auerbach (1993: 8), 'Students' native language can be used "as a meaning-making tool" and this makes language learning as "a means of communicating ideas rather than an end in itself."' In this context, Yuqing was not only creating 'inductive learning' by comparing the two languages, but also building a relationship by lowering the affective filter (Krashen, 1982) and creating a 'meaning-making tool.' This helped them build a friendly relationship, one certainly bolstered by the fact that Yuqing was not hesitant to 'share power' or create space for student agency as they exchanged roles and languages: he 'made me memorize' [Dari phrases]. Yuqing's willingness to share power is evidenced again in her discourse as she described how '*This* made us establish not only a friendly relationship but also a habit of thinking linguistically' (emphasis added). The unclear referent of the indefinite pronoun 'this' (perhaps it refers to Yuqing reminding the student of 'inductive learning') which acts upon them both ('made us') further equalizes their agency as they are equally objects of the sentence. In other words, Yuqing creates explicit space for the Afghan student to become the agent and share power during their interactions, but she also joins him as the object of the next sentence, each together '*made* to establish' 'a friendly relationship' and 'think linguistically.' They are subjects and objects alike, the latter occurring through 'grammatical metaphor' (Fairclough, 1992: 181) as the sentence is 'agentless' and as Yuqing and her tutoring partner share power. Broome and Collier (2012: 258) point out how intercultural dialogue can lead interactants to reproduce asymmetrical relations of power, but here we see how the tutoring pair trade off and share the role of agents (agency and structure are discussed in more depth in Chapter 6).

The constructive nature of *inter*religious dialogue to peacebuilding and relationship development has been explored in many studies (see, for example, Abu-Nimer, 2001; Mollov & Lavie, 2001). However, interreligious dialogue should be carefully structured and guided in order for it to remain constructive (Kefa & Ombuge, 2012). In the quote below, we see an example of *intra*religious dialogue which connects the tutor, Jamila, who was from Saudi Arabia, and the Afghan student, who share the same religion:

> We kept talking about her culture, specifically about marriage, relationships, and work. We found out that we share a lot of similarities in our cultures because we share the same religion. Before we finish this session, she told me that it was the best session because she talked a lot in English more than ever. (Jamila)

This time religion was the 'common point' that the tutor and student used as a basis for relationship building. As Jamila recalls this session in her reflective journal, we see a discursive evolution of their relationship in her word choice: while she starts with 'we,' she then reports on 'her [Afghan student's] culture,' with the pronoun 'her' marking a 'self/other' division, and 'culture' at first encompassing 'marriage, relationships, work.' Jamila is obviously open and curious (Deardorff, 2006b); moreover, the initial focus on the student's culture in this dialogue leads her to write of 'our cultures,' similarities between which are grounded in their shared religion. Here we see how a common religion led to relationship building through intrareligious dialogue, and how both members of this tutoring pair found within their shared religion a way to maximize mutual understanding (Lederach, 2003: 24).

Lisa's voice, as follows, reminds us of changes we explore in Chapter 4, as shifts in participants' beliefs and attitudes about themselves and others lead to transformations in group representations and identities:

> Through this experience I have been able to learn firsthand about an individual whose life is completely different than mine and I have learned that there is more that unites us than divides us as people and learners. (Lisa)

Although she describes her Afghan student as someone 'whose life is completely different than mine,' Lisa nevertheless discursively constructs an 'in-group' to which she and her interlocutor belong in her revelation that 'there is more that unites us than divides us as people.' In her words, we hear echoes of Tayba's declaration regarding her Afghan student: 'he is just like me, a human!' In addition, Lisa's statements remind us of another question of Lederach's (2003: 24) for us to consider when considering peacebuilding at the relational level: 'How do [interactants] perceive themselves, each other, and their expectations?' Lisa's perception through her tutoring experience tips the scale toward unity rather than division, another discursive indicator of peacebuilding which contributes to the accumulation and constellation of such indicators throughout the tutoring project. As well, Lisa's words evidence the intersectionality of peacebuilding and intercultural communication, as she reveals 'knowledge of self and other' and perhaps of both self and other to society (Byram, 1997), 'as people and learners.'

Structuring of Relationships: Embracing the Difference

So far, we have talked about how participants structured their relationships around similarities, but it does not mean that the quality of the relationship depends only on finding common ground. On the contrary, differences can also be a good starting point for relationship building. As Broome and Collier (2012: 251) observe, 'Dealing constructively with differences and disagreements' is another required component of peacebuilding at the relational level. In this section, we draw on participants' voices to illustrate how differences and disagreements may also discursively indicate peacebuilding.

Dialogue around differences has comprised the scope of many peacebuilding studies, whether these differences are around culture, religion or political ideologies (see, for example, Pentikainen & Rizk, 2019). Likewise, there are many intercultural communication studies focused around difference. Many subcomponents of intercultural frameworks such as awareness, knowledge, empathy and valuing (see, for example, Deardorff, 2004) start with becoming aware of and understanding dissimilarities, whether they are cultural, linguistic or behavioral differences. DeTurk (2006: 47) points out the importance of dialogue in intercultural understanding and alliance building and explains how talking about differences can contribute to intercultural understanding: 'Dialogue across differences, in sum, engenders intercultural understanding in terms of the experiences of others and the structures that shape those experiences.' In the examples below, we explore the reflections of some tutors who were concerned about cultural differences before they started tutoring, and other tutors who mentioned challenging times during their conversations when they had difficulty relating to the experiences of their Afghan students. We then consider how contending with 'difference' leads tutors to discursively build peace at the relational level.

In the previous section, we met tutor Jamila, who was comfortably engaged in intrareligious conversation with her student. In contrast, for tutors like Ionna, who was from Ukraine, coming from a different culture and religion from her student was of great concern to her before she started tutoring. She acknowledged this fact in her last journal entry:

> I worried if the difference between our cultures and religions could somehow influence our tutoring sessions. Fortunately enough, I did not have these issues at all. ... Frankly speaking, it did work and we had a good connection. Now I see that all those worries were in vain. The girl was very kind and respectful and thanked me for having lessons with her. (Ionna)

Referring to her student as 'the girl,' Ionna indicates that her initial 'worries were in vain' as 'the girl was very kind and respectful.' While the concern of religion and cultural difference might have created a wall between Ionna and her Afghan counterpart, the fact that the student was 'kind' and 'respectful' and 'thanked' her created for Ionna 'a good connection' and therefore a safe space to open up. What her discourse also reveals is that Ionna attributes her worries to 'the girl,' whom she doesn't name or individualize in her journals, who was 'kind' and 'respectful' and 'grateful.' While Ionna's worries were not realized, her discourse suggests in part an imbalance in status (did Ionna thank her student?). The status positioning of group members (in this case, a dyad) is unclear. Working toward and for equal status contributes significantly to peacebuilding at the relational level (Broome & Collier, 2012: 252).

In intercultural communication (and all communication), sometimes, it might be hard to control the flow of the conversation and that is why people may prefer to not take the risk of asking questions or pursuing some issues in greater depth. As a result, this might stop them from talking about controversial issues, many of which relate directly to issues of social justice, social inclusion and equity. The reason might be not being knowledgeable enough to discuss such topics or not being sure about how to take action in case the conversation takes participants in unexpected directions. However, Broome and Collier (2012: 257) cite the ideas of Galtung and Habermas to explain the value of such dialogue: 'For many scholars and practitioners, dialogue allows participants to penetrate deeper into a conflict (Galtung, 2004), overcoming the asymmetries in information and views that are inherent in conflict situations (Habermas, 1998).' In other words, talking about similarities and finding a common ground might contribute to relationship building; however, discussion of conflict situations can be just as, if not more, constructive. That is the reason why dialogue around differences has been the scope of many peacebuilding studies and has been highlighted as one of the most important components in reconciliation for the people involved (Lowry & Littlejohn, 2006; Mathieu, 2019).

In the following quotes, we can see some examples of how tutors anticipate topics of conversation that may be controversial, due to cultural and other differences; tutors were therefore reluctant to go into deeper discussions about them. The first quote is taken from Cassandra's first journal entry, written before she started tutoring. What she said about her student's expectations before she even met her is worth discussing:

> I anticipate that she would not want to discuss war, politics or religion and may be comfortable discussing certain aspects of culture (food, holidays, family, etc.), but not other aspects that may be controversial or where there is more potential for cultural differences in opinion (women's issues). (Cassandra)

If we remember Hall's (1976) iceberg analogy of culture, the topics Cassandra wants to discuss – or anticipates that her student wants to discuss – are from the tip of that iceberg, including obvious and observable characteristics of a culture like food, music or language. It is generally less risky when we talk about topics from the surface of the iceberg since they are not usually among core values. The risky part of the culture iceberg is what lies below the surface, which includes issues of deep culture like religion, gender roles, ethics, social position and privileges. These practices are generally the invisible part of a culture and can also be difficult to bring up during intercultural dialogue. That might be the reason why Cassandra assumed she and her counterpart would stay 'in the safe zone' – without talking about controversial issues or differences – and not run the risk of harming their relationship.

Cassandra writes about this assumption of her student in her first journal entry. In her third, she acknowledges that *she* may have been more hesitant than her student to discuss more sensitive issues:

> I find that Freshta is not shy and does not seem hesitant to discuss topics of a political nature. (She may even be more comfortable than I am on that front!) (Cassandra)

From Cassandra's parenthetical, it seems she was 'self protecting' by reducing 'self reflective honesty in favor of other reflective honesty' (Lederach, 2003: 50). Between the first and the third reflection, that is, Cassandra moves from validating her own feelings through what she imagined Freshta's would be, to being more honest with herself by directly reflecting on her feelings. '*Honesty* can never be forced,' says Lederach (2003: 50, italics in original); he goes on to state, 'We can, however, work toward the creation of process and spaces where people feel safe enough to be deeply honest with themselves and with others about their fears and hopes, hurts and responsibilities.' In short, while Cassandra initially projected her own concerns onto her student, Cassandra's reflections later show that she felt safe enough to be honest about her feelings, and in a relatively short period of time (three tutoring sessions over three weeks).

Turning to Afghan voices, we next hear what Afghan student Nadeem had to say when encountering difference. Nadeem said that he did not spend much time talking about cultural issues with his US counterpart.

Still, one day he asked a question and found out that his tutor and her boyfriend – not husband – were 'staying under a roof.' He had heard his tutor saying 'my partner,' but he had assumed 'partner' was a 'husband.' When he realized there was no marriage, he explains how the approach to this issue is different in his culture and caused him great surprise:

> In Afghanistan, it's not possible, you should marry with someone to stay under a roof, to spend the days and nights, actually, and since it is different with culture, maybe, because of that it was new for me, actually, I was amazed at that time, how it's possible that you're living/doing such a thing … I was awe-struck. (Nadeem)

As we mentioned before, starting conversations from similarities is easy; talking about the differences may require more courage and confidence. However, in sustained intercultural dialogue such differences may be unavoidable, expected and even vital for developing critical consciousness. We see in the tutoring project, then, an opportunity to practice respecting and valuing the 'different' thing in whatever form we come across it, what Byram (1997) describes as the ability to relativize (and decenter) self, and what Bennett (2004) terms 'ethnorelativism.' Nadeem is developing ethnorelativism as he recognizes that 'the experience of one's own beliefs and behaviors [is] just one organization of reality among many viable possibilities' (Bennett, 2004: 62); for Deardorff (2006b), too, an ethnorelative view is a desired internal outcome indicating intercultural communication competence. Lederach (2003: 13), in the field of peacebuilding, demonstrates another intersection with intercultural communication: 'We need multiple lenses to see different aspects of a complex reality.'

Understanding 'different,' 'complex' realities in Nadeem's situation initiated a dialogue between his tutor and him, which he explains in his interview. When asked if their relationship was at all affected by this new knowledge, he replied first by laughing and then by taking a very matter-of-fact tone:

> Most of the time we don't want to influence, actually, another's life. Therefore we just share our culture sometimes … it's her life, actually. (Nadeem)

Closeness and Distance

Tutor Mary and her student experienced something similar to Nadeem and his tutor. At the beginning stages of her communication with her Afghan student, Mary was nervous because she did not know how much to disclose in conversations with him. In her interview, she stated that she knew he would ask her about her family and she was not sure how much information she should share. She described her initial concerns in this way:

> How personal do I get? Am I going to offend him ... and why should I worry that he's offended by my culture? ... How soon do I come out with the fact that both my daughters are gay? (Mary)

Mary was clearly experiencing some uncertainty about how much she should share with her student because of her fear of 'offending' him, a word the repetition of which evidences the strength of this concern (Fairclough, 1989, 1992). Obviously, she had hopes of having a good relationship with him, and offending him would not serve this purpose. Mary did not stop at only admitting her concerns about her student, but she also started questioning why he would be offended. In both cases, she is struggling with how much information to self-disclose.

Mary's concerns about self-disclosure remind us of the important work of the social penetration theory of Altman and Taylor (1973). This interpersonal relationship theory uses the onion model metaphor to explain the layers of interpersonal communication in terms of self-disclosure. It starts with the superficial layer where people are cautious and share only general information about themselves without going into personal details. When people reach the core layer after regular contact for some time, they start to disclose more private information about themselves, similar to Hall's (1976) iceberg analogy of culture. Unsurprisingly, social penetration theory has been used in intercultural communication and studies related to peace (Chen & Nakazawa, 2009; Remland *et al.*, 2014), and it certainly evokes one of Lederach's (2003) questions related to the kinds of disclosures he construes as necessary for peacebuilding: 'How close or distant do people wish to be in their relationships?' (Lederach, 2003: 25). Furthermore, as Mary ponders how much to disclose of her life to her student, we may actually see her struggling with one of the most widely accepted indicators of intercultural communication competence: 'behaving and communicating effectively and appropriately (based on one's intercultural knowledge, skills attitudes) to achieve one's goal' (Deardorff, 2006b).

Clearly, Mary has to perform a balancing act between what it is appropriate to communicate and her desire to self-disclose. As she continues her interview, we find out that, like Cassandra, it took three to four sessions for her to feel comfortable enough to talk about herself with her student. As she 'created the connection' with her student, she shared more about her family. Here is what Mary said in her interview:

> I felt comfortable sharing with him that my daughter was married to another woman. He was like, 'Wow.' He wasn't shocked, but he was like surprised and he asked me if I agreed with that and I said, well, it's really not for me to agree or disagree. This is my daughter and this is her life and she chooses. ... It's not for me to disagree or agree. I just want my daughter to be happy. So. (Mary)

In this segment of transcript, we may hear an echo of Nadeem's words, after he learned his tutor was not married to the partner she lived with:

'it's her life, actually.' Mary takes quite a risk, which she acknowledges shortly thereafter, voicing her fears that 'in Muslim countries my impression is that gay people are put in prison.' She was naturally 'hesitant' (her word), but she did share based on her relationship with her student:

> [W]e talked about homosexuality and what his view was on it, what my view was on it, and we disagreed, but it was, you look what's going on out in the world right now and people can't even give their opinion without somebody slamming them, calling them Islamophobic, homophobic, whatever. It was nice that we have different points, but it's okay. ... I think he's, because he's educated and he comes from an educated home, he's open to more different viewpoints. (Mary)

From this segment of Mary's interview, it seems that she reached the core layer of the 'onion' model where she felt comfortable enough with her student to, through dialogue, agree to disagree. Obviously, she and her student had arrived at a place where they both felt safe to speak openly and, in Mary's view, 'it was nice.' We can even say that in this case, Mary and her student arrive at a view of 'conflict-as-opportunity' and the subsequent 'encouragement of creative change processes' (Lederach, 2003: 220) as they learn about each other and their views in the virtual intercultural borderlands of online exchange. Through their interactions and the risks each took expressing their views – that is, through increased open-mindedness, their willingness to engage with each other despite difficult topics, and their continued desires for closeness (Broome & Collier, 2012) – we see in their struggles and acceptance more discursive indicators of peacebuilding at the relational (and personal and structural) levels.

Use or Sharing of Power

We next turn back to Cassandra, since she brings up another important issue about power dynamics, not only at the structural level (e.g. the US and Afghanistan), but also at the relational level, as tutor and student. We saw from Yuqing how she discursively creates space for equal agency between her student and herself as they compare and have mini-lessons in Dari and Chinese. In a quote from Haroon, we see a similar example of shared agency:

> [S]ometimes she was giving me a homework and I was doing my homework ... I also give to her some homeworks, not just she, I can also give her, I could give her ... and I give her homework ... and we was like this. (Haroon)

Haroon and Yuqing each happily and actively demonstrate equal power and agency in their interactions with tutor and student, respectively. Lederach (2003: 51) emphasizes that 'we need to be attentive to people's perceptions of how identity is linked to power and to the systems and structures which organize and govern their relationships.' Cassandra's quote below shows how she is aware of and attentive to the power dynamics between her and her student:

> I am conscious of the power dynamics of the tutor – tutee relationship and those between our two countries. I hope to be sensitive to this and to keep her goals at the forefront of our time together, rather than my preconceived notions of how our tutoring sessions should look. (Cassandra)

Cassandra, who was from the US, demonstrates great sensitivity and awareness here to power at the structural and relational levels: she explicitly acknowledges the geopolitical relationships between their 'two countries' and the power dynamics of tutoring with 'tutor/tutee.' When Cassandra talks about 'tutor/tutee,' she functionalizes their roles in the interactions as she transforms verbs into nouns, each with implications: the suffixes in each case signaling the 'doer' (tutor) and the person who is being done unto '-ee' (tutee) (van Leeuwen, 2008: 42). Here we as authors need to be reflective and open, as we ourselves at times used the word 'tutee' with tutors (in interviews and classes), hence perpetuating the potentially unequally power dynamics between tutoring pairs. In the meantime, in Cassandra's explicit sensitivity to the dynamics, and in her desire to keep her Afghan counterpart's 'goals at the forefront,' she discursively evidences her willingness to share power by fronting the student's goals (Lederach, 2003: 52), another discursive indicator of peacebuilding at the relational level which becomes part of the accumulation and constellation of peacebuilding indicators across levels and between intercultural interactants. She is further well aware of and on the alert for her own preconceptions, demonstrating that she is working to 'maximiz[e] potential for individual changes in self-perceptions' (Broome & Collier, 2012: 251), an indicator of peacebuilding at the personal level (peacebuilding levels overlap), even as relationally she acknowledges the 'status positioning' of their relationship (Broome & Collier, 2012: 251). At a time when the hegemony of English as a global language remains under debate and scrutiny (see Chapters 3, 4 and 6), Cassandra provides a good example of how English language teaching can be used as a space to reflect on power dynamics and their impact on our relationships.

It is important to listen to the other side of this power dynamic as well, but before we share an Afghan perspective on power dynamics during tutoring, we should recall Hofstede's (1980) concept of power distance, the acceptance of the unequal distribution of power and its role in intercultural communication. If we think of this concept through an educator's lens, it means that the authority of teachers is expected and natural in high power distance cultures while in low power distance cultures, students are at the center of the educational system. Afghanistan is considered among the high power distance cultures (Gul *et al.*, 2018; Kibria, 2013) where teachers' authority is not questioned, but respected. In this context, Afghan participant Najibullah talks about his tutor, who was like a friend, not a tutor:

> She was a tutor, but ... she has been a really good friend of mine, I really loved this experience, and sometimes we ask each other, and I send her pictures I take from Afghanistan, this is very good, again, it's like finding a new friend. (Najibullah)

Contrary to the expected power dynamics between a teacher and a student in Afghanistan, Najibullah's tutor was *not* like a tutor, but 'a really good friend.' This is not only important in terms of building a bridge between them, but also for creating a space for Najibullah to reflect on power dynamics critically, indicating that *although* ('but') she was a tutor, she also became something else: 'a really good friend,' a relationship which came to transcend the tutor/student relationship in his view. One lesson we take from Najibullah's voice is stated clearly in Broome and Collier (2012: 260): 'Particularly in the arena of peacebuilding, we should be careful about essentializing members of cultural groups as "being" collectivistic, or "other face oriented," without qualifiers about contextual factors related to status and power relations, history, setting, the role of multiple identifications, and the potential for contestation.' Together, Najibullah and his 'really good friend,' his tutor, clearly created a safe space for more equitable relationships (Goodman, 2013) and alliance building. Accordingly, we should be careful about essentializing Najibullah as an 'Afghan English learner from a high power distance culture' (we might say the same about Haroon's tutor and Mary's student), just as Najibullah was obviously careful not to 'essentialize' his partner as 'teacher' or 'tutor.' She was something greater, 'a really good friend.'

At the relational level of peacebuilding, Lederach (2003: 25) describes one goal of positive change: 'to minimize poorly functioning communication and to maximize mutual understanding.' Mutual understanding, in turn, requires listening. Aijazi (2020: 3), in the context of humanitarian aid, peace and development work, discusses 'deep listening and power-sharing' both as equivalents and as acts of accountability. Among peacebuilding principles, Lederach (2003: 55) asserts, 'most essential is hearing and engaging the struggling, sometimes lost, voices of identity within the loud static of the conflictive environment.' While we do not construct the tutoring project as a 'humanitarian project' in Aijazi's (2020) terms, we do recognize the 'loud static of the conflictive environment,' and we have encountered throughout the voices of this project forceful evidence of the relationships between power and listening.

Jennifer provides a striking example of the power of a tutor listening, even as she struggles to understand and respond 'appropriately' to a student who was talking about the Taliban and war. Jennifer writes the following in her journal:

> Although our conversation was powerful, it was challenging for me to respond at times. Some of the discussion questions were around culture. When my tutee and I were discussing cultural norms and our perspective

on how the media can affect your perspective, the war in Afghanistan was brought up. The tutee spoke openly about the Taliban and how it has affected him and his family directly. This was challenging because I did not know how to respond. I wanted to make sure I said the right thing and did not offend him or his culture, and I was unsure how to respond. I just said I am sorry for what is happening and that I hope for peace. This was a difficult conversation to have, especially since I do not have many experiences that can relate to his. (Jennifer)

In this journal entry, we see that Jennifer clearly wanted to communicate effectively and appropriately, terms used to comprise the definition of intercultural communication competence in well-known models (e.g. Deardorff, 2006b). Her reference to the emotional impact of listening to her student as 'powerful' returns us to the personal level of peacebuilding (Lederach, 2003) (peacebuilding levels overlap), even as reference to and awareness of problematic media representations of conflicts evidence the structural level of peacebuilding (see Chapter 6). But relationally, by struggling to use the right words and not offend him by saying something wrong, we see Jennifer's mindful intentions as she listened, and 'hope for peace' as important perhaps as an 'appropriate' response: her reflection brings up her 'hope' (and her fears), and she explicitly shares her 'hope' with the student, discursive moves which Lederach (2003: 24) posits are essential to peacebuilding at the relational level. We read her reflection to be almost as powerful as her discussion with her Afghan student, and we read within it, too, another discursive indicator of peacebuilding at the relational level: that of empathy, which we explore next.

Maximizing Mutual Understanding: Empathy

Empathy among intercultural interactants is an essential component of a 'good' relationship. As Hodges and Klein (2001) observe, it is the price we pay for being human. But empathy for another may depend on the quality of the relationship we are in with that other. According to Broome and Collier (2012: 249–250), qualities 'such as empathy, communication style, and even motivation to engage in intercultural interactions ... emerg[e] from the quality of the relationship.' Empathy arises from our ability to perceive situations from others' points of view and develop an empathic understanding of the person we are interacting with, although as Lederach (2003: 43) describes it, empathy is also a 'discipline' we develop, allowing 'one to understand the situation of another (person or group) but not to be drawn into the spin of their anxieties and fears.' We find 'empathy' also as required for effective and appropriate intercultural communication (Arasaratnam, 2014; Deardorff, 2006b; DeTurk, 2001; Spitzberg & Changnon, 2009). At the same time, the importance of empathy goes beyond the relational level and into the structural. Stokke and Lybæk (2018: 82) write, '[I]nterculturalism opens a greater space for dialogue, and thus for minority voices to be heard and promote real integration, characterized by mutual understanding, mutual learning and empathy.'

All of these understandings of empathy should help us see it as central to peacebuilding as well. The lack of empathy has been described as a 'major threat to peace' (Grant-Hayford & Scheyer, 2017); the presence of empathy has been described as an 'invaluable natural resource for peace' (Abu-Akel *et al.*, 2019). Schmid's (2001) ideas on empathy add yet more to our understanding:

> Its [empathy's] relational dimension responds to the need of an individual in his or her search for being deeply understood and thus constituted as a person in their confusing position in the middle of a bewildering world. … Empathy is the ability, the challenge and the attempt to enter a solidary relationship to the Other, acknowledging diversity and yet trying to understand and to become aware of him or her. (Schmid, 2001: 10)

From Schmid's (2001) definition, key elements stand out. He highlights the links between identity and being/feeling 'deeply understood'; it is that sense of being deeply understood that allows us to feel we exist, as a person. To have such feelings, says Schmid (2001), we must have an ability for 'empathy,' a phrasing not unlike Lederach's (2003: 43) view of empathy as a necessary discipline peacebuilders work to develop. In both cases, we must take risks as we seek unity with another, we must recognize diversity and difference, and we must work to understand the other. For the work of peacebuilding as well as intercultural communication, empathy is thus a 'desired internal outcome' (Deardorff, 2006a) at the same level as ethnorelativism, not unlike Byram's (1997) notion of 'decentering' self, but we must (and can) seek evidence of empathy in behavior and in discourse (McAlinden, 2018).

Before we analyze the occurrence of empathy through the voices of our participants, we first offer an overview of definitions and types of empathy. Since the nature of empathy is complex, there have been various definitions in the literature; in fact, it is claimed that the meaning of 'empathy' might change from person to person (Kerem *et al.*, 2001). The complexity of the concept has led researchers to break it down into multiple types, such as cognitive, affective and multidimensional empathy (Davis *et al.*, 1994; Kerem *et al.*, 2001; Stephan & Finlay, 1999). Cognitive empathy – also called cognitive perspective taking – is the action of understanding others' feelings but not sharing those feelings, whereas affective empathy involves sharing the same feelings with the other person (de Vignemont & Singer, 2006). Multidimensional empathy works to fill the gaps between empathy as an internal process and empathy as it impacts communication behavior (Everett, 2005). Even though the definitions and types of empathy vary, the necessity for empathy in developing strong, positive relationships is indisputable (de Vignemont & Singer, 2006;

Stephan & Finlay, 1999): empathy is a critical component of peacebuilding (Lederach, 2003) and intercultural communication alike.

Turning to participants' voices, in this section we focus on the consequences and impacts of empathy on discourse and behavior and on how empathy affects relationship building so as to create greater equality and inclusive interaction between our research participants (Lederach, 2003). In the process, we take a step back to look at the bigger picture from the tutors' perspectives, especially as they, future teachers of English as an additional language (EAL), develop their abilities not only to engage empathetically in their classrooms, but also to contribute to the peacebuilding process. Empathy, on its own, is an essential skill for all educators and can be developed through experience especially with people from diverse cultures. Goodwin (2002: 161) claims that 'too many teachers or administrators lack any personal experience that might engender empathy and direct them to focus their attention on immigrant children,' reminding us of the importance of the concept for English language teachers who have daily interactions with students from diverse backgrounds. For our tutors and future teachers of EAL, we take hope from the fact that participants' discourses evidence how, in the virtual intercultural borderlands of online exchange, tutors and students clearly found a space where they could develop a deeper understanding of 'the other.' The following voices provide the foundations of this hope.

Valerie had tutoring sessions with her student during the month of Ramadan, the holy month for Muslims around the world. During Ramadan, for 30 days Muslims abstain from eating or drinking from dawn to sunset, or 'fast.' Ramadan is practiced in different months every year since it is based on the moon's natural cycles according to the Islamic calendar. When Valerie participated in this project, her student was fasting on a very hot day in Afghanistan. Even though they were only virtually together, Valerie seemed to feel the high temperature on the other side of the computer screen as she appeared to understand what her student was going through. She described the following in her interview:

> One day, he had a handkerchief and he kept on wiping his face and his head and I was just like, what's wrong? He's like, the air conditioner is not working here. I'm like, oh my god, that must be such an uncomfortable thing … on top of that fasting and everything. So the Ramadan, I think that was an issue, not so much for him because he never said it was. But I imagine it would have been, even if he didn't admit it, like being in an unairconditioned room sometimes not having water or anything. That is like not the best situation. (Valerie)

Here Valerie demonstrates empathy by trying to understand what is going on in her student's world. Although she has never fasted herself, she makes an effort to imagine how it feels to take an English class on a hot day without food, water or air conditioning. This kind of empathic understanding is also reflected in Valerie's behavior. In the same interview, she stated that she made some modifications to the lesson and asked her student if he wanted to cut the lesson short. Most importantly, Valerie paid extra attention not to eat or drink anything during the tutoring sessions so as not to make her student uncomfortable. Empathy, which started internally in Valerie's situation as she sought to understand the inner world of the other, ended up being externalized discursively as she expressed her concern and made the session length flexible based on her student's needs.

While Valerie described her empathetic feelings for her student, Kay, another tutor, experienced empathy *from* her student. Here we need to recall the eight-hour time difference between Afghan students and their US-based tutors. Tutors frequently had to make appointments to meet their students before 6:00 in the morning or after 10:00 at night:

> I'm pretty sure instead of [meeting for tutoring] at the school, he did it at his work, so he could come in earlier. Then when the school opened, he could go to his job, because he had computers at his job, so he was willing to work with me, and come in a little bit earlier, so I could get a little bit more sleep, which was very, which was very nice of him. It was very considerate. (Kay)

Sensing her student's empathetic feelings and efforts, Kay appreciated his change of behavior so she could sleep 'a little bit more.' The strength of her appreciation is enacted in discourse through repetition – 'which was very'; 'which was very'; 'It was very' (Fairclough, 2001: 115) – and she seems almost to struggle to find the right adjective: 'nice' doesn't seem quite strong enough, so she moves to 'considerate.' We value the way Kay realized and acknowledged this kind of empathy in her relationship. Sometimes, it is hard for us to become aware of the empathetic feelings of our students not only because we, as educators, have more students in our classrooms, but also because sometimes we feel so much empathy for them that we might miss how our students show empathy for us. There is no doubt that taking a moment to recognize our students' feelings and showing appreciation makes a big difference in our relationship building with them.

Resistance: Poorly Functioning Communication

Willingness to minimize poorly functioning communication is one of the components of the relational dimension of peacebuilding (Lederach, 2003). However, prejudgments and biases at the personal level can affect how open we are to the input from another person: 'we find it harder to really hear what others are saying – unless of course, they agree with us' (Lederach, 2003: 11). In the following reflection from Mary, from whom we heard earlier, we see an example of poorly functioning communication: one participant is not listening to or able to hear what the other is saying. In Chapter 4, we saw an example of the resistance Tayba displayed toward sharing personal information out of initial fear of her Afghan student. In the following passage, we observe a different type of resistance. Mary initially rejects information from her student, Nazir, which contradicts her own 'beliefs' about the world.

During one of their tutoring sessions, the discussion turned to the 13th century Persian scholar and poet Rumi:

> I really knew nothing about Rumi, so we talked about him ... [Nazir said] it could easily be seen that ... he is the bestseller poet in the U.S. and when I heard that ... well, I didn't know that. When Nazir told me that, I'm like ahh ... I don't think so. Then I went and researched ... Oh my God. He's right! (Mary)

Mary refuses to believe that the best-selling poet in the US could be from Afghanistan until she researches Rumi herself. After conducting her own research, however, Mary shares her surprise, perhaps at the discovery that Rumi is so well known and perhaps at the fact that Nazir possessed knowledge she did not: 'Oh my God. He's right!' When faced with information that contradicts previously held beliefs, 'positive change does not always happen,' Lederach (2003: 17) or it happens to varying degrees. In Mary's case, a transformative change did happen, but it was not without initial resistance:

> Also, he educated me. I really knew nothing about Rumi ... So we talked a little bit about his poetry and I had no idea such an enlightened man came from that ... you know. (Mary)

Acknowledging 'also, he educated me,' Mary offers evidence of increased open-mindedness (Lederach, 2003), a willingness to learn about and from her student. However, Mary continues to display resistance, questioning the accuracy of Nazir's description of the community in which he lives, and questioning the very possibility that 'such an enlightened man' could come from Afghanistan. Her resistance continues in the next quote from her interview:

> I asked him if his 14-year-old sister would be able to walk out on the street and he said yes. I'm not sure if that is exactly true, but I did not press the issue. (Mary)

Faced with information that contradicts her own perceptions, rather than initiating a discussion which might contribute to 'maximiz[ing] mutual understanding' (Lederach, 2003), Mary 'did not press the issue.'

Mary's resistance to learning more about the streets where her student, and his sister, walk serves as a reminder that when participants, like Mary and Nazir, come together, change is neither predictable nor inevitable. Nonetheless, through their online interactions our participants still learned about themselves, about each other and, as we explore next in Chapter 6, about each other's agency in the midst of structural forces at the structural level of person to person peacebuilding.

6 Person to Person Peacebuilding at the Structural Level

In this chapter, we turn our attention to the structural level of peacebuilding. As we discuss this level of peacebuilding, understanding of the terms 'agency' and 'structure' is key. We use the terms 'agency' and 'agent' according to standard sociological definitions, whereby 'agency' denotes the capacity to act, with intention, according to an actor's – or 'agent's' – mental state in relation to events (Schlosser, 2019). As for 'structure,' sociologists provide broad definitions, encompassing perceptible institutions (governments and political systems, education, healthcare, economics, law, the media) along with less visible, social-cultural structures (family structures, languages and language varieties, traditions, religions and other belief systems, rituals, social codes, etc.), all of which are organized through hierarchical patterns and relationships (Clarke-Habibi, 2014; Montiel, 2001; Parsons, 1951).

In reference to peacebuilding, understanding the power of social structures requires an understanding of the ongoing 'structure versus agency debate' in the social sciences. Within this debate there are three general positions. First, deterministic structural-functionalism posits that social structures exert powerful determining constraints on our actions so as to maintain social cohesion and order. In this view, the force of these structures renders them formidable and difficult to change, with human agency sorely delimited (Astley & Van de Ven, 1983; Clarke-Habibi, 2014; Parsons, 1951). A second, interpretive stance drawn from micro-sociology swings far in the other direction: this stance emphasizes how humans as individual agents create meaning and reality, and it is interactions between individuals that lead to the creation of social structures. As such, human agents are well positioned to enact social change through structural change (Barker, 2005). A third stance, that of Giddens' (1984) 'structuration theory,' contends that it is the dialectical interplay *between* social structures and human agency – the back and forth of who or what has the power – which both reproduces social systems and structures and which can also produce/create them anew. Structures and agents are hence interdependent. They both constrain *and* enable actions; individual actors create and shape these structures and, in turn, are profoundly shaped by them. It is this stance which reconciles: (1) the over-determination of structural-functionalism; and (2) the problematics of embracing free, agentive will without consideration of the restraints and constraints on individuals who are certainly positioned differently – and unequally – within structures.

Giddens' (1984) 'structuration theory' – and this more general background to structure, agency, and the relationship between the two – help us understand how Lederach (2003) and Broome and Collier (2012) view agency and the structural level of peacebuilding in their peacebuilding frameworks. Within these frameworks, we see what peacebuilders (our participants) should understand and be aware of; we see actions they should take or be prepared to take; and we see what to look for in participants' voices as discursive indicators of peacebuilding.

For this chapter, we combine the two frameworks as follows, with each component representing discursive indicators of peacebuilding at the structural level (see Table 6.1). We further order the basic sections of our chapter as follows, although there are times when multiple peacebuilding indicators are present in one quote or excerpt from tutors' written reflections:

(1) Participants' understandings of the causes and effects of conflicts (Lederach, 2003: 25), including how discourses, policies and practices create and enable: access to resources and status; levels of individual agency and equity; societal norms (Broome & Collier, 2012: 252).
(2) Participants' discussions of inclusion and decision making and means to more broadly include voices (Broome & Collier, 2012) in order to maximize the involvement of people in decisions that affect them (Lederach, 2003: 24–25).
(3) Participants' understandings of how policies, laws, public and media texts and discourses both enable and constrain individuals and groups (Broome & Collier, 2012: 252).
(4) Ways to create conditions and relations that contribute to social justice and peace (Broome & Collier, 2012: 252), including work to minimize and eliminate violence; and help in developing structures that meet basic human needs (Lederach, 2003: 24–25).
(5) Participant resistance in one participant as it relates to structural constraints.

Accordingly, in the analysis that follows, we show just how participants in the virtual intercultural borderlands availed themselves of the communication affordances present there to discursively manifest actions and changes needed for peacebuilding at the structural level. We posit, again, that the accumulation and constellation of these discursive indicators from intercultural interactants evidence the work of peacebuilding, a position grounded in the presuppositions of discourse analysis: that discourse

Table 6.1 Dimensions of peacebuilding: Positive change at the structural level of peacebuilding

At the STRUCTURAL level of peacebuilding, positive change in the following:

Lederach (2003)	Broome and Collier (2012)
Understanding the causes of conflict	How societal discourses, organizational policies and institutional practices create and enable differential access to resources and status, levels of individual agency and equity, and societal norms
Working to minimize and eliminate violence	
Working to foster social, economic, and institutional relationships to meet basic human needs and provide access to resources and decision making	Working for broader inclusion of diverse voices
	Creating conditions and relations that contribute to social justice and peace

constitutes, is constituted by and *is* social action (Hoffman, 2012; Wiggins, 2009); that discourse creates our worlds and our realities; and that meaning is made through the negotiations of social interaction (Berger & Luckmann, 1966; Cooper *et al.*, 2021; Cruikshank, 2012; Fairclough, 1989, 2001; Foucault, 1984; Laclau & Mouffe, 1985; van Dijk, 2000; Wodak, 2004). Throughout our analysis, we further highlight the integral intersections between intercultural communication and peacebuilding, thus shoring up a central thesis of Broome and Collier (2012: 246): 'the study of intercultural communication intersects with peacebuilding in fundamental and meaningful ways.'

Participants' Understandings of the Causes and Effects of Conflicts

Understandings of the effects of conflict were infused throughout participants' voices, most obviously (although not only) in transcripts of interviews with our Afghan participants, who live with these effects daily. There were brief references to the dangers of traveling in Afghanistan as compared to traveling in the US or Europe; there were direct discussions between tutors and their students about Afghan participants' desires to emigrate due to conflict. But the most prominent topic participants raised involved conflict's effects on the structural force of education in its various forms. For this reason, we first focus on conflict and education. Specifically, we share how participants talked and wrote about their understandings of the effects of conflict on the structural force of education, how participants exerted levels of agency in response to conflict, and how the force of conflict limits access to the resource of education.

Participants' understandings of the effects of conflict

We start with discursive constructions of how participants understand structural changes resulting from conflict, as these changes make up one significant part of the context and backdrop of the tutoring project. As discussed in Chapter 3, we remind readers here that context is not merely 'the scene' of peacebuilding, which Broome and Collier (2012: 253) make clear: 'it is a constitutive force and set of dynamic and material conditions ... both temporal and spatial, incorporating past, present and future.' From this definition of context, it follows that participants' discussions of the past, present and future (the before, during and after of their tutoring experiences) are essential to our analysis of peacebuilding at the structural level, particularly given another fundamental premise of discourse analysis: that participants' views ('beliefs, attitudes, attributions and perceptions') are not fixed or constant over time, but rather, are discursively constructed and shaped by their social, political, historical and cultural contexts.

Afghan participant Mirza depicts for us in some detail the landscape of the Afghan context in conflict. Throughout his interview, Mirza's discourse effectuates his understanding of conflict's impact on structures (Lederach, 2003) – and participants' lives – in Afghanistan. We also begin to see from Mirza how the structural force of war is brought to bear on the structural force of education, including how conflict limits access to education as a resource. At the same time, through his meetings with his tutor, he exerts his agency in response to conflict as he works toward a different, more peaceful future.

During his interview, Mirza, an English teacher in an Afghan university, was asked first why he wanted to study English with a US-based tutor. In his response, he begins to answer by explaining his aspirations for more education, but he quickly veers into talking about the war in Afghanistan and its stark impact on education:

> I am applying to continue my education, for instance, Master's degree or Ph.D. is my hope for that, I should have, my solution. When I see myself in Afghanistan, it is not possible, how can I change, or how should I work with this situation? Every day there is bomb explosion or attack or some days, the security is not good, and every day you are facing with many challenges, and because of that I am applying to finish my Master's degree or Ph.D., Inshallah, I'm trying to go overseas. ... When I am teaching at university, I see the security. ... This is the most challenging problem. When the security is not good, how you can learn? (Mirza)

Here, we hear how the palpable structure of conflict in the 'every day' – 'bomb explosion,' 'attack' – constrains opportunities for education generally and Mirza specifically, limiting his access to the resources of education: 'it is not possible, how can I change, or how should I work with this situation?'; and later, 'How you can learn?' Mirza constructs these effects as creating a nearly impossible situation, and his repetition ('every day,' 'every day') discursively stresses the 'continuity' – in this case, the seeming relentlessness – of violence (Fairclough, 2001: 94; Wodak *et al.*,

2009: 39). At the same time, as an English teacher striving to improve his English through the tutoring project, Mirza's discourse manifests contradiction: he is confronting the ostensibly hopeless effects of his conflict context – 'how should I work with this situation?' – while simultaneously exerting agency as he decides to work with his US-based tutor in the virtual intercultural borderlands to prepare for a future where he can pursue 'positive' change through education, 'to go overseas' and 'finish his Master's degree or Ph.D.' Both working with his tutor and the hope of future education thus become for Mirza a structural 'solution,' 'his hope' to overcome 'the most challenging' problem of security, the structural force of conflict. The hope we mention here goes beyond Mirza's personal desires, for (as we find out later in his interview) his goal for after his future higher education is to return to and work for Afghanistan: 'I want to be a good person in my country, and serve for my country, and because of that I'm applying to get scholarship.' While Mirza's goals are personal, for him they also hold the promise of structural change for *his* country, which he claims twice ('my country,' 'my country'), hence exerting in his discourse agency against the structural force of conflict: (1) through his repeated use of the possessive pronoun, which lays claim to what is his (van Leeuwen, 2008: 36); and (2) through his belief in his ability to effect structural change in the future. The agency Mirza has already exerted and will continue to exert, moreover, plays a crucial role in intercultural competence development and will serve him well in his future study 'overseas' and beyond, as he continues to learn about adapting his communication according to different cultural norms (Covert, 2014; Deardorff, 2006a). Even though this kind of agency is developed at the personal level, we can see that it also powerfully impacts relationship building (the relational level of peacebuilding) and, as we see here, change at the structural level of peacebuilding.

Mirza's desire for opportunities to study abroad – bolstered if not necessitated by the structural force of conflict and its effects – was echoed among Afghan participants. Tutor Lisa writes about her student in her reflective journal:

> I learned that Mustafa wanted to continue his education in America by completing his second masters program in order to increase the educational opportunities for the students of Afghanistan. One of the first things I asked him to do was to write a paragraph on any subject that he felt was interesting and relevant to his career goals. What I received was a very telling account of his feelings for his country and the importance of developing the infrastructure that would facilitate long lasting peace. (Lisa)

As with Mirza, Lisa's student, Mustafa, was seeking personal, relational and structural change (peacebuilding levels overlap) through more education, a structure which in Afghanistan remains woefully ill-equipped to meet most students' needs due to the impacts of intractable conflict (UNICEF, 2016). Mustafa's access to the resources he needs to fulfill his career goals is obstructed by the context of conflict in which he lives. Yet Mustafa had searched for (and in part, found) a means to go around this roadblock: first by completing a Master's degree in India (noted in another entry) and then by joining the tutoring program so his tutor could help him prepare to apply for scholarships in 'America,' just as Mirza's tutor had helped him. Here we see not only Mustafa's 'willingness to create new ways of interacting to build relationships' as he starts his work with tutor Lisa, but also his determination to help develop 'structures that look toward the future' (Lederach, 2003: 33). Lisa sums up Mustafa's words: he wants 'to increase the educational opportunities for the students of Afghanistan' as part of helping develop 'the infrastructure that would facilitate long lasting peace.'

Although we only learn about Mustafa's relationship with Lisa through her journal (we were unable to interview Lisa), it seems that he shares his life and experiences with her in some detail. He conveys to her, for instance, what he learns from his 'educator parents.' She writes:

> My favorite line stated that his educator parents taught him that peace will come through the ink in a pen rather than bullets from a gun. I told everyone this line. (Lisa)

In Lisa's lines, we see the reverse of what we have been exploring: conflict's impacts on education. Now we see at least one impact of education on conflict, as Mustafa's 'educator parents' encourage a way to resist conflict and contribute to creating the structural force of 'peace': through a pen. Furthermore, Lisa's decision to tell the discursively totalizing 'everyone' this line evidences her contributions to structural peacebuilding in two ways. First, her repetition of this line to 'everyone' launches a compelling 'chain of discourse.' As such, these words may grow in authority and strength with every new iteration and recontextualization and as 'everyone' Laura tells repeats them to others (Bakhtin, 1973; Blackledge, 2005: viii). Second, her repetition of the line is testament to how dramatically it impressed her: while the change *she* experiences from her interactions with Mustafa are obviously very personal, the substance of that change – 'that peace will come through the ink in a pen rather than bullets from a gun' – relates directly to Lisa's (and Mustafa's) understandings of structure, conflict and peace: structural peace is discursively embedded in structural literacy (literally, 'through the ink in a pen') (for more on the 'structural' force of literacy; see, for example, Brandt & Clinton, 2002), and in education more broadly.

Elsewhere in her journal Lisa shares the following about Mustafa's parents, a brief fact which allows us to infer that because of her work with her Afghan student, Lisa in all likelihood better – if more painfully – apprehends the effects of conflict on education:

> He wrote about the fact that his parents were both teachers but that his father had to leave Afghanistan when the Taliban gained control because they were beheading teachers. (Lisa)

With these words we return to conflict's brutal effects and to Lisa's (albeit indirect) encounter with the same through her intercultural interactions with Mustafa. The Taliban's ruthless campaign against the structure of education – by targeting teachers and students alike – illustrates how structures can clash, as the radical ideology of a group of insurgents attempts to destroy one of the most critical structures of *civil* society: education (see, for example, Ravitch & Viteritti, 2001). Through the tutoring project, Lisa must encounter this clash and its barbarism, if second hand, thereby certainly deepening her understanding of the impacts of conflict on education (as well as education's potential impacts on conflict).

While we infer Lisa's deeper understanding of the structural force of conflict through her reflective journal entry, tutor Carrie makes explicit her new comprehension of the effects of conflict through the clash between the structures of conflict and education. She writes in her journal:

> This has been an eye-opening experience on many levels. Education is taken for granted by those who have such quick and direct access to it. Andesha is willing to walk through the war torn streets of Afghanistan to sit at a computer and learn from someone halfway across the world. It is a humbling experience. (Carrie)

No doubt, this passage reflects, first, very personal change of the type we explore in Chapter 4, as Carrie's eyes have been opened 'on many levels' (peacebuilding levels overlap). What we take particular note of here is Carrie's assessment of the structure of education, access to which is 'taken for granted' by so many, and her student's determined agency (like Mirza's, like Mustafa's) to avail herself of the positive force of that structure despite the devastation wrought by another, conflict: 'Andesha is willing to walk through the war torn streets of Afghanistan' just to sit and learn. Of equal significance: while Carrie's description of 'the war torn streets' may be viewed as essentializing Afghanistan, defining it primarily and without nuance through the commonplace of 'war torn,' through those streets walks very much an individual (Andesha), whom Carrie nominates – or names specifically – and who is exerting her agency, an individual Carrie interacts with and who, in turn, is individualized, personalized, humanized (van Leeuwen, 2008: 50). This change at the personal dimension of peacebuilding as evidenced in her discourse leads Carrie to reflect on the gravity of what happens when structures (education, conflict) collide, and her description of the experience 'as humbling' highlights her newfound and profound understanding of structures, their power, and what it means – the responsibility – to be a part of them: even if 'halfway across the world' from her student.

Understanding of the type Carrie displays here is a result of raising awareness. Critical cultural awareness (CCA), which is described as reflecting on one's own and the other culture critically (Byram, 1997), creates a space for people to look at their cultures and contexts differently and anew, including the power, structures and privileges they experience. Based on critical reflection and evaluation, 'CCA might serve as a great tool for recognizing, evaluating and mediating between the myriad of identities, perspectives and meanings that interact "in-between," i.e. in the third place' (Cierpisz, 2019: 229; see also Chapter 3 for discussion of 'borderlands,' 'contact zones,' 'third space,' 'third place' and the virtual intercultural borderlands). Understanding of agency and empowerment and questioning of structures, including institutionalized hegemonic power, cannot exist without raising cultural awareness. Especially for privileged groups, this consciousness is crucial to raising awareness about inequalities and social/global injustice. Goodman (2011: 24) explains its importance: 'People from privileged groups tend to have little awareness of their own dominant identity, of the privileges it affords them, of the oppression suffered by the corresponding disadvantaged group, and they perpetuate it.' Without this critical awareness, there is little hope of expecting a structural change.

The demand for English as an effect of conflict

Another effect of conflict, understanding of which contributes to peacebuilding at the structural level (Lederach, 2003), is how conflict in Afghanistan has given rise, in large part, to both the perceived necessity of and demand for English among many Afghans. This is an effect we must look at critically and reflexively, given our own personal contributions to and benefits from the continuing dominance of English globally – and, for one author, in Afghanistan specifically. The presence of this effect in participants' discourses reminds us of the importance of raising CCA (Byram, 1997) – particularly awareness of the structural force of English and the pressures that urge its spread – among future project participants specifically in *English* language teaching and online intercultural exchange.

To explain the rise and spread of English as an effect of conflict, we turn to the work of Phillipson (1992, 2018), who initiated an ongoing conversation in the field of language teaching through his explorations of 'linguistic imperialism.' He asks:

> How can we, in a theoretically informed way, relate the global role of English, and the way in which language pedagogy supports the spread and promotion of the language, to the political, economic, military, and cultural pressures that propel it forward? How can analysis probe beyond individual experience and reflection to the processes and structures which are in operation at the international, national, group and personal levels? (Phillipson, 1992: 2)

While the analysis Phillipson entreats us to undertake is beyond the focus of this book, we do see clear-cut connections we must address: namely, in relation to 'the political, economic, military, and cultural pressures that propel [English] forward' (Phillipson, 1992: 2). These are structural pressures, and the pressures of politics, war and economics are evident in the following excerpt from our interview with Najibullah, who also goes on to describe a culture around English as it relates to these pressures:

> In Afghanistan, like when the U.S. army, the Europeans and their military came to Afghanistan, it had the effect on the job market, if a person knew English, ok ... he or she would have a good job, a good salary, this is one reason, and that effect is, like, it's become like a culture for us, for the students in Afghanistan, to learn English. (Najibullah)

Najibullah draws a fairly straight line from the presence of US and NATO forces in Afghanistan first to the 'job market' and then to English and 'a good salary,' an assertion supported by numbers: in 2010 alone, the International Security Assistance Force (ISAF) employed 60,000–80,000 Afghans, while USAID created between 31,000 and 60,000 jobs for Afghan civilians, numbers which do not include jobs financed by international aid money (Cordesman *et al.*, 2013), or numbers of Afghans killed by insurgent groups *because* they worked for NATO, US forces or international NGOs. While we do not know how many of those jobs required English, we do know that many of our Afghan participants pursued English so as to work for the military and/or various NATO contractors and NGOs in Afghanistan. Their thinking likely paralleled Najibullah's, who through repetition semantically builds on 'good,' 'good' – from job market, to job, to salary – discursively demonstrating the 'ongoing concept formation' of English (van Leeuwen, 2008: 19), as a 'good job' and a 'good salary' become semantically bound up in English. So too do 'the U.S. army, the Europeans and their military' – *where* the effect on the job market comes from – lead to 'good' and even a kind of 'culture' among Afghans who speak English, according to Najibullah. At the same time, we must remember what Tayba said about her tutor, as she 'learned that his life was in danger for being able to speak English and having previous experience with the U.S. Army.'

As another example of how the structural force of conflict in Afghanistan perpetuated a demand for English, we turn to Sadaf, who explains why she wanted to study English as follows:

> In Afghanistan, especially I'd like to work for an NGO that can help my people. ... To help my people. And have good salary also [she laughs] ... When I want to work for an NGO, basically it's working with Americans or maybe other foreign countries, when I want to interact with those countries, English is very important to speak with them. If I don't understand English, that would be hard for me to speak with them or say what I wanted to tell them. (Sadaf)

In this quote, Sadaf reinforces the connection between English, conflict and 'the job market' that Najibullah so eloquently explained, even though Sadaf's laugh suggests that she may be a little bit embarrassed by the afterthought (or perhaps she felt she was stating the obvious). Either way, salary was important to her, as was helping *her* people, a desire the strength of which she accentuates through repetition (Wodak *et al.*, 2009: 39). She even emphasizes 'To help my people' by making the thought its own (if incomplete) sentence. Sadaf further claims 'her people' twice, as 'her own,' with the possessive pronoun ('my people,' 'my people'). Discursively, that is, like Mirza wanting to serve ('my country,' 'my country'), Sadaf expresses a similar yearning, in the process exerting her agency in a way we find particularly meaningful, especially as we consider the effects of the structural force of conflict and the rise of English in Afghanistan.

To understand why Sadaf's exertion of agency here is important, we first need to quickly expand on Phillipson (1992) and the English linguistic imperialism debate (see also Chapters 3 and 4, where we briefly touch upon the effects of 'native speakerisms'). Scholars globally have lauded the importance of this conversation and simultaneously found fault with Phillipson's early 'deterministic' and 'reductive' positions, where learners and users of the language seemingly have no agency – no choice – against the imperialist, capitalist structure of English and all it connotes (Pennycook, 1994: 57; see also Canagarajah, 1999; Ferguson, 2006; Kumaravadivelu, 2014; Spolsky, 2004; Swan *et al.*, 2015). Instead, and returning to Giddens' (1984) views on agency and structure discussed at the start of this chapter, we can look to participants' discourses in order to see 'how people make sense of their lives and thus how human agency operates within global structures of inequality' (Pennycook, 1994: 57).

Sadaf's discourse substantiates her agency. Sadaf's repetition of 'my people,' 'my people' is one form of discursive agency she asserts as she claims the people of Afghanistan as *hers* (van Leeuwen, 2008: 23): moreover, the 'NGO' she imagines, which involves working with 'Americans or maybe other foreign countries,' is there in Afghanistan to help *her* people. She wants to work for that imagined NGO to help her people, too. But what we find most telling about her agency is *why* she perceives she needs English: 'English is very important to speak with them. If I don't understand English, that would be hard for me to speak with them or say what I wanted to tell them.' Sadaf's agency in relation to her future colleagues at her future, imagined, NGO is one where her voice matters: she needs English 'to speak *with* them' and 'say what *I* wanted to tell *them*.' Sadaf decidedly imagines her role in this NGO as an active, agentive one, for which she will use English 'to tell them' what she wants to say in reference to helping *her* people. Her agency is visible despite the perceived need for English in order to exert it: she understands and accepts it calmly as an effect of conflict, one which could constrain her work to help her people, her agency, but doesn't have to (she won't let it).

Participants' Understandings of the Causes of Conflict
Social actors and causes of conflict

While discussion of the effects of conflict were prevalent in participants' discourses, discussion of the *causes* underlying conflict – as explicitly linked to conflict – rarely probed beyond the surface level of violence. Poverty combined with a lack of development and limited access to the resource of education in Afghanistan were brought up frequently by both tutors and Afghans, although never as a direct cause of violence. Several participants – tutors and Afghans alike – did discuss, however, different groups of social actors to whom they attributed violence: Afghan participants expressed a lack of faith in the government and in elections to bring peace; they mentioned the more recent arrival of ISIS (or DAESH[1]) as causing more conflict; one US-based tutor quite fiercely questioned the legitimacy of the US invasion of Afghanistan in the first place.

But among social actors described as the cause of conflict, the Taliban were implicated most frequently. Recall, for instance, why Mustafa's educator father fled Afghanistan – out of fear of being beheaded. In Afghan participant Najibullah's discussion of the causes of conflict, he shares first how he views the impact of the tutoring project – and the potential affordances of the virtual intercultural borderlands – in relation to peacebuilding. During his interview, he begins discussing the causes of conflict while attempting to define 'peace':

> Defining peace. ... It's really a hard question. For me, peace is like when two humans with two different mindsets, different relationships ... can live in one neighborhood, or live even in one room. For me, that's the peace, because Afghans, they're not good with these things, but not all of them, I mean, like the Taliban, because they don't like our mindset, our way of living, that's why they kill innocent people ... here, since the Taliban, they don't, they're not on the same page with us, so that's why they kill the people. We have to learn that we can live and respect each other's opinions. (Najibullah)

In this passage, Najibullah moves from describing peace between two humans with different 'mindsets' and 'relationships' (the relational level of peacebuilding) to his view of one structural cause of conflict: 'the Taliban'; 'they don't like our mindset, our way of living.' While we do not hear details of that mindset or what it means 'to be on the same page,' we do learn more from Najibullah's ponderings over structural peace and violence through the pronouns he deploys. Specifically, Najibullah first discursively differentiates between individuals and groups, creating an us/them, self/other divide (van Leeuwen, 2008: 40), a discursive strategy we have also seen in Chapter 4. Najibullah tells us, 'Afghans, *they're* not good with these things [tolerating different mindsets], but not *all* of them' (italics added), discursively distancing himself from other Afghans. Significantly,

Najibullah does qualify his statement and avoids grouping *all* Afghans together here as he assesses their abilities to live together in peace in spite of their differences, thus belying a dangerous tendency which Broome and Collier (2012: 246) warn about: 'for opponents in such conflicts to attribute the causes of suffering or experiences of injustice *exclusively* to the other,' an 'essentialist view' which 'puts all the blame on others.'

This is what Najibullah does *not* do, and yet, despite the qualification in this statement, Najibullah (who is Afghan himself) still constructs himself initially as 'other' than other Afghans. Immediately following his discursive distancing from and explicit critique of Afghans and their 'mindset' generally, Najibullah makes another discursive us/them distinction: 'like the Taliban, because *they* don't like *our* mindset, *our* way of living, that's why *they* kill innocent people' (italics added). The 'they' he refers to now is 'the Taliban' and the structural force of their insurgency; in contrast to them, Najibullah now includes himself among those whose identities 'are forged in opposition' (Smith, 1992: 75, quoted in Hülsse, 1999): '*our* mindset,' '*our* way of living,' other Afghans, 'innocent people.' This second instance of 'othering' illuminates a linguistic strategy of laying blame and responsibility (Wodak *et al.*, 2009) on the 'other' – here, on the Taliban – for the 'not-peace' (the cause of structural conflict), as Najibullah discursively isolates the Taliban and accuses them of 'kill[ing] innocent people.' At the same time, we must remember that Najibullah's earlier othering of *Afghans* as separate from himself also attributes partial blame and responsibility to them, if 'not all of them.'

While Najibullah was being interviewed, the call to prayer could be heard through his open window. He had just explained how he viewed the structural causes of conflict, which he attributed in one part to an 'Afghan' 'mindset,' in larger part to the Taliban. This discussion coupled with the call to prayer likely prompted him to express the following, which moves from his understanding of the causes of conflict to how he sees the building of peace as linked with the tutoring project:

> [M]any of these [Afghan] students haven't had the experience to talk or communicate with a foreigner, like with an American or European, and in some areas, they are so religious ... they say bad things about you guys, honestly, but when students ... [are tutored] online with an American, then their idea changes, about you, they know that you are not bad, first, second, you're good [we laugh], they can share their happiness with you ... their mindset, ok, become positive, because when these students go home, he or she can share this experience to his family, to his mother, which is religious, to his father, which is religious, to his sister, and brothers, so it is not an effect on only one student, and the student, and his or her family, and his or her classmates. You have to add those too. (Najibullah)

In this passage, as Najibullah explicates his views on peace (indirectly) between 'Americans' ('you guys': the interviewer was from the US) and

Afghan project participants ('these students'), his reference to the structural force of religion is noteworthy: Najibullah implicates those who are 'so religious' (emphasis added) as at least part of the cause of conflict, but he does so with the belief that contact between groups (Allport et al., 1954; see also Pettigrew & Tropp, 2006) can remediate divisive relational perspectives. Ultimately, he suggests that contact and relationships between Afghan students and their tutors and the subsequent sharing of experiences with family members and classmates may be as powerful as 'the bad things' said about 'us guys' (others). Najibullah's last sentences, moreover, evidence the positive 'ripple' effects of the tutoring project, which we construe as another potent discourse chain (Blackledge, 2005) which can gain authority and legitimacy as it travels beyond the students' perspectives and is picked up, recontextualized and repeated: among family members, friends, classmates. For that discovery ('not bad'; 'good') to even have the potential to be shared so widely, we argue (with thanks to Najibullah), is a powerful testament to the peacebuilding capacities and action possibilities of the virtual intercultural borderlands which, as we see here, can spill beyond virtual borders and into others' lives.

Differential access to resources: Technology

Beyond the impacts of social actors, Broome and Collier (2012) delineate other, more specific causes of conflict at the structural level, awareness of which in participants' discourses joins the accumulation and constellation of discursive indicators of peacebuilding. Multiple tutors expressed concern over the Afghan students' access to the resources of technology, understandable since their tutoring sessions depended primarily upon videoconferencing. This recognition introduced for participants the critical connections between differential access to resources (Broome & Collier, 2012) and the structural barriers posed by factors underlying – and perhaps the cause of – conflict, such as poverty, politics and various societal norms. Understanding these factors, again, is a crucial component of building peace at the structural level (Broome & Collier, 2012; Lederach, 2003).

To illustrate concern over access to technology, in the first entry of her reflective journal, tutor Nadiya wrote:

> The only thing that I know is that (because of the political situation in their country) these students will have some problems with internet and electronic devices. (Nadiya)

Nadiya was an international student, a tutor originally from Ukraine who had experienced war in her own country. Her origins and experiences may well contribute to her certainty around 'the only thing' that she knows: that 'the political situation' will impact Afghan students' access to technology, which she states decisively.

In a similar fashion, tutor Hussein, an international student from Saudi Arabia, wrote in his reflective journal:

> I believe that it is very difficult to access to technology such as phones, computers, and the internet due to poverty. Also, due to this country had and still has many wars, this might be the reason why it is very difficult to access to technology. (Hussein)

Here Hussein attributes challenges in accessing technology first to poverty and *then* to war. He is not as definitive as Nadiya ('this might be the reason why') and he does not explicitly connect *poverty* to war (which he does have knowledge of, noting that the country 'had and still has many wars'). However, if loosely, we can begin to see reference to underlying causes of conflict (poverty, politics) from both Hussein and Nadiya, even if they are not constructed explicitly as such.

Another voice, Afghan student Sadaf again, explains her understanding of access to the resource of technology in Afghanistan:

> In some provinces in Afghanistan internet is available, in Kabul it's available, but it costs a lot, it costs an arm and a leg, it's not like America's culture, it's expensive here, so poor people and underprivileged people can't use internet that much easy. (Sadaf)

Sadaf's explanation indicates that she is clearly aware of the problems arising from differential access to resources, at least in Afghanistan, and in this case the resource of technology: internet availability in Afghanistan is limited and expensive, she states, making it difficult to access, especially for the 'poor' and 'underprivileged.' Through her comparison of internet access between Afghanistan and the US, Sadaf demonstrates Byram's (1997) critical cultural awareness; she also demonstrates her own keen awareness of the structural force of economic status. She acknowledges, that is, the specific difficulties faced by 'the poor' *and* the 'underprivileged,' whom she construes as equivalents through her use of syntactic parallelism; privilege comes with economic power, she implies, and so arguable necessities (technology) are unavailable to the '*under*privileged.' We should also mention that Sadaf *assumes* the internet is *not* expensive in America, with which many of our tutors who had limited (or no) home access to the internet would disagree.

'Technology as resource' comes in many forms, as we see with Soyoung, an international tutor from South Korea. She recounts, for instance, her tutoring partner's education in a terribly poor area of rural Afghanistan, and she does so in such a way as to vividly highlight differential access to resources (Broome & Collier, 2012):

> [S]he told me about how actually she studied with one pencil, for a whole entire like, year, one paper and one pencil, and she was just like writing, and erased it, and writing over again ... I still get a goosebump, it was so amazing. You know, when you see students [in the United States] ... they

just use it and throw the pencil and they look for a new one again, but she was talking about how she survived like a whole year with just one pencil, and try to write on the same paper over and over again ... it actually was very eye-opening. (Soyoung)

Soyoung, so plainly moved by her partner's account to the point of getting a 'goosebump,' is developing 'critical cultural awareness' (Byram, 1997) and ethnorelativism (Bennett, 1993) as she compares and contrasts access to resources (Broome & Collier, 2012) among students in Afghanistan and the US, a component of peacebuilding at the structural level which may be too often taken for granted by some, as she indicates: one pencil treasured while others are thrown away. The force of Soyoung's emotion as she comes to this awareness is discursively evidenced by her excited 'overwording' ('whole' *and* 'entire like, year') (Fairclough, 1992, 2001) and repetition ('one paper and one pencil'; 'and,' 'and,' 'and'; 'over and over again'); her choice of the word 'survived,' moreover, in reference to her student and the student's 'one pencil,' also evokes Lisa and Mustafa's discussion of structural peace as coming 'through the ink in a pen rather than bullets from a gun.' Literacy is peace; literacy is survival. Finally, like Carrie, Soyoung resorts to the familiar expression 'eye-opening' to convey the power of what she learned, which provoked both a physiological effect (goosebumps) and a metaphorical one representing her very new awareness of what differential access to resources can mean. According to Goodman (2011: 34), 'People are usually quite aware of their relative deprivation but refuse to acknowledge their relative privilege.' Therefore, creating opportunities to develop this consciousness through intercultural dialogue is crucial, as we see, through Soyoung's interactions, consciousness that contributes to peacebuilding at the structural dimension.

Differential access to resources: English and 'native speakers'

Earlier we saw how one effect of conflict in Afghanistan was the rise and spread of English, particularly as demanded by jobs for Afghans related to US and coalition forces and/or international and local humanitarian aid organizations and NGOs. It follows, then, that access to English language lessons can be construed as access to a resource which leads to *additional* resources and opportunities. Mirza, for example, framed English as vital to his pursuit of economics: '[A]ll the things ... that are *reliable* ... are in English ... It is not in Persian language.' For Fahim, a second Afghan participant, English also meant being able to access *more* resources: '[W]e can find a lot of information on Google with the English language ... there's a less amount of books with the Persian.' The dichotomies these participants construct between English and Persian are notable. Information in *English* is constructed as both more abundant and more reliable than resources in Persian; in turn, the perceived value of the information and of the English needed to access these resources is unmistakably elevated over information in Persian (Farsi or Dari).

Just as internet resources in English were perceived by some participants to have greater value than those in Persian, numerous Afghan participants expressed a great deal of excitement around having access to 'native speakers' of English as a resource through the tutoring project. This excitement reflects the ideology (again) that those deemed 'native speakers' are inherently more qualified than others to serve as teachers of the language, a myth and ideology clearly bound up in early arguments around English linguistic imperialism (see Chapters 3 and 4 for further discussion). This ideology perpetuates structural inequity, resulting in differential access to teaching positions, salaries and opportunities for professional advancement. Moreover, the belief that 'native speakers' are somehow more qualified than their 'non-native speaker of English' (NNSE) colleagues can have a profound impact on how future teachers of EAL are seen by others and how they see themselves. In our project, the fact that many of the tutors were not so-called 'native speakers' of English had profound personal ramifications (see also Chapter 4; Swan *et al.*, 2015).

Throughout this book we share examples of Afghan students who were changed by and profoundly grateful for their interactions with US-based tutors, including those for whom English was an additional language. Nonetheless, we recognize that for many Afghan participants, access to 'native speakers of English' was thought to be of particular value. Fahim expresses what we heard throughout the voices of many Afghan participants:

> Actually the main issue here in Afghanistan is that they don't have the native speakers, to speak with real English. … The people here who are studying English are really thirsty to speak with a native speaker. (Fahim)

The powerful metaphor of 'thirst' for access to 'native speakers' Fahim resorts to – comparing such access to something we need to *survive* – underscores the strength of his views by vitalizing 'real English' (Wodak *et al.*, 2009) as the 'main issue' in Afghanistan, as if 'English' were the cure for all national and social ills. The adjective 'real' further raises semantic questions around *what* is the 'real' English in a world where it is spoken by well over 500 million people in 101 countries, 35 of which list English as an 'official' language (Noack & Gamio, 2015). The same inequities and misconceptions posed by this myth are further perpetuated in our *tutors*' discourses as well, particularly from international students studying to become teachers of English as an additional language in their home countries. For example, in Chapter 4, we explore how a Chinese-born tutor felt that he would be discriminated against not only for his self-described lack of 'fluent English' but because of his 'face,' which was 'not American' and, notably, non-white.

Conflict and societal norms

As we see above, throughout the literature of English language teaching, discussion abounds as to how 'the native speaker of English' as teacher became a normative structural force leading to a stratified (if not rarified) contrast between 'natives' and 'non-natives,' against which there is now significant push-back although without real equity (in wages as but one example: see, for example, Achirri, 2017; Cook, 2012; Holliday, 2015; Kumaravadivelu, 2014; Swan *et al.*, 2015). This and other 'taken-for-granted norms' and assumptions, as Broome and Collier (2012: 262) argue, are 'structurally reproduced' and carry within them assumptions about power and privilege; reproduced without change or examples of change, such norms continue unchecked. Conversely, awareness of and a willingness to confront and work to change assumptions and norms become another means to work to build peace at the structural level.

Correspondingly, assumptions play an important role in the initial stages of intercultural interactants learning to communicate effectively and appropriately (Deardorff, 2006b). Assumptions are a significant part of any intercultural communication, and they can be strengthened or dismantled as interlocutors create new knowledge based on their communication. In a new cultural setting, interlocutors 'must be open to questioning these assumptions' and '"reflect radically" on the world, use their skills, knowledge, values, and perspectives, and draw on each other in doing so in order to invoke meaning so that new and fresh questions may be asked' (Fantini *et al.*, 2001: 65). This type of radical reflection and questioning not only contributes to the development of intercultural competence – and therefore to effective and appropriate communication – but also to considering structural norms from a social/global justice perspective.

Hofstede (2009) explains further:

> Different explicit rules hold in both societies, based on different unwritten cultural assumptions, and thus may seem strange to those from a different culture. This example applies to any other institution in society, including institutions as varied as companies, families, teams, governments, and armies. People are moral, but culture modifies that morality. (Hofstede, 2009: 86)

Tutor Soyoung confronts assumptions about societal norms and gender by working with her Afghan student; as a result, she re-examines her own experiences as a woman from South Korea. Soyoung tells us this:

> [S]he's really into women issues, well, injustice, for a female in Afghanistan … At the same time we had a … little bit of a similar cultural background, especially treating the women, in South Korea, I mean, it got a lot better but we still have limitations for women … females are specifically like, it's on the job … description, that you should be specific age … like a beginning position, it [your age] should be kind of lower than 26ish area, and if you're like, older older, you get a lot of weird questions about,

aren't you embarrassed about looking for a job on your age, with other younger people? (Soyoung)

Here we see that Soyoung's interactions with her partner lead her to reflect astutely on status (related to gender and age), equity and social justice (Broome & Collier, 2012; Goodman, 2013) as they play out in *South Korean* society as well as in Afghanistan. Her reflections emerge through 'ongoing concept formation' such as we saw with Najibullah's discussion of English: in Soyoung's discourse, she first adds on to 'women issues' through specification ('well, injustice, for a female in Afghanistan'), such that 'women's issues' become entangled with the larger semantic properties of 'injustice' (van Leeuwen, 2008: 19), which Soyoung embeds into their 'little bit' 'similar' cultural backgrounds. She builds on the concept further as she discusses how women are treated in South Korea, where age along with gender can lead to 'limitations' and shaming ('aren't you embarrassed about looking for a job on your age, with other younger people?'): age and gender intersect in a doubling of inequity and status diminished in and by societal norms. Shortly thereafter in her interview, after Soyoung recognizes the shared bond of gender inequity she and her partner face, inequity entrenched in the norms of both their societies, she arrives at this statement: 'we can actually understand each other *better*!'

Afghan student Mahtab also confronted societal norms related to gender through her work in the virtual intercultural borderlands with her tutor, who was an international student from China. When asked what surprised her most about her tutoring experience, Mahtab replies as follows (italics represent emphasis through syllable stress; capital letters indicate volume and stress):

> With my tutor there were a lot of surprises and a lot of important lessons for me, for example ... about the culture of China ... and I became shocked about *my* culture, about where I live. For example, she told me that in China people couldn't have two child. It was very strange and interesting for me, because in Afghanistan, people bring ten, twelve, thirteen, twenty, TWENTY-FIVE children and have two or three wives. ... I told her ... it is very strange, in my culture, men have a lot of work, can marry with a lot of women, in your culture, people just are only permitted to bring one child? This was AMAZING. ... Why we don't think about education, why we don't think about our situation of our life, just think about amount of children? ... I became shocked, where I live, I live in this kind of country. (Mahtab)

Mahtab's reply is impassioned, perhaps because of her work as a child protection officer for an international refugee organization. Human rights organizations have designated Afghanistan as 'the worst place to be born in the world' (IOHR, 2018). Looking back to Chapter 3, we recall again Mahtab's context: high child mortality rates; the lowest live birth expectancy rate globally; children forced into labor, marriage, sexual abuse;

and children even lacking legal identity and nationality (only 6% of births are officially recorded, leading to a complete lack of legal status) (IOHR, 2018). Knowing and living in this context, as Mahtab learns about China's (former) one-child policy through her tutor, it may be no wonder that she becomes 'shocked' about her own culture, the strength of which frames her answer (she is shocked at the start of the quote and shocked at the end). Then comes her list: 'people bring ten, twelve, thirteen, twenty, TWENTY-FIVE children and have two or three wives.' Mahtab's strong reaction, like Soyoung's, leads her to radically question her own culture ('Why we don't think about education? ... our situation of our life?'). Discursively, Mahtab's impugnment is a hard push back against *unjust* societal norms (Broome & Collier, 2012) which anger and bewilder her. What is more, what she learns from her tutor *is* a form of peacebuilding as she shares a new (if shocking) realization about her country, in the process, we believe, recognizing that her country (to which we add 'our world') can be/should be different, changed, and that it is possible. Mahtab, that is, is developing an ethnorelative view of the world (Bennett, 1993; Deardorff, 2006a) and critical cultural awareness (Byram, 1997). This new view and her new awareness are sure steps toward Mahtab reimagining and transforming her world.

Understandings of Inclusion, Decision Making and Means to More Broadly Include Voices

From taken-for-granted societal norms that preclude, exclude or diminish actors and their agency, we turn next to how Broome and Collier (2012) take great care to articulate the importance of understanding inclusion in the process of peacebuilding, which also results in increased status and participation in decision making for social actors historically *ex*cluded from such processes. Peacebuilders must, the authors write, work to 'enable broader inclusion of diverse voices' (Broome & Collier, 2012: 252), a position which Lederach (2003: 25) situates within 'the involvement of people in decisions that affect them (procedural justice).' Awareness and understanding of the importance of 'inclusion,' with its capacities for agentive decision making, and further attention to means to more broadly include voices, thus become discursive indicators of peacebuilding which we sought in participants' voices and which we encountered frequently and in multiple forms.

Tutor Jessica, for example, having conducted research before she started tutoring, discusses structural *ex*clusion of girls from education in Afghanistan:

> With ongoing war and poverty, student drop-out rates are incredibly high and access to qualified teachers is practically non-existent. Afghan girls were forced out of schools for years under Taliban rule and the country's literacy rates remain low. It's heartbreaking. (Jessica)

Tutor Harley expresses similar concerns:

> As I reflect on this experience, I can't help but contemplate the hurdles Afghan students encounter on a day to day basis and even more so the female students, who risk their lives to attend school. (Harley)

These quotes echo what we examined earlier: the impacts of conflict on the structural force of education, but here, especially, for girls and women, and for the tutors (Jessica, Harley) confronting these impacts, if secondhand. Thinking back to Chapter 3, we may be reminded that just as Afghanistan has been described as 'the worst place to be born' in the world, so also has it been described as 'the worst place in the world to be a woman' by multiple human rights organizations (see, for example, Amnesty International, 2017), given that the vast majority of girls and women are illiterate (87%), are forced into child marriage (70–80%), have experienced domestic abuse (more than 90%), and have the highest suicide rates (80% of all suicides) (Bohn, 2018). Jessica references access directly along with how 'Afghan girls were forced out of schools' and hence excluded from higher levels of literacy (if they achieve literacy at all), the significance of which was proclaimed by Mustafa's educator parents: 'peace will come through the ink in a pen.' That peace *depends* upon literacy and the inclusion of girls and women in society's decision-making processes, claims advanced consistently by UNESCO (2019), which promotes 'the cause of education as the strongest foundation for peace.' Education is pivotal to inclusion. Scholars, too, have been particularly vocal in emphasizing the importance of literacy for women and girls: Pousada (2016), for instance, defines literacy as a 'prerequisite for world peace,' going on to deplore how 'longstanding patriarchal ideologies' have valued men's literacy over women's (and men over women), perpetuating patriarchal hegemony globally while excluding women and girls from the process and products of peace.

But we did not hear about the importance of inclusion only in tutors' voices or in the voices of Afghan women students. Afghan participant Fawad speaks directly to the importance of inclusion as it relates to gender, beginning with our tutoring program:

> Girls are very important to join this program, in Afghanistan ... 'cause families do not give many privileges to girls. That's what my family does. ... I'm allowed to go everywhere and to study and to go far away from my home, and ... my sister is sitting at home and doing only the schoolworks. ... In Afghanistan, girls, they basically don't allow girls to educate, to, finish a college, to discover the world, they don't let them to go overseas, or go abroad to learn, it's really difficult, even if they send they will ... like, they're 'on the eye' by her family. (Fawad)

Here, Fawad first speaks quite personally as he laments the difference in 'privilege' he and his sister experience, a difference he then extends to girls generally in Afghanistan. Fawad goes on to list the many social constraints on girls, and his syntactic parallelism of infinitive clauses ('to educate'; 'to finish' 'to discover'; 'to go overseas') accentuates the breadth of difference he constructs between 'girls' and 'boys' (and women and men) and the social constraints on the former (Wodak *et al.*, 2009: 36). Ultimately, Fawad's point – that 'Girls are very important to join' the tutoring program – illustrates not only his understanding of the importance of inclusion as it relates to girls, but also his willingness to advocate for the same, as he encouraged *us* to find ways to include more girls and women in our tutoring program. When Fawad was asked at the interview's close if he had any final words or comments, he ended this way, with a smile and a fist in the air:

Afghan women's empowerment!

There were anomalies in Fawad's and other participants' understandings of inclusion and gender, which will also be important to share with future tutors and students in future iterations of this project, as these exceptions suggest: (1) a country and context struggling toward positive transformation as well as undergoing political upheaval; and (2) the necessity of nuance and open-mindedness in our intercultural interactions, always.

Tutor Janie, for instance, learns this about her Afghan student, Maryam, who was raised in Iran by Afghan parents:

[S]he also enjoys quite a bit of support from her family and has much more autonomy than I assumed at the start of this project, knowing that she was a young woman in Afghanistan. Maryam lives alone in Afghanistan, where she moved to attend university. (Janie)

Here we see Janie explicitly acknowledging the risks of presuppositions as she learns about Maryam's autonomy and family, who clearly support her choices and upend Janie's assumptions. As Janie continues in her reflective journal, she (and we) learn more about Maryam, who complicates further (if not circumvents) assumptions most tutors held about Afghanistan and Afghan women:

Her degree is in public administration and from our conversation, I garnered that her new job involves traveling to meet with community groups, providing education and information about voting. (Janie)

Janie's account of Maryam's new job reminds us of the great courage present in the voices of the virtual intercultural borderlands. The act of voting in a democracy as young and fragile as that of Afghanistan's is already perilous, with polling places and voters alike frequently the targets of attacks. Imagine, then, Maryam traveling and meeting community groups to educate voters. It is dangerous to live and work in Afghanistan; it is far more dangerous to live and work in Afghanistan as a woman. And yet, through Janie, we see an example of peacebuilding as her partner works to maximize the involvement of people in decisions affecting them (Lederach, 2003): there may be no greater decision-making act or act of inclusion than that of voting. Indeed, importantly, by her journal's end, we hear Janie admit, 'I suppose this course has also called to my attention, my privilege,' and in such a way as to call into question her thinking about her teaching: she writes that she is 'fulfilled' by her tutoring experience and inspired such that she is considering moving away from teaching children in public schools to teaching adult refugee and immigrant students, despite the more challenging hours and the dramatically lower salaries. For Janie, this change is possible because of *her* 'privilege.' Janie declares, 'I have the option to choose.'

Understanding How Structural Discourses Enable and Constrain Individuals and Groups

Janie's interactions with Maryam in the virtual intercultural borderlands helped her confront and complicate her assumptions about societal norms, specifically gender norms in Afghanistan as she understood them. In their peacebuilding framework, Broome and Collier (2012: 252) draw our attention to how societal discourses perpetuate these norms, 'enabl[ing] and constrain[ing] individuals and groups' through mandates, rules and laws as well as through representations in the media, all structural forces with additional impacts at the personal and relational levels of peacebuilding. Neither tutors nor their Afghan counterparts directly addressed specific policies or laws in their discourses. We do see, however, abundant reference in participants' discourses to media representations of Afghanistan and, indirectly, of Afghans. In this section we show how participants arrive at a deeper understanding of how media discourses can both enable and constrain perceptions of others (Broome & Collier, 2012). As Broome and Collier (2012) explain, cultivating a more critical reception of media representations is another potent form of – and another discursive indicator of – peacebuilding at the structural level.

Tutor Jennifer discusses this topic openly with her student. We first heard from Jennifer in Chapter 5, in relation to empathy and the relational level of peacebuilding. We return to her voice now to consider how media discourses constrain and enable perceptions:

> When my tutee and I were discussing cultural norms and our perspective on how the media can affect your perspective, the war in Afghanistan was brought up. The tutee spoke openly about the Taliban and how it has affected him and his family directly. This was challenging because I did not know how to respond. (Jennifer)

Here we see that Jennifer and her partner are aware both of cultural norms (as discussed in the previous section) and of how the media can enable or constrain their perspectives, a discussion which led to discussing the 'war in Afghanistan.' While Jennifer's Afghan student feels free to speak openly about the 'Taliban,' Jennifer herself initially does not know how to respond, her discomfort likely contributing to the discursive deletion of agent/subject in the first sentence ('the war in Afghanistan was brought up').

Still, not knowing how to respond to her student's narrative did not stop Jennifer from connecting with him (the relational level of peacebuilding) or challenging the perceptions that the media had established in her mind (the structural level of peacebuilding). In her last journal entry, Jennifer writes:

> This project allowed me to connect with someone who is living in a different, a completely different culture and society than myself. I found that this experience has changed my perspective on how I view Afghanistan and the culture. It is hard to understand what life is truly like in Afghanistan because of the media and this experience allowed me to understand and see the truth. (Jennifer)

From Jennifer's awareness of the impact of the media on her perspectives of Afghanistan, we see that she recognizes how the media constrains views (in distorting 'what life is truly like in Afghanistan'). On the other hand, work with her student in the virtual intercultural borderlands allows her to 'to understand and see the truth' (which she does not expand on) or, at the very least, to come to a more fine-grained understanding of what life in Afghanistan is like.

Tutor Kay is more specific as to how the project transformed her perceptions as created through the media:

> [I]t [the tutoring project] actually did a lot for me, to create some empathy, for him, for people of Afghanistan, for people of the Middle East, because the stuff you mostly hear about the Middle East is, not positive, especially when it's coming from American news, but I got to meet this real person and make real connections, and really care about him, and so like now whenever I hear someone say something negative about Afghanistan, or Afghan people, I'm like, Hey! I know someone. He's amazing. Don't say that kind of stuff. (Kay)

Kay's words here are uplifting as they launch a direct and personal counter-discourse in response to media portrayals and 'American news' as recontextualized by the words of someone, anyone. Kay shuts down that discourse chain (Blackledge, 2005), and in so doing, her discourse powerfully actualizes peacebuilding as specified by Broome and Collier (2012: 252) at the structural level: awareness of and attention to how 'media texts and discourses, both enable and constrain individuals and groups.' Kay recognizes the limits of what is coming 'from American news,' but her new empathy is in no way limited as she moves from her student, 'to the people of Afghanistan,' to 'people of the Middle East' (although geopolitically Afghanistan is part of Central Asia; see also

Chapter 5). We see here, too, overlaps *between* peacebuilding levels: Kay's willingness to speak out against stereotypes and on behalf of her student is as personal and relational as it is structural.

Ways to Create Conditions and Relations that Contribute to Social Justice and Peace

Thus far in this chapter we have focused primarily on change in participants' understandings and awareness of different components from our peacebuilding frameworks, including understandings of: (1) the effects and causes of conflict; (2) the powers of inclusion, decision making and advocacy for inclusion of voices; and (3) the role media and other discourses play in constraining and enabling perceptions of individual groups. In this section, we look specifically to how participants' discourses evidence work which contributes to social justice and peace (Broome & Collier, 2012), including work to minimize if not eliminate violence and help developing structures that meet 'basic human needs' (Lederach, 2003).

For Soyoung, the international tutor we met earlier in this chapter, her work in the virtual intercultural borderlands with her Afghan student leads her to transform her professional goals. She had been a nursing student, but here Soyoung explains how she always wanted to be something like an 'educational volunteer' and how her tutoring experience with this project helped her back to that path:

> [A]s soon as I started my Ph.D., I am working with ... my advisor professors, who are working in villages and building schools in undeveloped areas ... So I am working with them ... and I guess this experience in Afghanistan, meeting her, my student, I guess I will just call her my friend ... it gets me like more concrete ideas about how actually I can do it. (Soyoung)

To restate Soyoung's words: by collaborating with her advisors, and inspired by her tutoring partner, who discursively shifts from 'student' to 'friend' (as we saw with Najibullah's tutor in Chapter 5), we now see how she, too, will work to meet basic human needs (Lederach, 2003) – defined as food security, clean drinking water, shelter, healthcare, sanitation, contagious disease prevention and education (WFP, 2020) – such a vital component of peacebuilding. Her work with the tutoring project in conjunction with her professors has provided her with 'more concrete ideas' about how to actually realize the work she imagines, beginning with 'building schools in undeveloped areas.'

Afghan student Sadaf also imagines work in the future to meet basic human needs, like Soyoung, related to education. Previously we heard Sadaf talk about her desire to work with a tutor as a step toward working for an NGO, in her words, 'to help my people.' As she continues, she states:

> I want to bridge the gap between privileged and underprivileged girls in Afghanistan. ... I want to make a school ... in other provinces in Afghanistan to provide an education for those girls, for those underprivileged girls. (Sadaf)

When asked if she wanted to teach English, her answer addresses basic needs in a critically important way:

> Yah, I think that English and also provide education for them. At first education is very important, and after that I will try to help them develop English skills, and understand a foreign language that will help them to find work in other countries or maybe in their own province. (Sadaf)

Like Soyoung, Sadaf imagines her future work as serving the basic need of education, particularly in the more remote provinces and particularly for 'underprivileged girls.' She makes a key distinction as she expounds upon her answer: 'at first *education* is very important, and *after that* ... English' (emphasis added). In other words, she smartly notes that 'English' and 'foreign language' should be secondary to 'education,' to what we assume are more basic learning needs as defined by UNESCO such as literacy in the first/primary language, numeracy, oral expression and problem solving (IBE-UNESCO, 2020).

Soyoung and Sadaf are talking about the future, about goals that their work in the virtual intercultural borderlands inspired or facilitated, goals in both cases which lead to work that helps meet basic human needs. Their re-envisioning of their futures reminds us that Broome and Collier (2012) construct context as temporal as well as spatial, and so their visions have a bearing on future peacebuilding (in Afghanistan and elsewhere).

Other Afghan participants were already working directly for peace. Afghan participant Jaweed was likewise inspired to envision a new future, after he and his tutor discussed 'conflict resolution' during one of their tutoring sessions. As a result of that discussion, his imagined future involves working to minimize or eliminate violence (Lederach, 2003). He shares with us:

> I need to know about more, so meet with someone who mediates between two people ... in Afghanistan, our people, they are always fighting, and I want to be a mediator, to solve fighting between my peoples. (Jaweed)

Jaweed's new goal – to become a conflict mediator – is a compelling indicator of just how interactions in the virtual intercultural borderlands can lead to the affordance of peacebuilding. His words further evince how peacebuilding levels overlap: his desire and hope is personal; the work he describes ('between two people') may be seen as more relational than structural; but the work ultimately in his mind leads him to want 'to solve fighting between my peoples.'

Also working to meet basic human needs and eliminate violence (Lederach, 2003) is Mahtab, an Afghan 'child protection officer' who works for an international NGO where she frequently has to speak – and read – English. At the beginning of her interview, she talks about her job with great enthusiasm:

> It is a very good job I think, and I love to work for a refugee organization. In my idea it is a big honor for me to work for such an organization and to do such kind of work, because I like to be in the society a lot, between my people, and work. (Mahtab)

Mahtab's desire to 'be in the society,' 'between [her] people' is decidedly reminiscent of Mirza's desire to 'serve for' his 'people' – and Sadaf's desire to work for hers ('my people,' 'my people') – the possessive pronouns each participant uses reinforcing their agency and how we have already seen participants' desires and plans to work to meet basic human needs (Lederach, 2003) in a variety of ways.

Mahtab has begun this work. She loves her job and is honored to take it on, but it is challenging, especially as her supervisor does not speak Dari. She describes how she felt when she started:

> I had a lot of stress, my supervisor, I can't talk to her, and when she talk, I can't talk, I know English, I speak English, but I can't talk, because I'm not relaxed! (Mahtab)

Mahtab had studied English at university, 'but not a lot,' and when any 'foreign person' came into her office (which was frequent), especially her supervisor, she grew extremely anxious. This was the reason why Mahtab joined the tutoring project, a decision which eased her 'stress' and raised her confidence considerably, as we saw in Chapter 4: personally, we see Mahtab's confidence and self-esteem grow as she works with her tutor in English (see also Rubio, 2007); relationally, it is through continuous interaction that she grows comfortable with her tutor. Confidence and interaction are obvious affordances present in the virtual intercultural borderlands of online exchange. What we attend to in this chapter, however, is the unexpected affordance of peacebuilding at the *structural* level, which Mahtab demonstrates throughout her interview. As she goes on, for instance, we see more of her work to meet basic human needs and to minimize violence (Lederach, 2003) supported by the tutoring project.

One very consequential responsibility of Mahtab's position as a child protection officer is that of 'Father Daughter Hours,' an initiative intended to counteract the long and brutal tradition in Afghanistan of valuing sons over daughters. As we explore in more detail in Chapter 3, some Afghan fathers barter or sell their daughters in marriage to relieve debt or enrich their families (Nawa, 2013); women are abused for giving birth to daughters (Fahimullah, 2017); and hundreds of girls and women are murdered each year as a result of 'honor killings,' often by fathers or brothers (Ahmadi & Bezhan, 2020). There are, of course, many exceptions, some of which we have seen in this book. At the same time, knowing this context, we can see both Mahtab's courage in her work with the 'Father Daughter Hours' program and how her work seeks to minimize if not eliminate violence.

Although Mahtab was 'honored' to take part in this work and she 'loved' her job, she nevertheless struggled to understand how to operationalize the program, even though she was given guidelines. The guidelines, however, were in English. Challenging though these guidelines were for Mahtab, she goes on to explain how, with the help of her tutor, she was able to work through and understand them; as a result, she was able to talk with more comfort and confidence about those guidelines and the program.

In her interview, Mahtab first explains the initiative with pride:

> Father Hour Program is for father and daughter, it is a program as I studied in guidelines, we have father and daughter with us in our place, and in this place we try to talk with father, with daughter, and we use game and arts between father and daughter, and they play together, they help each other, and I can understand from these guidelines that my work is that. (Mahtab)

Significantly, Mahtab was given the responsibility of this initiative only after her participation in the tutoring project, only after, that is, she moved from 'I can't talk, I know English, I speak English, but I can't talk!' to the point where she 'removed' her 'stress' and became 'a different person.' Put another way, we can see the combined efforts of Mahtab with the support of her tutor as leading to direct interventions intended to eliminate violence (Lederach, 2003) – specifically, against violence toward girls in Afghanistan. Mahtab's work for this program – with help from her tutor – reveals once again the profound possibilities on offer through the unexpected affordance of peacebuilding in the virtual intercultural borderlands, affordances of which Mahtab availed herself in order to attain her goal:

> When I learn English and I understand English better and better, and learn some new vocabulary, new things, I can use my English in some way, for example, studying these guidelines, helping these fathers and daughters, and what behavior should I have with these father and daughter, and I think it has important effect for peace. (Mahtab)

'It' – an all-encompassing pronoun without a clear referent – has an incontestable 'effect for peace.' She attributes much of that effect to her improvement in English, to what she has learned through the tutoring program, in the virtual intercultural borderlands, and to how her work with her tutor helped her study 'these guidelines' and help 'these fathers and daughters.'

We see another, less immediate connection to peacebuilding in Mahtab's discourse as she continues. Mahtab is talking about an English-medium leadership training course she attended which was sponsored by an international NGO. This training course took place after her work with her tutor, which leads us back to Broome and Collier's (2012) construction of context as temporal as well as spatial. In other words, we believe it matters if we share what participants say before, during and *after* (as we see here) the tutoring project, just as we believe their discourses about the past, present and future are all relevant to peacebuilding in the virtual intercultural borderlands. Here is what Mahtab says about the 'educated' people in the class, starting with men, and here also is what she does (capital letters indicate volume and emphasis):

> Even they [the men in the class] don't talk about their wife and they don't tell the name of his wife to another man, because they think that it's a shame for him, to talk about his wife, to talk about his family. ... I told him, YOU ARE STUDYING LEADERSHIP! You shouldn't be ashamed of this, you should be good leader. ... They told me, no no no, leadership is good, but our culture don't permit us to do this ... we can't change. But they CAN change, they CAN change, and when I talk with them, and laughing with them, most of my colleagues, my classmates come and told me, oh, you shouldn't laugh with these men. Why? Because it is not good, it is not good for a women, and I told them, no, it IS good. ... When I laugh with other person, it is NOT bad. It is GOOD. (Mahtab)

In this quote we see clear evidence of Mahtab's courage and confidence: we see how her work for peace and an end to violence against girls (Broome & Collier, 2012; Lederach, 2003) extends beyond her field work and 'Father Daughter Hours.' She is willing, that is, to stand up to men directly and call them out on behalf of their wives and families, face to face, in the middle of class, with the belief that they can change (and, in turn, that her country/our world can change). We also see her tell her women colleagues that laughter – even with men – is good. Certainly, laughter in this very tense situation is a nonviolent means to reduce adversarial interaction (Lederach, 2003: 24); certainly, she resists unjust societal norms (Broome & Collier, 2012) of Afghanistan directly in her discourse and her laughter. She is defiant, confident with 'should' and 'shouldn't'; she is no longer someone who 'can't talk.' Indeed, we see Mahtab fiercely offering an alternative to the current realities and problems of Afghanistan. We see Mahtab beginning to discursively rescript her world.

Resistance and the Structural Level of Person to Person Peacebuilding

To end this chapter, we share the experience of Janis, a US-based and US-born graduate student who demonstrated consistent resistance to person to person peacebuilding throughout the tutoring project. In Chapter 4, we saw Tayba's resistance based on fears of Afghan culture. In Chapter 5, Mary resisted listening to and believing what her Afghan student told her. Here is what we learned about Janis' resistance, well after the project had ended for her, when she agreed to be interviewed.

At the time when she served as a tutor, Janis and her Pakistani-born husband were in the process of applying for him to become a US citizen. When we interviewed her about her participation in the project, Janis shared that from the outset she was concerned about how her work one on one, online, with someone from Afghanistan might be perceived by the US government:

> As soon as [the instructor] said 'Afghanistan,' I said shit. I mean. It's not that I have anything against Afghani people at all. It's just the government's perception of what I could be doing. (Janis)

Janis' concern over the US 'government's perception' of what she could be doing should not be surprising: at the time she was a tutor, former President Trump was fighting in the courts to ban travel from (primarily, although not only) Muslim-majority countries to the US, and his list of specific countries seemed to grow longer each week. Because of the difference in time zones, moreover, Janis was logging on at midnight to meet her student, Aalem. Janis was fearful that her interactions might not only be tracked by but raise the suspicion of US government officials, particularly given the regularity and late hour of the weekly online meetings. Hence, Janis' first reaction: 'Shit.' We find it telling, too, that she starts the next two sentences with 'It': 'It's not that I have anything'; 'It's just the government's perception.' This use of indetermination through 'it' without a referent functions to 'endow social actors with a kind of impersonal authority' ('the government's perception') and/or to anonymize what Janis doesn't have: 'anything against Afghani people at all' (van Leeuwen, 2008: 40).

As she elaborated on the reasons for her concern, Janis shared with the interviewer an experience she and her husband had had:

> I know it sounds paranoid, but we've had the FBI [the Federal Bureau of Investigation] come to our house and question my husband without a warrant because he's Pakistani. (Janis)

Such events, she explained, made her fearful of what information might be gathered about her and about her husband in the course of their citizenship application, a process which, under the Trump administration, became substantially more difficult for applicants (Narea, 2020). As with the authority she ascribes to 'the government's perception' earlier, here the construction 'we've had the FBI come to our house' (as opposed to 'the FBI came to our house'), by fronting 'we've' at the start of the sentence, underscores the vulnerability and struggle for agency she and her husband experienced through a form of grammatical metaphor (Fairclough, 1992). While it seems that 'we' is the agent of the sentence, she is discussing what had happened to her husband and her, a struggle attributable to her sense of how she and her husband were objects being acted upon rather than subjects exerting agency.

While Janis fulfilled the requirements for the project and for her graduate course, her resistance to establishing a close relationship beyond the tutoring sessions – and the pain from that resistance – is evident in her recollections:

> I love my tutee. Our interactions were lovely, but she always, like, wanted more. She wanted to connect on social media. She wanted to come over [to the US] and talk to me and I had never in my life had that moment of refusing connections to a human because I was scared of my government. (Janis)

Aalem's goal was to attend a US university; she was eager to learn as much about the US as she could and to engage with Janis outside of the online classroom. For Janis, however, the series and syntactic parallelism of Aalem's 'wants' piled up so as to overwhelm her, leading her to confront a very harsh truth: 'I had never in my life had that moment of refusing connections to a human because I was scared of my government.'

Contact with Aalem represented a potential threat, one that Janis clearly agonized over as she pondered the possible ramifications of the tutoring project to her and her husband, personal ramifications undergirded by structural and geopolitical forces:

> In order for her to be in this exchange program in the first place, her family had to have some kind of security and money. And to have security and money in Afghanistan, you're probably connected to some political sphere, right? ... I kept thinking, she's probably middle class. She probably has a brother or a father or an uncle; that's why she's gotten into this program. ... So if you have someone affluent over there, you just don't know the connections. So I just kept holding her at bay, which is something that I've really never done before, because of sheer worry. (Janis)

Aalem was an individual but also, for Janis, a representative of an imminent danger. The linguistic choices Janis makes when explaining her experience to the interviewer suggest her fears were linked not to information she gained from Aalem but rather to what Janis was imagining about her student, as she qualifies through a series of worrying 'probabilities': 'she's probably middle class'; 'she probably has a brother or a father or an uncle [with economic or political power]'; 'probably connected to some political sphere.' Janis' almost frantic speculation is also reflected in her use of conditional forms to describe Aalem and her family: 'her family had to have some kind of security and money' and 'if you have someone affluent over there, you just don't know the connections.' Here especially, with 'someone affluent *over there*' (italics added), we see Janis spatialize and recontextualize 'Afghanistan' such that 'over there' grows larger, more fluid, amorphous and monolithic in its lack of geographic and discursive boundaries. In other words, 'over there' could include Pakistan as well as Afghanistan – at least – particularly given the specificity of Janis' conjecture.

Finally, despite the resistance Janis shares, we note too the power and complexity of the emotions she describes; as she reflects on her experience, she expresses regret at not having built a stronger relationship with Aalem. An experienced EAL teacher, Janis shared with the interviewer that she usually prided herself on building close bonds with her students. In the case of her Afghan student, however, and due to structural forces directly related to conflict (markedly, in the US as well as Afghanistan), she leaves us with this sentence: 'I just kept holding her at bay,' she says of Aalem, 'which is something that I've really never done before, because of sheer worry.'

Conclusion

In this chapter, we have focused on how participants' voices have discursively brought to life the unexpected affordance of peacebuilding at the structural level in the virtual intercultural borderlands of online exchange. We have seen US-based tutors and Afghan participants alike share the harrowing effects of conflict in depth, such as constraints on access to resources (particularly, education) and status (particularly, for women); we have seen them exert their agency powerfully and profoundly, and we have seen them push for greater equity and inclusion and push back against unjust norms. Participants demonstrated evolving awareness of how media discourses constrain perceptions of individuals and groups (primarily, Afghanistan); perhaps most profoundly, we saw how participants, US-based tutors and Afghan students alike, found multiple ways to create conditions and relations that contribute to social justice and peace. They worked to eliminate violence, they worked to meet basic needs, and/or they were planning such work for the future, part of central motivations for participants to join the tutoring program in the first place.

From this chapter, as with Chapters 4 and 5, we have learned so much from participants' voices. From the insights gained and lessons gleaned, we seek next, in Chapter 7, to show how – in future iterations of this or similar projects – we can more deliberately leverage the unexpected affordance of peacebuilding evidenced in the discourses of tutors and students working together in the virtual intercultural borderlands of online exchange.

Note

(1) DAESH is the transliterated Arabic acronym equivalent to the English ISIS.

7 Fostering Person to Person Peacebuilding While Teaching Language and Intercultural Communication

In Chapters 4, 5 and 6, we have shared and analyzed participants' voices, showing how pre-service teachers of English as an additional language (EAL) and Afghan learners of English availed themselves of the unexpected affordance of peacebuilding as they met and interacted in the virtual intercultural borderlands of online exchange. This *unexpected* affordance – mapped through the accumulation and constellation of discursive indicators of peacebuilding – evidences how person to person peacebuilding is *already*, in many instances, a fundamental part of the language teaching and intercultural communication experience, whether 'peacebuilding' is formally and explicitly acknowledged as part of the curriculum or not.

Now, in this last chapter, we share how what we have learned from our participants can help us more *deliberately* leverage the affordance of peacebuilding while teaching language and intercultural communication and/or preparing future teachers of language and intercultural communication. We do so by returning to some of the most compelling, most salient insights to emerge from participants' voices as they pertain to classroom instruction and/or work between tutors and students in the virtual intercultural borderlands of online exchange. Specifically, we consider what they teach us about: (1) the necessities of reflection; (2) differential access to resources and global inequities; (3) the reconfiguration of identities; (4) the roles of agency and power; and, finally, (5) the relationships between agency and emotions. In what follows, we discuss each of these themes briefly, share the voices of participants who bring them to life, and provide suggestions for practical activities that can help us more purposefully leverage these particular affordances which contribute to the larger affordance of peacebuilding.

Given the context of our study, where US-based tutors who were candidate teachers of EAL worked with Afghan learners of English, throughout this book we have placed special emphasis on projects that partner with students in conflict countries. Due to the vast structural and dynamic complexities of conflict, however, we anticipate and hope that the lessons we have learned and share here will be useful and adaptable to a wide array of contexts, including both virtual and in-person projects, not only in the fields of language teaching and teacher education but in other arenas in which intercultural communication and education play a role.

Reflection, Writing and the Reflective Practitioner

The overarching lesson we take from the tutoring project is the criticality of reflection to peacebuilding. Certainly, we would not have thought to focus on peacebuilding within this study had it not been for the wealth of reflective writing produced by pre-service teachers of EAL tutoring Afghan learners of English – and the abundant references to peace and war throughout their journal entries. The power resounding in tutors' written reflections both inspired this book and then spurred us on to gather the perspectives of Afghan participants, whose voices join those of the tutors in guiding us through the terrain of their learning and lives. Hence the first 'lesson' we highlight here, one we knew beforehand but which we must reiterate: reflection is as critical to peacebuilding as it is to teacher education, language learning and intercultural communication. And one of the most salient ways to trace and cultivate reflection is by reflective writing, within which we can seek evidence of change: what Lederach (2003: 35) describes as 'positive' change processes toward 'the horizon of preferred [more peaceful] future.' Guided by our participants, in this first section we discuss how changes that contribute to peacebuilding can be fostered more deliberately through reflection and reflective writing.

Reflection and reflective writing provide opportunity and time for what Dewey (1910: 6) described as 'the active, persistent and careful consideration of any belief or supposed form of knowledge' according to support for that belief or knowledge, *along with* an embrace of uncertainty and a willingness to inquire *beyond* one's belief or knowledge. Kolb (1984) and Schön (1983) carry Dewey's ideas forward in order to help us see how learning through reflection is especially bolstered by reflection on *experience*, with Schön's construct of a 'reflective practitioner' – one who reflects on, learns from and *changes* action and thought as a part of problem solving, typically in a professional context – becoming a benchmark for teacher education programs internationally (see, for example, Richards & Farrell, 2011). Slade *et al.* (2019) explain the significance for teacher education, noting how critical reflection invites teacher candidates to regularly examine their thinking and attitudes, their preconceptions, their biases, the actions they take. Hence, in their words, 'reflective practice facilitates the development of new knowledge, skills, and dispositions in teacher candidates by fostering critical contemplation of actions in a real-world environment' (Slade *et al.*, 2019: 1). More directly linked to our purposes in this book and as discussed in Chapter 1, Rothman and Sanderson (2018), in their exploration of the 'Language of Peace Approach' (Oxford, 2013) through a 'Global Issues' course in Japan, touch briefly upon the role of reflection in developing the critical thinking skills they believe language students need in order to recognize and use the language of peace. Freire's (1970: 51) 'critical praxis' – 'reflection and action upon the world in order to transform it' – may be the simplest yet most powerful statement on the importance of reflection and reflective practice, with the transformations upon the world that Freire imagines – or, in Lederach's (2003) words again, 'positive,' 'preferred' changes – leading us forward toward the horizon of peace.

It is thus not surprising that the idea of a reflective practitioner has powerfully informed not only education, but peacebuilding in 'real-world' environments such as Slade *et al.* (2019) might not even have imagined. In their *Reflective Peacebuilding* toolkit, Lederach *et al.* (2007: iii) describe reflective practice as a means of 'enhancing peacebuilders' capacity to design and impact transformative change, and track and improve upon those changes over time,' in varied, volatile and often uncertain contexts (such as, in the case of our project, Afghanistan). As for their definition of the reflective peacebuilding practitioner, they write: 'This is the ***reflective practitioner***: a person who includes time to dig into and elaborate the too-often ***implicit theories of change*** that guide his or her daily activity and projects' (Lederach *et al.*, 2007: 3, emphases in original). They then set out ways to 'demystify' what they mean 'by theories of change,' as they suggest we undertake the following:

> Mak[e] explicit the underlying assumptions about how things work, about how particular actions or processes create consequences, in environments of conflict and change. For example, we want to learn about how we impact social phenomena such as participation, trust, violence, respect, and so forth. (Lederach *et al.*, 2007: 4)

It is just such 'transformative change' – through unearthing assumptions and connecting consequences to actions – that we seek also in pre-service teachers, in English learners, in intercultural interactants and in ourselves as teacher educators and lifelong learners – especially in our goal of fostering peacebuilding. And we *did* find evidence of transformative change through the tutoring project: let us recall, for instance, from Chapter 6, Carrie's wonderment as her partner, Andesha, walked 'through war-torn' streets to sit at a computer and learn from her, which 'opened' Carrie's eyes and world to understanding agency in the midst of the structural force of conflict; or Soyoung learning about inequity and access to resources while 'getting a goosebump' as she discovers her student has one pencil, only, to use for a whole school year.

These examples of reflection – which vivify the unexpected affordance of peacebuilding emerging from language teaching and intercultural communication – also profoundly illustrate the power of reflection: for peacebuilding and for *all* learning. Therefore, as we focus on how teacher educators and candidates might specifically leverage the affordance of peacebuilding in their work, we envision reflection as the umbrella arching over this chapter, our project and all teaching and learning. More specifically, inviting pre-service teachers (who were, in our case, also tutors) to keep a reflective journal and write about their tutoring sessions over time is the first pedagogical recommendation we make – and it is a recommendation that helps us begin to identify ways to more deliberately leverage the affordance of peacebuilding in language teaching and intercultural communication.

Activities: Guided reflection, modeling, sharing

To invite reflection that fosters person to person peacebuilding, we propose providing guided reflection questions for pre-service teachers which encourage thinking across personal, relational and structural peacebuilding levels (Broome & Collier, 2012; Lederach, 2003). Lederach (2003: 25), for instance, discusses the relational level of peacebuilding as including questions that discern 'what are [people's] hopes and fears for their lives and relationships, their patterns of communication and interaction?' The graduate TESOL instructor in our project did, indeed, invite tutors to write about their 'hopes and fears for the project' as part of their first reflective entry. In turn, pre-service teacher Lisa composed the following, which helps us see the enormous potential of guided reflection questions for more deliberately fostering peacebuilding:

> My only frame of reference of Afghanistan is that which is presented to me by the media, which presents a country in constant turmoil and war. Through this experience I will be able to learn first hand about an individual whose life is completely different than mine yet I hope that we will see that there is more that unites us than divides us as people and learners.
> (Lisa)

In this entry and through her response to a guided reflection question about hopes and fears, Lisa leads us to recognize the following:

- She is actively and carefully considering one 'supposed form of knowledge' (Dewey, 1910: 6) – that which is presented to her by the media, 'a country in constant turmoil and war,' her '*only* frame of reference of Afghanistan' (emphasis added). In her awareness of the one-dimensional limits of media representation, she shows a distinct readiness to

challenge (at the structural level of peacebuilding) 'how structures such as ... media texts and discourses, both enable and constrain individuals and groups' (Broome & Collier, 2012: 252).
- Recognizing that her own knowledge has heretofore been constrained by media representations of Afghanistan, Lisa is willing to probe beyond the constraints of the structural force of the media 'to learn first hand about an individual whose life is completely different from [hers].' We thus see at the personal level of peacebuilding Lisa's 'willingness to engage with the other through dialogue' (Broome & Collier, 2012: 251), a process she believes will 'maximize' her 'potential for growth' (Lederach, 2003: 24).
- In her hope that she and her Afghan counterpart will discover that 'there is more that unites us than divides us as people and learners,' Lisa demonstrates her desire 'to maximize mutual understanding' in addition to 'bring[ing] to the surface explicitly the relational fears, hopes, and goals of the people involved,' part of the relational level of peacebuilding (Lederach, 2003: 25): in this case, Lisa's hopes and fears for her relationship with her Afghan student.
- In Lisa's hope that 'we will see that there is more that unites us than divides us as people and learners,' she constructs her future student and herself as equally 'people,' equally 'learners,' in the process connoting an equal relationship in their use and sharing of power, one more element at the relational level of peacebuilding (Lederach, 2003: 25) which can be fostered by carefully crafted, carefully guided reflection questions.

From Lisa's reflection alone, we not only see topics and themes worth delving into with future teachers of language and intercultural communication (critical media literacy, especially representations of others; what it means to exert individual agency and push past media representations; the importance of equity-mindedness; the potency of hope), but we also see how guided reflection questions lay the groundwork for the emergence and ownership of these themes from the voices of teacher candidates themselves.

As we suggest that participants engage in guided reflective writing, we further encourage teacher educators to take the time to model reflection (and all activities), a scaffolding necessity which should be familiar to most educators but especially to those who work with language learners. In our work, 'self-confidence,' for instance, provided another example of a topic for guided reflection given that: (1) most tutors revealed a lack of self-confidence at the outset of the project; (2) self-confidence has been an integral component of models and theories of intercultural communication and language learning alike (see, for example, Ghasemi *et al.*, 2020); and (3) developing self-confidence is closely related to developing 'self-esteem' and 'self-perception' in conflict transformation at the personal level (Broome & Collier, 2012; Lederach, 2003) and thus one key indicator of peacebuilding which we can more deliberately leverage through reflection.

Modeling reflection on self-confidence might look something like this:

As I prepare to assign these reflection questions, I myself wonder: Will students recognize the value of reflection? Will they be able to explain why they feel more confident (hopefully) working with their 'student'? Will anyone feel less confident? Will they see connections between self-confidence and our relationships with others? I remember my own early days teaching as a Peace Corps Volunteer in a country the US had once been at war with: the nerves, the questions, the what-ifs, my complete lack of self-confidence. I remember thinking I would get sick before the class even started. But when I smiled, my students smiled back, and when I showed them my shaking hands, we all laughed before we got started on the lesson plan and I experienced my first inkling of self-confidence. ...

As tutors track (in this case) their levels of self-confidence from session to session, we might also invite them to reflect on what happens and why their confidence level changes over time (or how their hopes and fears for their relationships with students are evolving, or how actively they are helping students – if not themselves – to meet basic human needs). The reasons they identify will likely inspire additional guided reflective questions which invite tutors to 'dig into and elaborate the too-often implicit **theories of change** that guide his or her daily activity and projects' (Lederach et al., 2007: 3, emphasis in original), just as we saw Lisa come to recognize how the media constrained her perceptions of Afghanistan to a 'country in constant turmoil and war.' We focus here on 'self-confidence,' but questions could be added and easily adapted according to specific issues pre-service teachers write about in their journals, to what the teacher educator wants to focus on, and to the elements in our peacebuilding frameworks (Broome & Collier, 2012; Lederach, 2003): from tutors' changing emotions (Lederach's 'emotional stability' at the personal level of peacebuilding); to hopes and fears for ensuing relationships as we saw with Lisa (Lederach's 'relational level of peacebuilding'); to examining decision-making processes and the inclusion of others' perspectives (from Lederach's 'structural level of peacebuilding').

Candidate teachers should further be encouraged to share reflections with each other. In small-group work or whole-class discussions, in person or online, 'theory building' can begin to emerge as participants develop an understanding of (for instance) critical media literacy or the role of self-confidence in teaching, language learning, intercultural communication, peacebuilding, in *all* learning. Lederach et al. (2007: 4) provide useful parameters for group discussion which help 'demystify' theory and bring it into the realm of reflective practice, parameters that can easily be adapted as instructions for group discussion. We thus could invite students to:

- describe why (or why not) activities go as planned;
- 'be annoyingly inquisitive,' asking always why why why and how how how;

- predict cause and effect relationships between activities and outcomes;
- think systematically, including about the wider social, historical, political, cultural, economic and other contexts that bear down on actions and decisions;
- compare experiences with one another in search of both patterns and variations;
- 'be wild' and suggest ideas/explanations for experiences which are not only outside of the box, but *break the box*. (Lederach *et al.*, 2007: 4)

Discussions guided by these parameters create space for yet richer reflection on practice and 'critical praxis' – 'reflection and action upon the world in order to transform it' (Freire, 1970: 51). We add, too: inviting student teachers to invite guided reflections from their language learners will further engender the value and importance of reflection to the learning process generally (see, for example, Allwright & Hanks, 2009; Hanks, 2015). Pre-service teachers might brainstorm and craft reflective prompts together during their coursework, which they then invite their students to write in response to: possibly at the beginning of lessons (a 'do now' warm-up activity) or at the end (in the form of reflective 'exit tickets' in which the student identifies critical takeaways or favorite moments from the lesson or session). Nor does reflection necessarily mean 'writing': Villamizar and Mejía (2019) discuss, for instance, how a digital reflection journal in video format supported more creative learning and teaching, enhanced critical thinking and augmented language learners' oral and written proficiency in the target language. We have also found that teacher candidates and language students alike take pleasure in drawing or doodling their thoughts – another form of reflection which can lead discussion and teaching in important new directions.

Clearly, there are myriad ways pre-service teachers, teacher educators, intercultural interactants and language learners alike can reflect and share with one another, all and always with the goal to uncover what is working, describe what is not, and imagine what steps we each need to take to more deliberately leverage the affordance of peacebuilding as we work with one another.

Understanding Differential Access to Resources

One notable indicator of peacebuilding we heard in participants' voices involved their efforts at understanding a world where resources are unequally distributed and unequally available. We revisit next how the promotion of equity – a constituent part of peacebuilding – is predicated on the recognition of inequity, or how structures enable 'differential access to resources and status' (Broome & Collier, 2012: 252). In Chapter 6, which focused on the structural dimension of peacebuilding, we saw how heightened and sudden awareness of such differential access to resources had a tremendous impact on one tutor, Soyoung. Here she describes what she learned from her Afghan student:

> She told me about how actually she studied with one pencil, for a whole entire like, year, one paper and one pencil, and she was just like writing, and erased it, and writing over again ... I still get a goosebump. (Soyoung)

Soyoung's realization led her to directly compare access to resources in Afghanistan and the US, where she had witnessed students throwing away pencils and looking for new ones without so much as a care:

> Like, a lot of kids in here [in the US] ... they want, like, 'I want a *cute* pencil, I don't want, like, yellow ones,' and some students don't have even a *single* yellow pencil. (Soyoung)

Impelled by Soyoung's words, as we think again about how to more deliberately leverage peacebuilding in work with future teachers of languages and intercultural communication, we draw additional inspiration from Smith (2019: 5), who proposes that learning more about the conditions of people experiencing war and conflict can lead to a better comprehension of the roots of the conflict:

> Flipping our attention from the commanding heights of the state and leading market players to the places where people struggle to survive and thrive, we can not only better understand the forces driving conflicts, but we also observe efforts at what we might call 'counter-hegemonic peacebuilding'. (Smith, 2019: 5)

This quote reminds us that many of the tutors did attend 'to the places where people [the Afghan English learners] struggle to survive and thrive.' In Smith's words, we might also see their work as a form of 'counter-hegemonic peacebuilding,' as tutors gain knowledge of the resources and conditions of the learners they work with, much like Soyoung learning about her student. Gaining such knowledge is another pivotal component of the peacebuilding process. We might even say that all efforts to build peace start with this understanding and consciousness.

Activity: Access to resources

Our next recommendation, therefore, is to work with future teachers to raise awareness of differential access to resources, particularly (although not only) when working with students from conflict countries. While videos, readings, guest speakers and lectures can provide valuable background and information on conflict contexts – along with ensuing discussions – for future teachers who may work with or in those contexts, we also encourage activities that allow future teachers to experience, through simulation, what it means to have unequal access to resources. The next activity we share, experienced by one of the authors in an orientation for a Global Citizenship seminar in Salzburg, Austria, has ignited critical conversations regarding links between inequities and conflict:

- Without sharing the purpose of the activity, begin by dividing participants into pairs or small groups. Each group is given resources to complete a project such as creating a map for their future students. While the project for each group is the same, the resources they receive are not. For example, Group A may have crayons, scissors, glue, colored paper and stickers; Group B receives only crayons, scissors and paper; Group C is given pencils and one piece of white paper.
- Now groups can begin working on their projects. At this point, expect to get some objections from the groups who received the most limited supplies. Some may even try to make use of resources they have brought with them or find around the classroom. Participants should be encouraged to complete the project with only the resources provided.
- At the end of the time allotted for the activity, each group can present what they created with their resources. Participants might even rank or judge the maps (or other artifacts).
- After the group presentations are over, participants can be asked to share how they felt when they needed to finish the same project but had different resources from their classmates, whether they had the most or the least resources.

This activity can prompt in-depth discussions regarding inequities in a variety of areas, including education, healthcare, and basic human needs such as clean water, clean air and food. Raising awareness of and reflecting on global inequities and unequal access to resources can further help future teachers begin to understand a central *cause* of conflict, one of the elements of peacebuilding which, in participants' discourses, rarely went beyond discussing the surface level of violence. Such awareness may also help instill in future educators the important possibilities of their work, as happened in Soyoung's case: later in her interview, she spoke of working with her doctoral advisors to help build schools in India and Jordan.

Exploring Identity, Leveraging Peacebuilding

Throughout the voices of pre-service teachers of EAL and Afghan English learners, we have heard time and again how they asserted various aspects of their social identities in their reflective writing and in interview transcripts. In Chapter 4, we heard Sangmu worry about whether she could 'change' her 'role from being a long-time student to an instructor.'

Jiang worried about being 'just a Chinese English speaker' who doesn't have 'an American face.' Iraqi-born Tayba, who at first feared her Afghan counterpart, in the last reflection arrived at this conclusion: 'I was upset that I had judged him and learned that he is just like me, a human!' These voices and others lead us next to consider how reflection on identity and identities serve as another means to more deliberately leverage person to person peacebuilding through language teaching and intercultural communication.

The voice of Nadiya from Chapter 4, a tutor who was also an international pre-service teacher from Ukraine, helps illuminate the roles of identity in peacebuilding. She began her reflection journal from a place of difference and othering – along with a desire for change – as she imagined the project ahead of her:

> I want to learn more about this country and its people, about their culture and education. I want to change my stereotypes (that are in my mind) about Afghani and change my attitude toward Afghanistan. (Nadiya)

Nadiya was upfront about confronting the 'stereotypes' and 'attitude' that were initially in her mind about the people (Afghani) and place (Afghanistan) she sought to learn more about. Shortly thereafter, we discover what those concerns were: 'I was afraid that they may be rude, or impatient, or unable to learn anything.' But as we read further, we find in Nadiya's final journal entry ample evidence of transformation and just how this transformation takes place: through the reconfiguration of social identities. Here is but one example evidencing change in the configuration of her identity, where she describes interactions with her Afghan student, Hassan:

> We were talking about wars in our countries, about politics and government, system of education, cultures and traditions, American people and their way of living. (Nadiya)

As discussed in Chapter 4, we find in this sentence that Nadiya and her Afghan counterpart have now become a 'we' rather than an 'us'/'them,' a social in-group constituted from a stark fact: they both are experiencing 'war in [their] countries,' with 'American people and their way of living' now an out-group worthy of discussion from their decidedly 'un'- American viewpoints. Nadiya and her student's new in-group remind us: one's willingness to *change* group membership and/or widen a group so as to join an in-group of the 'other' is a powerful indicator of peacebuilding at the personal, relational and structural levels of peacebuilding as interactants demonstrate a willingness to engage in dialogue with another, personally (Broome & Collier, 2012: 251); as they structure and restructure relationships including inter-group and intra-group, relationally (Lederach, 2003: 25); and as they discuss 'wars,' 'politics,' 'government,' 'systems of education' – in other words, 'how social structures, organizations, and institutions are built, sustained, and changed by conflict' (Lederach, 2003: 25).

This example from Nadiya highlights the importance of our next recommendation: that we create opportunities to explore notions of 'identity' – and the fluidities of identities – with pre-service teachers (who may then explore with students). Such a step is vital to leveraging peacebuilding personally, relationally and structurally, just as we find identity intertwined with language learning (see, for example, Norton, 2000; Norton & Toohey, 2011; Tamimi Sa'd, 2017) and intercultural communication (see, for example, Corbu *et al.*, 2014). In the 'Language of Peace Approach' as examined and implemented by Rothman and Sanderson (2018: 58; see also Oxford, 2013), the authors highlight the significance of exploring identity, arguing that 'increasing our students' awareness of how their identity influences their language, and how their language shapes a dialogue, widens the students' capacity to anticipate misunderstanding, empathize with the listener, and communicate constructively rather than destructively.' From their viewpoints, too, Nadiya's final reflections about her Afghan counterpart indicate her abilities to empathize (at the relational level of peacebuilding) and 'communicate constructively' as they discover the in-groups to which they both belong.

In thinking about how to address identity in teacher education, language teaching and intercultural communication classrooms, we find it useful to draw from the goals bound up in what is described in the US K-12 context as 'culturally responsive pedagogy,' one principle of which is that awareness of and respect for another's identities (ethnic, cultural, religious, linguistic – identities in all iterations and forms) play a central role in: (1) the processes of becoming culturally (and interculturally) responsive; (2) the processes of teaching and learning; and (3) the processes of becoming socially informed agents of change (Gay, 2010; Ladson-Billings, 1995; NYSED, 2018; Paris & Samy Alim, 2017; Walker, 2019). Indeed, Walker (2019: 4) is categorical when summing up the role of identity in pedagogy, noting how it is imperative that teachers who aim to be culturally responsive must first be conscious of their own identities and biases and how these may impact their pedagogical practices. These imperatives dovetail with the 'musts' of person to person peacebuilding: Nolden and Kostić (2017: 7), for instance, in their training manual for *Strengthening Resilience – Building Peace from Within*, remind us of the importance of explicitly reflecting on identity: they state unequivocally that a person's understanding of their identit(ies) powerfully impacts their abilities to transform conflict and build peace.

Activities: Exploring identities

We encourage, then, inclusion of context-sensitive and context-appropriate activities that invite reflection on identity. For instance, teachers in US classrooms may create opportunities for their students to explore their identities as members of racially and linguistically minoritized groups. In the context of our project and inspired by Tayba, Nadiya and other voices from this study, we offer a relatively simple activity for exploring 'shared identity,' one borrowed and adapted from the Greater Good Science Center (GGSC, n.d.) at the University of California-Berkeley. We mention the GGSC in particular as all resources and activities they offer are accompanied by research-based articles, the site offers podcasts related to the theme of each activity, and there are also online interactive quizzes related to activity themes – all rich, multimodal resources which can supplement language teaching and intercultural communication lessons and curriculum in ways that further leverage the peacebuilding potential therein.

This 'shared identity' activity can be done with candidate teachers of EAL in a classroom, and it can also be adapted for tutors to do with their students one-on-one.

- Start by inviting students to think of someone in their lives who is very different from themselves: model and brainstorm *with them* so that they can imagine 'difference' in many ways (physical appearance, gender, nationality, age, language, dialect, etc.; someone who has different political affiliations, different hobbies or passions, belongs to different clubs or groups, etc.). Encourage a lengthy list and, again, model and brainstorm with students.
- Once this list is complete, next ask students to list everything they have in common with this person: Did you or do you both go to school? Hold a job? Have brothers and sisters? Speak the same language? Hate (or love, or fear) math? Again, encourage a lengthy list. Students could even create a Venn diagram of overlapping circles, with commonalities listed in the center overlapping areas and differences listed in the outer rings.
- When students have finished their lists, ask them to focus on the commonalities, the social 'in-groups' to which they and their 'person' belong. Ask students if they 'see' the person differently from before, when they focused only on differences. Do they see the person more as an individual than as a member of a 'group' (which may be an 'out-group')? Discussions should be rich, and during discussion listen for and highlight evidence of changing impressions of 'others,' changes that demonstrate the fluidity of boundaries around our differing social identities.

While this activity may seem relatively simple, the conversations it can spark may be profound. Moreover, creating opportunities for reflection and discussion of stereotypes and prejudgments can further maximize opportunities for cognitive change around thinking about identity. Such conversations can, and should, push participants out of their comfort zones. It is equally crucial that the instructors/facilitators acknowledge that all people have biases and harbor stereotypes, including themselves, and that, while such conversations might be uncomfortable, participants should recognize the importance of examining their feelings and beliefs.

Such conversations can be enhanced yet more profoundly by using the voices in this book as examples to start the conversation. Share, for instance, Nadiya's initial attitudes before she came to realize that she and her student belonged to the in-group of belonging to a country engaged in war, or Sangmu discovering that she and her student both learned from the grammar translation method, or even Tayba's discovery that they were both, indeed, human: as the GGSC (n.d.) points out, 'At the broadest level, you both [we all] belong to the human species, which means that you [we] share 99.9 percent of your DNA.' One more note in relation to the GGSC (n.d.): in their abundance of supplementary materials, they also provide concise readings that explain the importance of such activities. Regarding the 'Shared Identity' activity and why we might try it, for example, we find the following explanation:

> Although people generally want and try to be altruistic, they may also feel competitive toward people outside of their 'in-group,' and the boundaries of their in-group might shrink at times when resources seem scarce or they are fearful for their safety. Reminding people to see the basic humanity that they share with those who might seem different from them can help overcome fear and distrust and promote cooperation. Even small similarities, like recognizing a shared love of sports, can foster a greater sense of kinship across group boundaries. Importantly, recognizing commonalities doesn't mean negating differences, but may in fact help people value differences rather than feeling threatened by them. (GGSE, n.d.)

This 'Shared Identity' activity is but one example. Pre-service teachers might also begin by writing in response to the questions: 'What is identity? What does it mean to you? What constitutes your identity?' Nolden and Kostić (2017: 7–9) propose these questions as the start of a more formal discussion on identity and its relationship to peacebuilding, which could easily be extended to teaching language and intercultural communication. Another example is an activity called 'Circles of My Multicultural Self,' in which participants first identify various aspects of their identity (teacher, student, scholar, daughter, husband, mechanic, etc.). Then they write and reflect on stories when they were proud to experience one aspect of identity (I am proud to be fluent in Hungarian, English, Portuguese) and when one aspect of their identity brought them pain (during the terror attacks of 9/11, one author from the US who was working in another country was told repeatedly that 'America had it coming'). The goals, ultimately, are that activities 'foster' 'kinship across group boundaries' and help participants 'valu[e] differences rather than feeling threatened by them' (GGSC, n.d.; for related activities, see also Mahalingappa *et al.*,

2021). These concepts are infused throughout models of peacebuilding and conflict transformation – including the two we rely on in this book (Broome & Collier, 2012; Lederach, 2003) – and they resound in the voices of our participants.

Agency and Power

In Broome and Collier's (2012: 252) peacebuilding model – built from Lederach's (2003) work and connected by culture and communication – they show the intersections between peacebuilding and intercultural communication, in the process drawing our attention to how 'individual levels of agency and equity' (at the personal, *individual* level of peacebuilding) are often experienced as what 'structures' (discourses, policies and practices of organizations and institutions – and the decision-makers behind them) allow (see also Giddens, 1984). Stated more broadly, 'power' matters and is evidenced in: who can act, and how; what is allowed, what isn't; and who is doing the allowing, who is making the decisions.

Having just discussed the relevance of 'identity' to peacebuilding, we find a quote from Lederach (2003) especially fitting as we start this section related to agency and power:

> [W]e need to be attentive to peoples' perceptions of how identity is linked to power and to the systems and structures which organize and govern their relationships. This is particularly important for people who feel their identity has historically been eroded, marginalized, or under deep threat. (Lederach, 2003: 60)

In addition to the interweaving of peacebuilding elements within this quote across personal, relational and structural levels, what we also take from Lederach's words is that work with teacher candidates to understand and work against forces that threaten and marginalize others (including the forces of armed and deadly conflict, terror) is also work *for* agency and power. Accordingly, as we push forward in our search for ways to more deliberately leverage peacebuilding in the work between future teachers, language learners and intercultural interactants, we turn again to what we have learned from our participants – including now the voices of Afghan participants along *with* tutors – in order to contemplate how leveraging participants' perceptions and awareness of agency and power provides us with further footholds into peacebuilding.

We start with what we have seen so far in relation to agency and power. In Chapter 5, Afghan student Haroon described his work with his tutor as follows:

> [S]ometimes she was giving me a homework and I was doing my homework ... I also give to her some homeworks, not just she, I can also give her, I could give her. ... and I give her homework ... and we was like this. (Haroon)

Here we see that Haroon's relationship with his tutor clearly harbored space for him to step up and claim his own agency ('I also give to her some homeworks, not just she'). Five times in this excerpt he discursively stepped into the subject position of the sentence and acted *upon* his tutor ('her'), demonstrating his perception of his own agency, his sense of being an 'equal' in the tutoring/learning relationship, and how he believed they shared power ('not just she, I can also give her').

Tutor Yuqing experienced something quite similar with her Afghan counterpart:

> He even asked me how to say something in Chinese. He is also proud of his first language, when I showed him some simple Chinese and he translated to Dari and made me memorize them. (Yuqing)

Yuqing's student, like Haroon, must have perceived his own agency and power as he 'made' her memorize phrases or words he had translated from Chinese into Dari. Shortly thereafter, Yuqing ascribed the 'friendly relationship' that they established as due in part to this exchange of their home languages, a relationship certainly bolstered by the fact that Yuqing was not hesitant to 'share power' when her student, like Haroon, stepped into the subject position of the clause ('he translated to Dari and made me memorize'), exerting his agency as he did so.

In both of these examples, we begin to discern the affordance of peacebuilding in participants' discourses again, with agency exerted and power shared. In Chapter 5, tutor Cassandra made the potential imbalance of power between tutor and 'tutee' explicit, demonstrating once more how peacebuilding is already in many instances a fundamental component of language teaching and intercultural communication:

> I am conscious of the power dynamics of the tutor – tutee relationship and those between our two countries. I hope to be sensitive to this and to keep her goals at the forefront of our time together, rather than my preconceived notions of how our tutoring sessions should look. (Cassandra)

Here Cassandra makes the leap from the micro- and meso-interactions (personal, relational) of tutoring to the macro (structural) implications, which we see in her awareness of 'the power dynamics of the tutor-tutee relationship *and* those between our two countries' (italics added). She is aware, in other words, of the possible geopolitical tensions of a graduate student from the US tutoring an Afghan English learner, even if she was too young to remember the events of 9/11. Her words and her desire to place her Afghan counterpart's goals at the forefront of her tutoring attest not only to her awareness of power dynamics, but also to her commitment to ensuring that her student's agency guides their work together.

So how might we more deliberately leverage opportunities to raise awareness of and ensure space for agency and a balanced sharing of power? We approach this question in three parts: first, by looking at agency in the classroom and/or in the virtual intercultural borderlands; second, by looking at agency for work and issues beyond and outside the teaching and tutoring context; and third and finally, by considering agency as it relates to emotions.

Activities: Agency in the classroom and in the virtual intercultural borderlands

Cassandra's intention to keep her student's goals at the forefront of their work reifies how we think of agency. As we work with pre-service teachers of language and intercultural communication, we should likewise explore and enact 'choice' with them as much as possible, so they too become ever more aware of their own agency and power. We should also encourage teacher candidates to consider how they will ensure that their students have choices. Hull-Sypnieski and Ferlazzo (2016) affirm Cassandra's focus on agency by reiterating the importance of students' goals as curriculum and lesson drivers, along with scaffolding learning and strategies so students know what they need to do to achieve their goals, developing a 'growth mindset' as they try different approaches and take different paths in their work to achieve those goals (Dweck, 2015). MacKenzie (2020) urges us to nurture agency with students, as much as possible, through '*genuine* decision-making' (italics added); he then propounds a series of practical activities which can cultivate student agency within the classroom and which can be adapted and adopted for work in the virtual intercultural borderlands:

- Invite learners to reflect on learning preferences (Alone, in pairs, through groups? Through writing, drawing, acting out? And how much time do they believe they can stay focused on an activity before doing something else?). Let their answers guide the teaching or tutoring process.
- Support and celebrate their curiosities and passions by including them in curricular and assignment decisions, making real-world connections between course content, their passions and the world beyond the classroom (or beyond the virtual intercultural borderlands).
- Pose (and invite students to pose) what MacKenzie (2020) calls 'big, unGoogleable questions,' which lead to other questions, which infuse the room and the course and/or the virtual intercultural borderlands with curiosity, curiosities and an understanding of how questions drive learning.
- Provide students the tools and possibilities to take part in how they are assessed and how they give feedback to others (allow students to create rubrics for assignments, for example, and encourage self-assessment, to be included in grades).

- Furnish students with options (MacKenzie uses a 'Choice Board') of how they will learn (Through reading texts? Looking at images? Watching videos? Listening to podcasts?), including choice in how students will document learning (Through timelines? A poster? An essay? A poem? A demonstration?).
- Finally, Mackenzie (2020) asks us to find ways that help students become what they want to be, even as we encourage 'empathy and equity' along the way. This strategy reaffirms Cassandra's intention and the charge of Hull-Sypnieski and Ferlazzo (2016), both of which advocate for agency, again, by using student goals as the driving force behind curricular and lesson goals.

To these strategies, we add the following ideas as informed by our experiences with students' and tutors' experiences in the virtual intercultural borderlands. The exchange of languages between tutors and their Afghan counterparts (from Chinese to Dari, and Dari to Chinese, as just one example) could easily become a regular practice, a form of 'reciprocal peer tutoring' or 'tandem learning,' where tutors and students exchange roles (tutors become students, students tutors), essentially taking turns to teach one another their languages, even if it is just for a few minutes at the beginning or end of a tutoring session. Some of the benefits of this practice include the stimulation of more active learning and oral interaction, the reinforcement of learning content for both members of the tutoring dyad, increased levels of comfort and openness, and other affective qualities which make up our peacebuilding models, including 'more supportive relationships; greater psychological well-being, social competence, communication skills and self-esteem' (Briggs, 2013). Teacher educators might ask tutors or candidate teachers to track and reflect on what they are learning about their students' languages and cultural practices, knowledge of which is instrumental in fostering the teaching of languages. For those teacher educators who want to focus explicitly on peace in their curriculum, following, for instance, Kruger's (2012) and Gomes de Matos' (2014) 'linguistics of non-violence' (see also Chapter 1) or Rosenberg's (2003) 'nonviolent communication,' reciprocal tutoring or tandem learning could explore cross-linguistic terms for peace, conflict, compassion, positive feelings, negative feelings, and so on, discussions of which should continue to drive forward the goals of balanced power and mutual agency.

Activities: Agency beyond the classroom, beyond the virtual intercultural borderlands

As we consider agency beyond the confines of the classroom and beyond the virtual intercultural borderlands, we first recall how many of our Afghan participants were exerting their agency in the face of one of the most controlling structures possible to imagine: that of conflict, that of war. Thus, as examined in Chapter 6, participants like Mirza and Lisa's student Mustafa sought to leave Afghanistan for further education in order to return better prepared to 'serve' their country (Mirza) and help 'develop[ ] the infrastructure that would facilitate long lasting peace' (Mustafa). Sadaf said, 'I'd like to work for an NGO that can help my people'; Mahtab's work endeavored to eliminate violence against children and especially girls in Afghanistan by creating programs for fathers and daughters to play and work together. We heard also from Fawad, expressing concern over how his sister did not have the same rights and opportunities as he had. His interview ended with a fist in the air and these last words: 'Afghan Women's Empowerment!'

Given these students' aspirations and work and drawing from our experiences with tutors and students both, to more deliberately foster agency and the peacebuilding possibilities of such projects, we enjoin those working with pre-service language teachers to undertake the following:

- Work with teachers/tutors to conduct a context-sensitive needs analysis to develop curriculum (or plan several sessions) around that analysis (Nation & Macalister, 2010; Richards, 2002; Songhori, 2008) based on the language learners' needs. Nation and Macalister (2010) – writing about language curriculum development – provide a step by step guide and questions to think through to help with these processes: from identifying environmental constraints (such as internet access and broadband speed) to distinguishing between objective and subjective needs. In the case of our project, tutors were encouraged to find out: do/will/might their students need to work on application writing for scholarships, grant writing, statements of purpose, academic writing, English for specific purposes, or something else?
- Integrate, as much as possible, the inclusion of authentic materials their students may already be working with, such as Mahtab's 'Guidelines' for implementing the 'Father Daughter Hours' (with permissions, if necessary, to use and possibly even make these materials available to future tutors and students).
- Work with tutors to undertake genre analysis (Cheng, 2018; Hyland, 2013; Swales & Feak, 2012) so that, in turn, tutors can help their students with genre analysis. In this way tutor and student alike can discover and adapt genre conventions of specific texts according to audience, purpose, context and language conventions of specific genres. Tutors and students will also come to see how genre conventions are just that – conventions, not rules – and they can likewise explore how they might adapt/adopt/transform or resist conventions, all of which are acts of agency which highlight their abilities to choose what they want to say/do, and how.
- Invite analysis of such materials between tutors/pre-service teachers and students. Tutor and student might consider whether guidelines (as

in the case of Mahtab) are locally created or 'handed down' from international NGOs and donors, are appropriate for the local context, and/or are workable as written, as tutor and student explore together the possibilities of suggestions, adaptations, adoptions, transformations – and perhaps resistance.

Such exercises can not only enhance individual agency, but also provide pre-service teachers with consequential lessons into: NGO/international donor relationships with local community partners, and whether those partnerships are mutual and equal as projects are implemented; whether projects are locally owned and contextualized; and/or whether they place '"developed nations" ahead of "developing" nations; support[ing] the reproduction of linguistic, colonial, and patriarchal discourses and hierarchies' (Appleby, 2010: 4).

Agency and Emotion

In their exploration of the emotional dynamics of conflict transformation, Bramsen and Poder (2018: 2) object to the vast attention paid to negative emotions in peace and conflict studies. They ask us to attend instead to the 'emotional energy' around conflict and its transformation (peace), which impacts interactants' sense of agency. Ideally, the authors contend, interactions will be 'cooperative,' as 'cooperative interaction engenders positive EE [emotional energy] such as confidence and trust, promoting *productive* agency' (Bramsen & Poder, 2018: 2, italics added). Emotional energy can occasion and generate not only 'cooperative interaction' but subsequent positive emotions, namely, trust, hope and forgiveness (Bramsen & Poder, 2018: 6), many of the elements, we add, that are present in our peacebuilding frameworks (Broome & Collier, 2012; Lederach, 2003).

Activities

For our final recommendations in this chapter, then, we consider agency again, but now as it relates to the emotional dynamics of conflict and how to create 'cooperative interaction' (Bramsen & Poder, 2018: 7). Bramsen and Poder draw on the work of Collins (2004), who explored interaction ritual (IR) chains, 'during which a mutual focus of attention, common rhythm, and a shared mood generate positive EE [emotional energy] in individuals and solidarity among them.' Through Collins' work on interaction rituals, Bramsen and Poder (2018: 13) argue, we can begin to identify and then create conditions for the emergence of elements of successful interaction which may so often seem 'coincidental, mysterious or arbitrary, namely when interaction "works".' In their subsequent discussion of the practical implications of cooperative interaction and interaction rituals, Bramsen and Poder (2018: 14) provide us with important advice which we see as being as useful to language and intercultural communication teachers as it is to more formally recognized peacebuilders:

- Encourage tutors to establish focus and engagement immediately, at the start of the session. For an introductory session, tutor and student can each complete a getting-to-know-you questionnaire, for instance, which can allow each half of the tutoring pair to get a handle on their nerves before detailed interaction begins and they start talking more freely. An easy first topic to write, talk and answer questions about is language. Why do you want to speak English? How long have you been learning English? What is your home language? What other languages do you speak? What is your favorite word in your language? What is your favorite word in English? And so on.
- For subsequent sessions and in order to continue developing the 'interaction ritual' (Collins, 2004) so helpful for peacebuilding, tutors can prepare a 'warm-up' activity for each session which reviews prior learning, checks on background knowledge and/or helps the pair continue to build their relationships with each other as well as with the larger communities to which they belong (English learners in Afghanistan; tutors of EAL for the graduate TESOL course). Not only (again) are warm-up activities considered 'best practices' of language teaching more generally (see, for example, Echevarria *et al.*, 2016), but such activities 'build momentum' and help tutor and student mutually focus on the lesson at hand, two more actions that substantially contribute to cooperative interaction and ultimately peacebuilding at the micro-level of engagement (Bramsen & Poder, 2018: 14).
- Intriguingly, a part of interaction rituals which contributes to the strength of cooperation between interactants is some form of demarcation, a barrier to outsiders (Bramsen & Poder, 2018: 5; Collins, 2004). In the case of our tutoring project, barriers were provided by the limits of videoconferencing as participants met 'face to face,' if virtually. This is not to say that 'outsiders' cannot interrupt interactions (as we know all too well now, after teaching online throughout the first long years of a global pandemic): from either side of the virtual intercultural borderlands, children and pets may push their way in; other students may walk past and behind interactants; other lessons may be going on in a computer lab, contributing to noise and distraction. We must therefore encourage tutors to find ways to 'shelter' and focus their interactions in the virtual intercultural borderlands of online exchange, although 'flexibility' can also lead to rich tangents. As one author experienced while tutoring an Afghan student, the conversation went something like this: 'This is my dog'; 'I'm afraid of dogs. He lives in your house?'; 'Yes.'; 'Why do Americans let

dogs live inside? Dogs are haram in my culture.'; 'Why?' And together tutor and student tracked down a simple article in English addressing and discussing – with curiosity, with openness, without judgment, developing 'critical cultural awareness' (Byram, 1997) – what Islam says about dogs (for instance, hunting and guard dogs are acceptable, but not inside the house, etc.). We have also heard tutors and students alike share with excitement what they experienced with their counterpart during their sessions: fireworks through the window on the Fourth of July (US Independence Day); the smiling face of 'Aunt Gul' who wants to say 'hi' in English; an Afghan living room; a student dorm in the US.

There is a certain irony in this last recommendation: there needs to be a 'barrier' creating a safe, focused space for interaction in the virtual intercultural borderlands, a barrier which further allows for the opening up of liminal, hybrid and metaphorical spaces for participants to share, interact and build peace, person to person. At the same time, these borderlands can be intentionally and literally 'opened up' (with permission of all parties, of course) to provide a glimpse of the backdrops to interaction: to a rooster crowing on a Kabul rooftop; to posters of sport stars on a dorm wall; to a thin black cloud of smoke rising on the horizon.

In this chapter, we have focused on the most salient and compelling insights we have taken from project participants and how those lessons help us more deliberately to leverage the affordance of peacebuilding. We recognize that there are many more lessons contained herein, discussions of which go beyond the possible length and scope of this book. We hope the activities we have shared provide enough of a light forward for teachers and teacher educators to start their own projects with students – especially in conflict countries or regions – wherever there might be the need and desire to work at the intersections of language learning, intercultural communication and person to person peacebuilding.

Concluding Remarks

As we end this book, we face, still, the profound and persistent need for peacebuilding and the actions and changes it requires and makes possible (Broome & Collier, 2012; Lederach, 2003). We face, still, the 'chaos that surrounds' (Rose). Daily, we encounter reminders of the inequalities that exist in access to economic, political and social capital. In spite of the development and distribution of vaccines in the world's wealthier nations, a global pandemic continues to take a deadly toll on countries and regions with less access to resources, laying bare existing inequities around the world. In the US, the closing of school buildings has revealed how many students rely on schools not only for education but also for the daily sustenance of breakfasts and lunches provided at no cost. In the meantime, while technology has made possible projects like the one at the heart of this book, the move from in-person classrooms to online learning has made it impossible for school and government officials globally to deny the existence of a deep and ongoing digital divide between those who have access to technology and reliable internet and those who do not. Moreover, for some, the transition from office-based jobs to working from home has been relatively easy; however, for others, especially immigrants and members of racially and linguistically minoritized communities, working in the era of COVID-19 has meant facing daily risks to their health and that of their families, leading to proportionally higher rates of infection and death among these communities.

Conflict, too, persists – across the globe and in the home countries of our participants, tutors and students alike. In occupied Crimea, Ukrainians grapple with Russians over oil, gas, water. During recent Israel-Gaza violence, at least 12 Israelis died and more than 230 Palestinians, among them 67 children (Cohen, 2021). In the US, the horrific death of George Floyd (2020), a black man whose murder by a white police officer was filmed for all the world to see, has forced an acknowledgment of long-standing, systemic racism and the entrenchment of white supremacist groups, like those that overran the US Capitol on January 6. Finally, Afghanistan, home to so many of our participants, remains mired in violence and upheaval. Months before the complete withdrawal of US troops, the Taliban continues to wrest control of villages, districts and provinces across the country. In May 2021, a car bomb targeting girls killed more than 90 people outside a high school in Kabul.

Despite atrocity, disparity, brutality, the voices of our participants convince us of the profound power and potential of person to person peacebuilding, and we hope that teachers and teacher educators will deliberately leverage the affordance of peacebuilding in their work. We hope that teachers, teacher educators and researchers alike will continue to listen to and learn from the voices of participants, in virtual exchange or in traditional classrooms, engaged in intercultural communication and building peace, person to person. We hope that researchers will take up questions that are beyond the scope of this book: How might the peacebuilding frameworks we have used inform the design and implementation of projects in other languages and content areas? How can we ensure that those who design and participate in EAL projects do not lose sight of the hegemonic power and presence of English in the world? What kind of teacher identities and roles does peacebuilding in language and intercultural communication classrooms assume, need and/or require? How might peacebuilding principles and practices (formal and informal) from around the world complicate, interrogate, enrich and inform our (predominantly North American, European) understandings of peacebuilding? We look forward to further conversations.

We hope, too, that the voices of our participants stay with readers as they stay with us – from Tayba's recognition that her student is human, 'just like us'; to Mary's fear of disclosing to her student that her daughters were married to other women; to Mahtab insisting that laughing with men 'is NOT bad. It's GOOD,' especially in a leadership class. From these individual voices, moreover, we hope it is clear how the discursive indicators of peacebuilding we have identified at the personal, relational and structural levels (Broome & Collier, 2012; Lederach, 2003) intersect with and are embedded in intercultural communication. From the totality of these voices – one on one – we have shown how these peacebuilding indicators accumulate and constellate within the shelter of the virtual intercultural borderlands. We hope that these voices both inform and inspire other language teachers, teachers educators and researchers, as they have informed and inspired us.

Afterword: August 2021

As we prepare to send this book to press, we do so with the knowledge that Afghanistan has fallen to the Taliban. We do so having spent the last days and weeks working with Afghans on visa applications, proofreading threat statements, and fielding phone call after phone call (many from the voices in this book, including tutors) in desperate search for help or ways to help. Mirza was hiding in the foothills of the Hindu Kush and trying to determine which refugee camp to walk to: Iran? Tajikistan? Najibullah was fleeing with two girls and two journalists to Pakistan. Perhaps more chilling, the women in Afghanistan we spoke to have mostly gone silent, have disappeared from social media, have deactivated their Facebook and WhatsApp accounts: wise moves, certainly, but now? Radio silence.

We are left in that silence with a terrible reality. We are afraid for our Afghan colleagues and we are also boundlessly grateful to them: the tutoring project which inspired this book led participants to make not only connections, but profound connections which will continue to inspire, we hope, work for peace: in Afghanistan, in the US, in the world.

References

Abdallah-Pretceille, M. (2003) *Former et éduquer en contexte hétérogène: Pour un humanisme du divers* [*Teaching and Education in a Heterogeneous Context: For a Humanism of Diversity*]. Paris: Anthropos.

Abu-Akel, A., Armour, E., Baron-Cohen, S., Charnalia, N., Leckman, J., Rounthwaite, D. and Staiti, H. (2019) *Empathy: An Invaluable Natural Resource for Peace* (White Paper). Toronto: Empathy for Peace. See https://www.researchgate.net/publication/339135921_Empathy_An_Invaluable_Natural_Resource_for_Peace#fullTextFileContent (accessed 8 August 2020).

Abu-Lughod, L. (1991) Writing against culture. In R.G. Fox (ed.) *Recapturing Anthropology: Working in the Present* (pp. 137–162). Santa Fe, NM: School of American Research Press.

Abu-Nimer, M. (2001) Conflict resolution, culture, and religion: Toward a training model of interreligious peacebuilding. *Journal of Peace Research* 38 (6), 685–704.

Achirri, K. (2017) Perceiving identity through accent lenses: A case study of a Chinese English speaker's perceptions of her pronunciation and perceived social identity. *Semantic Scholar*, paper. See https://www.semanticscholar.org/paper/Perceiving-Identity-through-Accent-Lenses%3A-A-Case-a-Achirri/a4d9de849cd1e74b179bdd2e8a26b6a564700b61?p2df (accessed 5 March 2020).

Adams, J.P. (1991) *Peacework: Oral Histories of Women Peace Activists*. Boston, MA: Twayne Publishers.

Ahmadi, N. and Bezhan, F. (2020) Horrific murder of teenage girl again puts spotlight on Afghanistan's 'honor' killings. *Radio Free Europe: Radio Liberty*, article, 7 May. See https://www.rferl.org/a/horrific-killing-of-teenage-girl-puts-spotlight-on-afghanistans-honor-killings/30599545.html (accessed 21 June 2020).

Aijazi, O. (2020) Why technocratic understandings of humanitarian accountability can harm local communities. *Canadian Partnership for Reconstruction and Development*. See https://cprd.ca/wp-content/uploads/2020/03/Understanding-humanitarian-Acountability.pdf (accessed 2 June 2021).

Alias, A.M. (2015) Reinventing the role of children and youth in post-conflict peacebuilding. *Capstone Collection* 2787. See http://digitalcollections.sit.edu/capstones/2787 (accessed 6 April 2020).

Allen, M. (2011) Political representation. In D. Chatterjee (ed.) *Encyclopedia of Global Justice* (pp. 877–880). Dordrecht: Springer.

Allport, G.W., Clark, K. and Pettigrew, T. (1954) *The Nature of Prejudice*. New York: Addison-Wesley.

Allwright, D. and Hanks, J. (2009) *The Developing Language Learner: An Introduction to Exploratory Practice*. London: Palgrave.

Alred, G., Byram, M. and Fleming, M. (2003) *Intercultural Experience and Education*. Clevedon: Multilingual Matters.

Alsop, R. (2005) Empowerment: If it matters, how do we measure it? *International Poverty Centre, Brasilia*, conference paper, 29–31 August. See http://www.ipc-undp.org/conference/md-poverty/papers/Ruth_.pdf (accessed 20 September 2020).

Altman, I. and Taylor, D.A. (1973) *Social Penetration: The Development of Interpersonal Relationships*. New York: Holt, Rinehart & Winston.
Amnesty International (2017) *The World's Worst Places To Be A Woman*, web page, 17 June. See https://www.amnestyusa.org/the-worlds-worst-places-to-be-a-woman/ (accessed 26 July 2020).
Anzaldúa, G. (1987) *Borderlands/La Frontera: The New Mestiza*. San Francisco, CA: Spinsters/Aunt Lute Books.
Appleby, R. (2010) *ELT, Gender and International Development: Myths of Progress in a Neocolonial World*. Bristol: Multilingual Matters.
Arasaratnam, L.A. (2014) Ten years of research in intercultural communication competence (2003–2013): A retrospective. *Journal of Intercultural Communication* 35 (7), 1–12.
Ashworth, M. (1991) Internationalism and our strenuous family. *TESOL Quarterly* 25 (2), 231–243.
Astley, W.G. and Van de Ven, A.H. (1983) Central perspectives and debates in organization theory. *Administrative Science Quarterly* 28 (2), 245–273.
Auerbach, E.R. (1993) Reexamining English only in the ESL classroom. *TESOL Quarterly* 27 (1), 9–32.
Avruch, K. (1998) *Culture & Conflict Resolution*. Washington, DC: US Institute of Peace Press.
Avruch, K. (2003) Type I and type II errors in culturally sensitive conflict resolution practice. *Conflict Resolution Quarterly* 20 (3), 351–371.
Avruch, K. (2006) Culture, relativism, and human rights. In J.A. Mertus and J.W. Helsing (eds) *Human Rights and Conflict: Exploring the Links Between Rights, Law, and Peacebuilding* (pp. 97–120). Washington, DC: United States Institute of Peace.
Bakhtin, M. (1973) *Mikhail Bakhtin: The Duvakin Interviews, 1973* (S.N. Gratchev and M. Marinova, eds). Lewisburg, PA: Bucknell University Press.
Bakhtin, M. (1981) *The Dialogic Imagination*. Austin, TX: University of Texas Press.
Bakhtin, M. (1984) *Problems of Dostoevsky's Poetics* (C. Emerson, trans.). Manchester: Manchester University Press.
Baldwin, J. (2017) Murky waters: Histories of intercultural communication research. In L. Chen (ed.) *Handbook of Intercultural Communication* (pp. 19–43). Berlin: De Gruyter Mouton.
Bamber, P.M. (2016) *Transformative Education through International Service-Learning: Realising an Ethical Ecology of Learning*. New York: Routledge.
Barcelos, A.M.F. (2021) Revolutionary love and peace in the construction of an English teacher's professional identity. In R.L. Oxford, M.M. Olivero, M. Harrison and T. Gregersen (eds) *Peacebuilding in Language Education: Innovations in Theory and Practice* (pp. 96–109). Bristol: Multilingual Matters.
Barker, C. (2005) *Cultural Studies: Theory and Practice*. London: Sage.
Belz, J. (2003) Linguistic perspectives on the development of intercultural competence in telecollaboration. *Language Learning & Technology* 7 (2), 68–99.
Bennett, M.J. (1993) Towards ethnorelativism: A developmental model of intercultural sensitivity. In R.M. Paige (ed.) *Education for the Intercultural Experience* (pp. 21–71). Yarmouth, ME: Intercultural Press.
Bennett, M.J. (1998) Intercultural communication: A current perspective. In M.J. Bennett (ed.) *Basic Concepts of Intercultural Communication: Selected Readings*. Yarmouth, ME: Intercultural Press.
Bennett, M.J. (2004) Becoming interculturally competent. In J.S. Wurzel (ed.) *Toward Multiculturalism: A Reader in Multicultural Education*. Newton, MA: Intercultural Resource Corporation.
Bennett, M.J. (2018a) Developmental model of intercultural sensitivity. *The International Encyclopedia of Intercultural Communication* (pp. 1–10). Hoboken, NJ: Wiley Blackwell.

Bennett, M.J. (2018b) Intercultural communication. *IDR Institute: Intercultural Development Research*, web page. See https://www.idrinstitute.org/resources/intercultural-communication/ (accessed 13 September 2020).

Berger, P.L. and Luckmann, T. (1966) *The Social Construction of Reality*. Harmondsworth: Penguin Books.

Bhabha, H.K. (2006) *The Location of Culture*. New York: Routledge. (Original work published 1994.)

Biden, J. (2021) Remarks by President Biden on the way forward in Afghanistan. *The White House*, 14 April. See https://www.whitehouse.gov/briefing-room/speeches-remarks/2021/04/14/remarks-by-president-biden-on-the-way-forward-in-afghanistan/ (accessed 30 May 2021).

Blackledge, A. (2005) *Discourse and Power in a Multilingual World*. Amsterdam: John Benjamins.

Bohm, D. (1996) *On Dialogue*. London: Routledge.

Bohn, L. (2018) 'We're all handcuffed in this country.' Why Afghanistan is still the worst place in the world to be a woman. *Time*, 8 December. See https://time.com/5472411/afghanistan-women-justice-war/ (accessed 22 September 2020).

Boot, M. (2020) Peace talks have begun in Afghanistan, major pitfalls await. *Council on Foreign Relations*, 15 September. See https://www.cfr.org/in-brief/peace-talks-afghanistan-taliban-pitfalls-await (accessed 24 September 2020).

Botes, J. (2003) Conflict transformation: A debate over semantics or a crucial shift in the theory and practice of peace and conflict studies? *International Journal of Peace Studies* 8 (2), 1–27.

Boulding, E. (1990) *Building a Global Civic Culture: Education for an Interdependent World*. New York: Syracuse University Press.

Boulding, K.E. (1957) Organization and conflict. *Conflict Resolution* 1 (2), 122–134.

Boulding, K.E. (1962) *Conflict and Defense: A General Theory*. Oxford: Harper.

Boulding, K.E. (1977) Twelve friendly quarrels with Johan Galtung. *Journal of Peace Research* 14 (1), 75–86.

Boulding, K.E. (1990) *Three Faces of Power*. Newbury Park, CA: Sage.

Bourdieu, P. (1989) Social space and symbolic power. *Sociological Theory* 7 (1), 14–25.

Boutros-Ghali, B. (1992) *An Agenda for Peace: Preventive Diplomacy, Peacemaking and Peace-keeping*. New York: United Nations. See https://digitallibrary.un.org/record/145749?ln=en.

Brahimi Report (2000) Identical letters dated 21 August 2000 from the *Secretary-General to the President of the General Assembly and the President of the Security Council: Report of the Panel on United Nations Peace Operations*, A/55/305-S/2000/809. New York: UN General Assembly.

Braine, G. (1999) *Non-Native Educators in English Language Teaching*. Mahwah, NJ: Lawrence Erlbaum.

Bramsen, I. and Poder, P. (2018) *Berghof Handbook for Conflict Transformation, Online Edition*. Berlin: Berghof Foundation. See https://www.berghof-foundation.org/fileadmin/redaktion/Publications/Handbook/Articles/bramsen_poder_handbook.pdf (accessed 1 September 2020).

Brandt, D. and Clinton, K. (2002) Limits of the local: Expanding perspectives on literacy as a social practice. *Journal of Literacy Research* 34 (3), 337–356.

Brantmeier, E.J. (2007) Everyday understandings of peace and non-peace: Peacekeeping and peacebuilding at a US Midwestern high school. *Journal of Peace Education* 4 (2), 127–148.

Brantmeier, E.J. (2008) Building intercultural empathy for peace: Teacher involvement in peace curricula development at a U.S. midwestern high school. In J. Lin, E.J. Brantmeier and C. Bruhn (eds) *Transforming Education for Peace* (pp. 67–89). Charlotte, NC: Information Age Publishing.

Bratić, V. (2006) Media effects during violent conflict: Evaluating media contributions to peace building. *Conflict & Communication Online* 5 (1). See http://www.cco.regener-online.de/2006_1/pdf_2006-1/bratic.pdf (accessed 23 March 2020).

Briggs, S. (2013) How peer teaching improves student learning and 10 ways to encourage it. *InformEd*, 7 June. See https://www.opencolleges.edu.au/informed/features/peer-teaching (accessed 22 May 2021).

Brock-Utne, B. (2012) The centrality of women's work for peace in the thinking, actions, and writings of Elise Boulding. *Journal of Peace Education* 9 (2), 127–137.

Broome, B.J. and Collier, M.J. (2012) Culture, communication, and peacebuilding: A reflexive multi-dimensional contextual framework. *Journal of International and Intercultural Communication* 5 (4), 245–269.

Bumiller, E. (2009) Remembering Afghanistan's golden age. *The New York Times*, 17 October. See https://www.nytimes.com/2009/10/18/weekinreview/18bumiller.html (accessed 24 September 2020).

Burde, D. (2014) *Schools for Conflict or for Peace in Afghanistan*. New York: Columbia University Press.

Byram, M. (1997) *Teaching and Assessing Intercultural Communicative Competence* (1st edn). Clevedon: Multilingual Matters.

Byram, M. (2009) Intercultural competence in foreign languages: The intercultural speaker and the pedagogy of foreign language education. In D.K. Deardorff (ed.) *The Sage Handbook of Intercultural Competence* (pp. 321–332). Los Angeles, CA: Sage.

Byram, M., Golubeva, I., Hui, H. and Wagner, M. (eds) (2017) *From Principles to Practice in Education for Intercultural Citizenship*. Bristol: Multilingual Matters.

Byrd, W. (2012) Lessons from Afghanistan's history for the current transition and beyond. *United States Institute of Peace*, special report, 12 September. See https://www.usip.org/publications/2012/09/lessons-afghanistans-history-current-transition-and-beyond (accessed 24 September 2020).

Bystydzienski, J.M. (2011) *Intercultural Couples: Crossing Boundaries, Negotiating Difference*. New York: New York University Press.

Canagarajah, A. (1999) *Resisting Linguistic Imperialism in English Teaching*. Oxford: Oxford University Press.

Carté, P. and Fox, C. (2008) *Bridging the Culture Gap: A Practical Guide to International Business Communication*. London: Kogan Page.

Chakraverti, M. (2009) Deliberate dialogue. In J. deRivera (ed.) *Handbook on Building Cultures of Peace* (pp. 259–272). New York: Springer.

Chen, G.M. and Starosta, W.J. (1996) Intercultural communication competence: A synthesis. *Annals of the International Communication Association* 19 (1), 353–383.

Chen, Y.W. and Nakazawa, M. (2009) Influences of culture on self-disclosure as relationally situated in intercultural and interracial friendships from a social penetration perspective. *Journal of Intercultural Communication Research* 38 (2), 77–98.

Cheng, A. (2018) *Genre and Graduate-level Research Writing*. Ann Arbor, MI: University of Michigan Press.

Chiluwa, I. (2019) *Discourse Analysis and Conflict Studies*. London: Sage.

Chow, R. (2014) *Not Like a Native Speaker: On Languaging as a Postcolonial Experience*. New York: Columbia University Press.

Chua, R.Y., Morris, M.W. and Mor, S. (2012) Collaborating across cultures: Cultural metacognition and affect-based trust in creative collaboration. *Organizational Behavior and Human Decision Processes* 118 (2), 116–131.

Chughtai, A. and Qazi, S. (2020) From the 2001 fall of the Taliban to 2020 Afghan peace talks. *Aljazeera*, 12 September. See https://www.aljazeera.com/indepth/interactive/2020/02/war-afghanistan-2001-invasion-2020-taliban-deal-200229142658305.html (accessed 24 September 2020).

Cierpisz, A. (2019) Dismantling intercultural competence: A proposal for interpreting the concept of critical cultural awareness in an L2 teaching context. *Neofilolog* 52 (2), 227–243.

Clarke-Habibi, S. (2014) *Exploring the Structure-Agency Debate in Peacebuilding Through Education*, blog, 20 November. See https://saraclarkehabibi.weebly.com/blog/exploring-the-structure-agency-debate-in-peacebuilding-through-education (accessed 3 June 2020).

Cohen, R. (2021) An Israeli death and the tangled conflict left behind. *The New York Times*, 28 May. See https://www.nytimes.com/2021/05/28/world/middleeast/israel-gaza.html?action=click&module=Well&pgtype=Homepage&section=World%20News (accessed 29 May 2001).

COIL Institute for Globally Networked Learning in the Humanities (n.d.) *SUNY COIL Center: Collaborative Online International Learning*. See https://coil.suny.edu/global-network/ (accessed 20 September 2020).

Coll, S. (2021) Leaving Afghanistan, and the lessons of America's longest war. *The New Yorker*, 15 April. See https://www.newyorker.com/news/daily-comment/leaving-afghanistan-and-the-lessons-of-americas-longest-war (accessed 30 May 2021).

Collins, N.L. and Miller, L.C. (1994) Self-disclosure and liking: A meta-analytic review. *Psychological Bulletin* 116 (3), 457–475.

Collins, R. (2004) *Interaction Ritual Chains*. Princeton, NJ: Princeton University Press.

Common Acronyms (2018) *Common Acronyms in the TESOL Profession*. See https://www.tesol.org/enhance-your-career/career-development/beginning-your-career/a-guide-to-common-acronyms-in-the-tesol-profession (accessed 25 September 2020).

Confortini, C.C. (2006) Galtung, violence, and gender: The case for a peace studies/feminism alliance. *Peace & Change* 31 (3), 333–367.

Confortini, C.C. (2012) *Intelligent Compassion: Feminist Critical Methodology in the Women's International League for Peace and Freedom*. New York: Oxford University Press.

Conole, G. and Dyke, M. (2016) What are the affordances of information and communication technologies? *Research in Learning Technology* 12 (2), 113–124.

Cook, V. (2012) Going beyond the native speaker in language teaching. *TESOL Quarterly* 33 (2), 185–209.

Cooper, K.L., Luck, L., Chang, E. and Dixon, K. (2021) The application of Schneider's critical discourse analysis framework for a study of spirituality in nursing. *International Journal of Qualitative Methods*, January. doi:10.1177/1609406921998912.

Corbu, N., Popescu-Jourdy, D. and Vlad, T. (eds) (2014) *Identity and Intercultural Communication*. Newcastle Upon Tyne: Cambridge Scholars Publishing.

Cordesman, A.H., Gold, B. and Hess, A. (2013) *The Afghan War in 2013: Meeting the Challenges of Transition*. Washington, DC: Center for Strategic and International Studies.

Cossey, K. and Fischer, H. (2021) *COVID-19 Impact Research Brief: Virtual Exchanges at Community Colleges*. Washington, DC: NAFSA. See https://www.nafsa.org/sites/default/files/media/document/covid-19-impact-virtual-exchanges.pdf (accessed 1 June 2021).

Covert, H.H. (2014) Stories of personal agency: Undergraduate students' perceptions of developing intercultural competence during a semester abroad in Chile. *Journal of Studies in International Education* 18 (2), 162–179.

Croucher, S.M., Faulkner, S.L., Oommen, D. and Long, B. (2010) Demographic and religious differences in the dimensions of self-disclosure among Hindus and Muslims in India. *Journal of Intercultural Communication Research* 39 (1), 29–48.

Croucher, S.M., Holody, K.J., Anarbaeva, S. and Spencer, A. (2012) Religion and the relationship between verbal aggressiveness and argumentativeness. *Atlantic Journal of Communication* 20 (2), 116–129.

Croucher, S.M., Sommier, M. and Rahmani, D. (2015) Intercultural communication: Where we've been, where we're going, issues we face. *Communication Research and Practice* 1 (1), 71–87.
Crozet, C., Liddicoat, A. and Lo Bianco, J. (1999) Intercultural competence: From language policy to language education. In J. Lo Bianco, A. Liddicoat and C. Crozet (eds) *Striving for the Third Place: Intercultural Competence through Language Teaching* (pp. 1–17). Melbourne: Language Australia.
Cruickshank, J. (2012) The role of qualitative interviews in discourse theory. *Critical Approaches to Discourse Analysis across Disciplines* 6 (1), 38–52.
Cummins, J. and Sayers, D. (1995) *Brave New Schools: Challenging Cultural Literacy Through Global Learning Networks*. New York: St Martin's Press.
Darhower, M. (2008) The role of linguistic affordances in telecollaborative chat. *CALICO Journal* 26 (1), 48–69.
Davies, A. (2003) *The Native Speaker: Myth and Reality*. Bristol: Multilingual Matters.
Davies, L. (2004) Building a civic culture post-conflict. *London Review of Education* 2 (3), 229–244.
Davis, M.H., Luce, C. and Kraus, S.J. (1994) The heritability of characteristics associated with dispositional empathy. *Journal of Personality* 62 (3), 369–391.
Deardorff, D.K. (2004) The identification and assessment of intercultural competence as a student of international education at institutions of higher education in the United States. PhD dissertation, University of North Carolina.
Deardorff, D.K. (2006a) Identification and assessment of intercultural competence as a student outcome of internationalization. *Journal of Studies in International Education* 10 (3), 241–266.
Deardorff, D.K. (2006b) Theory reflections: Intercultural competence framework/model. *Journal of Studies in International Education* 10, 1–6.
Deardorff, D.K. (2009) How do I approach my role in teaching students with very different cultural backgrounds? *Presentation at University of North Carolina-Chapel Hill*, PowerPoint, 12 August. See https://docplayer.net/49127941-How-do-i-approach-my-role-in-teaching-students-with-very-different-cultural-backgrounds.html (accessed 5 May 2019).
Deardorff, D.K. (2015) *Demystifying Outcomes Assessment for International Educators: A Practical Approach*. Sterling, VA: Stylus Publishing.
Deardorff, D.K. (2017) The big picture: Reflections on the role of international educational exchange in peace and understanding. In J. Mathews-Aydinli (ed.) *International Education Exchanges and Intercultural Understanding* (pp. 11–20). Cham: Palgrave Macmillan.
Deardorff, D.K. (2018) Theories of cultural and educational exchange, intercultural competence, conflict resolution, and peace education. In C.P. Chou and J. Spangler (eds) *Cultural and Educational Exchanges in Rival Societies* (pp. 23–38). Singapore: Springer.
Dervin, B. (1997) Given a context by any other name: Methodological tools for taming the unruly beast. In P. Vakkar and R. Savolainen (eds) *Information Seeking in Context. Proceedings of an International Conference on Research in Information Needs: Seeking and Use in Different Contexts, Tampere, Finland* (pp. 13–38). London: Taylor Graham.
Dervin, F. (2008) *Métamorphoses identitaires en situation de mobilité*. Turku, Finland: University of Turku, Humanoria.
Dervin, F. (2010) *Lingua francas*. Paris: L'Harmattan.
de Sousa, G.U. (1999) *Shakespeare's Cross-Cultural Encounters*. London: Palgrave MacMillan.
DeTurk, S. (2001) Intercultural empathy: Myth, competency, or possibility for alliance building? *Communication Education* 50 (4), 374–384.

DeTurk, S. (2006) The power of dialogue: Consequences of intergroup dialogue and their implications for agency and alliance building. *Communication Quarterly* 54 (1), 33–51.

de Vignemont, F. and Singer, T. (2006) The empathic brain: How, when and why? *Trends in Cognitive Sciences* 10 (10), 435–441.

Dewey, J. (1910) *How We Think: A Restatement of Reflective Thinking to the Educative Process.* Boston, MA: D.C. Heath.

Dormer, J.E. and Woelk, C. (2018) *Teaching English for Reconciliation: Pursuing Peace through Transformed Relationships in Language Learning and Teaching.* Pasadena, CA: William Carey Library.

Dorronsoro, G. (2007) Kabul at war (1992–1996): State, ethnicity and social classes. *Open Edition Journals.* See https://journals.openedition.org/samaj/212 (accessed 14 August 2020).

Duncan-Andrade, J.M.R. (2009) Note to educators: Hope required when growing roses in concrete. *Harvard Educational Review* 79 (2), 181–194.

Dweck, C. (2015) Carol Dweck revisits the 'growth mindset'. *Education Week*, 22 September. See https://www.edweek.org/leadership/opinion-carol-dweck-revisits-the-growth-mindset/2015/09 (accessed 22 May 2021).

Echevarría, J., Vogt, M. and Short, D.J. (2016) *Making Content Comprehensible for English Learners: The SIOP Model.* Boston, MA: Pearson.

Ekici, D. (2018) Developing intercultural competence through online English language teaching. Doctoral dissertation, University of San Francisco.

Elo, S. and Kyngäs, H. (2008) The qualitative content analysis process. *Journal of Advanced Nursing* 62 (1), 107–115.

Elosúa, M.R. (2015) Intercultural competence in the education process. *Journal of Education and Learning* 4 (1), 72–83.

European Commission (2020) *The Digital Education Action Plan 2021–2027.* See https://ec.europa.eu/education/sites/default/files/document-library-docs/deap-communication-sept2020_en.pdf (accessed 1 June 2021).

Everett, M.K. (2005) Communicating empathy: A multidimensional approach to dispositional and situational variables in constructing person-centered messages. PhD dissertation, Kent State University.

Fahimullah (2017) Afghanistan: The shame of having daughters. *Institute for War and Peace Reporting*, 30 January. See https://iwpr.net/global-voices/afghanistan-shame-having-daughters (accessed 19 July 2020).

Fairclough, N. (1989) *Language and Power.* London: Longman.

Fairclough, N. (1992) *Discourse and Social Change.* Cambridge: Polity Press.

Fairclough, N. (2001) Critical discourse analysis as a method in social scientific research. In R. Wodak and M. Meyer (eds) *Methods of Critical Discourse Analysis* (pp. 121–138). London: Sage.

Fairclough, N. (2013) *Critical Discourse Analysis: The Critical Study of Language.* London: Routledge. (Original work published 1995.)

Fantini, A.E., Arias-Galicia, F. and Guay, D. (2001) *Globalization and 21st Century Competencies: Challenges for North American Higher Education.* Boulder, CO: Western Interstate Commission for Higher Education.

Farini, F. (2008) Intercultural and interlinguistical mediation in the healthcare system: The challenge of conflict management. *Migracijske i etničke teme* 3, 251–271.

Feng Teng, M. (2019) *Autonomy, Agency, and Identity in Teaching and Learning English as a Foreign Language.* Singapore: Springer.

Ferguson, G. (2006) *Language Planning and Education.* Edinburgh: Edinburgh University Press.

Firchow, P., Martin-Shields, C., Omer, A. and Ginty, R.M. (2017) PeaceTech: The liminal spaces of digital technology in peacebuilding. *International Studies Perspectives* 18 (1), 4–42.

Flanagan, C. and Levine, P. (2010) Civic engagement and the transition to adulthood. *The Future of Children* 20 (1), 159–179.
Foucault, M. (1984) The order of discourse [L'ordre du discours, 1971]. Reproduced in M. Shapiro (ed.) *Language and Politics* (pp. 108–138). New York: New York University Press.
Freire, P. (1970) *Pedagogy of the Oppressed* (M. Bergman Ramos, trans.). New York: Seabury.
Galtung, J. (1964) Peace: Research. *Journal of Peace Research* 1 (1), 1–4.
Galtung, J. (1969) Conflict as a way of life. *New Society* 14 (368), 590–592.
Galtung, J. (1970) Why a bulletin of peace proposals? *Bulletin of Peace Proposals* 1 (1), 5–8.
Galtung, J. (1975) Three approaches to peace: Peacekeeping, peacemaking and peacebuilding. In J. Galtung (ed.) *Essays in Peace Research, Vol. 2: Peace, War and Defense*. Copenhagen: Christian Eljers.
Galtung, J. (1984a) On the dialectic between crisis and crisis perception. *International Journal of Comparative Sociology* 25, 4.
Galtung, J. (1984b) Transarmament: From offensive to defensive defense. *Journal of Peace Research* 21 (2), 127–139.
Galtung, J. (1985) Twenty-five years of peace research: Ten challenges and some responses. *Journal of Peace Research* 22 (2), 141–158.
Galtung, J. (1990) Cultural violence. *Journal of Peace Research* 27 (3), 291–305.
Galtung, J. (1996) *Peace by Peaceful Means: Peace and Conflict, Development and Civilization*. Newbury Park, CA: Sage.
Galtung, J. (2004) *Transcend and Transform: An Introduction to Conflict Work*. London: Pluto Press.
Galtung, J. (2010) Peace: Negative and positive. In N.J. Young (ed.) *The Oxford International Encyclopedia of Peace*. Oxford: Oxford University Press.
Galtung, J. (2011) Peace: Positive and negative. In D. Christie (ed.) *The Encyclopedia of Peace Psychology*. Malden, MA: Wiley-Blackwell.
Gandomi, J. (2008) Lessons from the Soviet occupation in Afghanistan for the United States and NATO. *Journal of Public and International Affairs* 19, 51.
Gay, G. (2010) *Culturally Responsive Teaching: Theory, Research, and Practice*. New York: Teachers College Press.
Gee, J.P. (2004) *An Introduction to Discourse Analysis: Theory and Method*. London: Routledge. (Original work published 1999.)
GGSC (Greater Good Science Center) (n.d.) Shared identity. *Greater Good In Action: Science-Based Practices for a Meaningful Life*. See https://ggia.berkeley.edu/practice/shared_identity.
Ghasemi, A.A., Ahmadian, M., Yazdani, H. and Amerian, M. (2020) Towards a model of intercultural communicative competence in Iranian EFL context: Testing the role of international posture, ideal L2 self, L2 self-confidence, and metacognitive strategies. *Journal of Intercultural Communication Research* 49 (1), 41–60. doi:10.1080/17475759.2019.1705877
Gibson, J.J. (1979) The theory of affordances. In *The Ecological Approach to Visual Perception*. Boston, MA: Houghton Mifflin.
Giddens, A. (1984) *The Constitution of Society: Outline of the Theory of Structuration*. Berkeley, CA: University of California Press.
Gkonou, C., Olivero, M.M. and Oxford, R.L. (2021) Empowering language teachers to be influential peacebuilders: Knowledge, competencies and activities. In R.L. Oxford, M.M. Olivero, M. Harrison and T. Gregersen (eds) *Peacebuilding in Language Education: Innovations in Theory and Practice* (pp. 29–42). Bristol: Multilingual Matters.
Gomes de Matos, F. (2011) *Communicative Dignity: A Checklist*. Recife: Associação Brasil América. See http://www.humiliationstudies.org/documents/MatosWDU.pdf.

Gomes de Matos, F. (2014) Language, peace, and conflict resolution. In M. Deutsch, P.T. Coleman and E.C. Marcus (eds) *The Handbook of Conflict Resolution: Theory and Practice* (pp. 158–175). San Francisco, CA: Jossey-Bass.

Goodman, D.J. (2011) *Promoting Diversity and Social Justice: Educating People from Privileged Groups*. London: Routledge.

Goodman, D.J. (2014) Cultural competence for equity and inclusion: A framework for individual and organizational change. *Understanding and Dismantling Privilege* 10 (1). See https://dianegoodman.com/wp-content/uploads/2020/05/CulturalCompetencefor EquityandInclusionDianeGoodman.pdf (accessed 15 September 2020).

Goodwin, A.L. (2002) Teacher preparation and the education of immigrant children. *Education and Urban Society* 34 (2), 156–172.

Gould, J. (2008) *Thinking Outside Development: Epistemological Explorations 1994–2008*. Helsinki.fi. See https://www.academia.edu/2302357/Thinking_outside_development (accessed 15 August 2020).

Grant-Hayford, N. and Scheyer, V. (2017) On the lack of empathy as a major threat to peace. *Galtung-Institut for Peace Theory and Peace Practice*, 8 November. See https://www.galtung-institut.de/en/2017/lack-of-empathy-as-a-major-threat-to-peace/ (accessed 29 September 2020).

Gudykunst, W.B. (1994) *Bridging Differences: Effective Intergroup Communication*. London: Sage.

Gudykunst, W.B. (2003) *Cross-cultural and Intercultural Communication*. Thousand Oaks, CA: Sage.

Gudykunst, W.B. (2004) *Bridging Differences: Effective Intergroup Communication*. Thousand Oaks, CA: Sage.

Gudykunst, W.B. and Hammer, M.R. (1988) The influence of social identity and intimacy of interethnic relationships on uncertainty reduction processes. *Human Communication Research* 14 (4), 569–601.

Gudykunst, W.B. and Kim, Y.Y. (1984) *Communication with Strangers: An Approach to Intercultural Communication*. New York: Random House.

Gul, H., Usman, M., Liu, Y., Rehman, Z. and Jebran, K. (2018) Does the effect of power distance moderate the relation between person environment fit and job satisfaction leading to job performance? Evidence from Afghanistan and Pakistan. *Future Business Journal* 4 (1), 68–83.

Gulliver, P.H. (1979) *Disputes and Negotiations: A Cross-Cultural Perspective*. New York: Academic Press.

Guth, S. and Helm, F. (eds) (2010) *Telecollaboration 2.0: Language, Literacies and Intercultural Learning in the 21st Century*. New York: Peter Lang.

Habermas, J. (1998) *On the Pragmatics of Communication*. Cambridge, MA: MIT Press.

Hackert, S. (2013) *The Emergence of the English Native Speaker: A Chapter in Nineteenth-Century Linguistic Thought*. Berlin: De Gruyter Mouton.

Hahn, A. (2018) Communication for peacebuilding. In *Salem Press Encyclopedia*. Hackensack, NJ: Salem Press.

Haines, K.J. (2015) Learning to identify and actualize affordances in a new tool. *Language Learning & Technology* 19 (1), 165–180.

Hall, E.T. (1959) *The Silent Language*. New York: Anchor Books.

Hall, E.T. (1976) *Beyond Culture*. Garden City, NY: Anchor Press.

Hall, E.T. and Hall, M.R. (1990) *Understanding Cultural Differences*. Boston, MA: Intercultural Press.

Halperin, E. (2016) *Emotions in Conflict: Inhibitors and Facilitators of Peace Making*. New York: Routledge.

Hanks, J. (2015) Language teachers making sense of exploratory practice. *Language Teaching Research* 19 (5), 612–633.

Hansen, L. (2006) *Security as Practice: Discourse Analysis and the Bosnian War*. London: Routledge.

Harjanne, P. and Tella, S. (2007) Foreign language didactics, foreign language teaching and transdisciplinary affordances. In A. Koskensalo, J. Smeds, P. Kaikkonen and V. Kohonen (eds) *Foreign Languages and Multicultural Perspectives in the European Context; Fremdsprachen und multikulturelle Perspektiven im europäischen Kontext. Dichtung – Wahrheit – Sprache* (pp. 197–225). Berlin: LITVerlag.

Hartl, S. and Chavan, M. (2016) Culture – the imperceptible influence shaping conflict management and dispute resolution strategies in transnational business relationships: A conceptual framework to improve communication skills with international counterparts. In A. Tirpitz and R.R. Schleus (eds) *Communication in International Business* (pp. 257–288). Berlin: Epubli.

Hayward, F.M. (2015) *Transforming Higher Education in Afghanistan: Success amidst Ongoing Struggles*. Ann Arbor, MI: Society For College And University Planning.

Heleta, S. and Deardorff, D.K. (2017) The role of higher education institutions in developing intercultural competence in peace-building in the aftermath of violent conflict. In D.K. Deardorff and L.A. Arasaratnam-Smith (eds) *Intercultural Competence in Higher Education* (pp. 53–63). London: Routledge.

Hodges, S.D. and Klein, K. (2001) Regulating the costs of empathy: The price of being human. *Journal of Socio-Economics* 30, 437–452.

Hoffman, C.R. (2012) *Cohesive Profiling: Meaning and Interaction in Personal Weblogs*. Amsterdam: John Benjamins.

Hofstede, G.J. (1980) *Culture's Consequences: International Differences in Work-related Values*. Beverly Hills, CA: Sage.

Hofstede, G.J. (2009) The moral circle in intercultural competence: Trust across cultures. In D.K. Deardorff (ed.) *The Sage Handbook of Intercultural Competence* (pp. 85–99). Thousand Oaks, CA: Sage.

Holliday, A. (2005) *The Struggle to Teach English as an International Language*. Oxford: Oxford University Press.

Holliday, A. (2010) *Intercultural Communication and Ideology*. London: Sage.

Holliday, A. (2015) Native-speakerism: Taking the concept forward and achieving cultural belief. In A. Swan, P. Aboshiha and A. Holliday (eds) *(En)Countering Native-speakerism: Global Perspectives* (pp. 11–25). New York: Palgrave Macmillan.

Huber, J. and Reynolds, C. (2014) *Developing Intercultural Competence Through Education*. Strasbourg: Council of Europe. See https://rm.coe.int/developing-intercultural-enfr/16808ce258 (accessed 15 January 2019).

Hull-Sypnieski, K. and Ferlazzo, L. (2016) How to cultivate student agency in English language learners. *Mindshift*, 4 April. See https://www.kqed.org/mindshift/43376/how-to-cultivate-student-agency-in-english-language-learners (accessed 22 May 2021).

Hülsse, R. (1999) *The Discursive Construction of Identity and Difference: Turkey as Europe's Other?* See https://citeseerx.ist.psu.edu/viewdoc/download?doi=10.1.1.200.9166&rep=rep1&type=pdf (accessed 7 April 2020).

Hyland, K. (2013) Genre and discourse analysis in language for specific purposes. In C. Chapelle (ed.) *The Encyclopaedia of Applied Linguistics*. Oxford: Wiley-Blackwell.

IBE-UNESCO (2020) *Basic Learning Needs*. See http://www.ibe.unesco.org/en/glossary-curriculum-terminology/b/basic-learning-needs (accessed 18 June 2020).

iEARN (n.d.) *iEARN*. See https://www.iearn.org/ (accessed 20 September 2020).

Im, E., Page, R., Lin., L., Tsai, H. and Cheng, C. (2004) Rigour in cross-cultural research. *International Journal of Nursing Studies* 41 (8), 891–899.

Ingram, L., Kent, L. and McWilliam, A. (eds) (2015) *A New Era? Timor-Leste After the UN*. Acton, ACT: ANU Press.

IOHR (International Observatory of Human Rights) (2018) Afghanistan – the worst place to be born in the world. *International Observatory of Human Rights*, 10 December. See https://observatoryihr.org/blog/afghanistan-the-worst-place-to-be-born-in-the-world/ (accessed 7 March 2020).

Iriye, A. (2004) *Global Community: The Role of International Organizations in the Making of the Contemporary World*. Oakland, CA: University of California Press.

Jackson, N. (2017) The great game revisited: Afghanistan in the 1970s. *Adam Matthew*, 1 December. See https://www.amdigital.co.uk/about/blog/item/the-great-game-revisited-afghanistan-in-the-1970s (accessed 22 September 2020).

Jakar, V.S. and Milofsky, A. (2016) Bringing peacebuilding into the English language classroom. In C. Hastings and L. Jacob (eds) *Social Justice in English Language Teaching* (pp. 39–46). Alexandria, VA: TESOL Press.

Johansen, J. and Jones, J. (2010) *Experiments with Peace: Celebrating Peace on Johan Galtung's 80th Birthday*. Cape Town: Pambazuka Press.

Johnson, J.L. and Callahan, C. (2013) Minority cultures and social media: Magnifying garifuna. *Journal of Intercultural Communication Research* 42, 319–339.

Karlberg, M. (2005) The power of discourse and the discourse of power: Pursuing peace through discourse intervention. *International Journal of Peace Studies* 10 (1), 1–25.

Karn, J.M. (2016) Building hope: An experiential, interfaith and peacebuilding leadership curriculum design for American, Israeli and Palestinian teenagers. Unpublished capstone paper, School for International Training, Brattleboro, VT.

Kefa, A.K. and Ombuge, M.M. (2012) *Manual for Interreligious Dialogue*. Limuru: Franciscan Kolbe Press.

Kennett, P. (2011) Language, disasters, and development. In H. Coleman (ed.) *Dreams and Realities: Developing Countries and the English Language* (pp. 1–15). London: British Council.

Kerem, E., Fishman, N. and Josselson, R. (2001) The experience of empathy in everyday relationships: Cognitive and affective elements. *Journal of Social and Personal Relationships* 18 (5), 709–729.

Khan, A. (2015) Ghost students, ghost teachers, ghost schools. *Buzzfeed News*, 9 July. See https://www.buzzfeednews.com/article/azmatkhan/the-big-lie-that-helped-justify-americas-war-in-afghanistan (accessed 20 September 2020).

Kibiswa, N.K. (2019) Directed qualitative content analysis (DQlCA): A tool for conflict analysis. *The Qualitative Report* 24 (8), 2059–2079.

Kibria, M.G. (2013) The magnitude of cultural factors that affect school enrolment and retention in Afghanistan: An analysis through Hofstede's cultural model. *Canadian Social Science* 9 (6), 161–168.

King, M.L. (1963) *Letter from a Birmingham Jail*. See https://www.africa.upenn.edu/Articles_Gen/Letter_Birmingham.html.

Kolb, D.A. (1984) *Experiential Learning: Experience as the Source of Learning and Development*. Englewood Cliffs, NJ: Prentice-Hall.

Kopka, A. (2017) Mediacja jako sposób rozwiązywania sporów gospodarczych o charakterze transgranicznym na przykładzie Polski i Niemiec [Mediation as a way of solving cross-border economic disputes using Poland and Germany as an example]. *Political Science Review/Przegląd Politologiczny* 2, 79–98.

Kramsch, C. (1993) *Context and Culture in Language Teaching*. Oxford: Oxford University Press.

Krashen, S. (1982) *Principles and Practice in Second Language Acquisition*. Oxford: Pergamon Press.

Kruger, F. (2012) The role of TESOL in educating for peace. *Journal of Peace Education* 9 (1), 17–30.

Kubota, R. (2002) The impact of globalization on language teaching in Japan. In D. Block and D. Cameron (eds) *Globalization and Language Teaching* (pp. 13–28). London: Routledge.

Kumaravadivelu, B. (2014) The decolonial option in English teaching: Can the subaltern act? *TESOL Quarterly* 50 (1), 66–85.

Kyngäs, H. and Kaakinen, P. (2020) Deductive content analysis. In H. Kyngäs, K. Mikkonen and M. Kääriäinen (eds) *The Application of Content Analysis in Nursing Science Research* (pp. 23–30). Cham: Springer.

Laclau, E. and Mouffe, C. (1985) *Hegemony and Socialist Strategy: Towards a Radical Democratic Politics*. London: Verso.

Ladson-Billings, G. (1995) But that's just good teaching! The case for culturally relevant pedagogy. *Theory Into Practice* 34 (3), 159–165.

Landis, D., Bennett, J. and Bennett, M. (2004) *Handbook of Intercultural Training*. Thousand Oaks, CA: Sage.

Larson, D. (1990) TESOL's role in global understanding: A possible agenda. *TESOL Newsletter* 24 (1), 21.

Larson, D. (1992) Peace, justice and sustainable development: Ingredients for an emerging world order. *TESOL Matters* 1, 19.

Lawrence, Q. (2010) Chaos after Soviet withdrawal gave rise to Taliban. *National Public Radio*, 7 December. See https://www.npr.org/2010/12/07/131884473/Afghanistan-After-The-Soviet-Withdrawal (accessed 10 September 2020).

Lederach, J.P. (1995) *Preparing for Peace: Conflict Transformation Across Cultures*. New York: Syracuse University Press.

Lederach, J.P. (1998) *Building Peace: Sustainable Reconciliation in Divided Societies*. Washington, DC: United States Institute of Peace.

Lederach, J.P. (1999) The challenge of the 21st century: Just peace. *Peace, 35 Inspiring Stories from Around the World*. Utrecht: European Centre for Conflict Prevention.

Lederach, J.P. (2003) *Little Book of Conflict Transformation*. Intercourse, PA: Good Books.

Lederach, J.P. (2006) *Building Peace: Sustainable Reconciliation in Divided Societies*. Washington, DC: United States Institute of Peace.

Lederach, J.P. and Appleby, R.S. (2010) Strategic peacebuilding: An overview. In D. Philpott and G.F. Powers (eds) *Strategies of Peace: Transforming Conflict in a Violent World* (pp. 19–44). Oxford: Oxford University Press.

Lederach, J.P., Neufeldt, R. and Culbertson, H. (2007) *Reflective Peacebuilding: A Planning, Monitoring and Learning Toolkit*. Davao: Joan B. Kroc Institute for International Peace Studies and Catholic Relief Services.

Leeds-Hurwitz, W.L. (1990) Notes in the history of intercultural communication: The Foreign Service Institute and the mandate for intercultural training. *Quarterly Journal of Speech* 76, 262–281.

Lo Bianco, J., Liddicoat, A. and Crozet, C. (eds) *Striving for the Third Place: Intercultural Competence through Language Teaching*. Melbourne: Language Australia.

Lowry, C. and Littlejohn, S. (2006) Dialogue and the discourse of peacebuilding in Maluku, Indonesia. *Conflict Resolution Quarterly* 23 (4), 409–426.

Lune, H. and Berg, B.L. (2007) Focus group interviewing. In B.L. Berg (ed.) *Qualitative Research Methods for the Social Sciences* (pp. 144–170). Boston, MA: Pearson Education.

Lustig, M.W. and Koester, J. (2010) *Intercultural Competence: Interpersonal Communication across Cultures*. Boston, MA: Pearson.

Lynch, E.W. and Hanson, M.J. (1998) *Developing Cross-Cultural Competence: A Guide for Working with Children and their Families*. Baltimore, MD: Brookes Publishing.

MacKenzie, T. (2020) How can teachers nurture meaningful student agency? *Mindshift*, 9 November. See https://www.kqed.org/mindshift/56946/how-can-teachers-nurture-meaningful-student-agency (accessed 22 May 2021).

Macrina, A. (2015) The Tor browser and intellectual freedom in the digital age. *Accidental Technologist* 54 (4). See https://journals.ala.org/index.php/rusq/article/view/5704/7093 (accessed 5 May 2018).

Mahalingappa, L., Rodriguez, T.L. and Polat, N. (2021) Promoting peace through social justice pedagogies for students from immigrant Muslim communities: Using critical language awareness in second language classrooms. In R.L. Oxford, M.M. Olivero, M. Harrison and T. Gregersen (eds) *Peacebuilding in Language Education: Innovations in Theory and Practice* (pp. 162–176). Bristol: Multilingual Matters.

Mahan, L.N. and Mahuna, J.M. (2017) Bridging the divide: Cross-cultural mediation. *International Research and Review* 7 (1), 11–22.

Maier, A., Zhang, Q. and Clark, A. (2013) Self-disclosure and emotional closeness in intracultural friendships: A cross-cultural comparison among U.S. Americans and Romanians. *Journal of Intercultural Communication Research* 42 (1), 22–34.

Maizland, L. and Laub, Z. (2020) The Taliban in Afghanistan. *Council on Foreign Relations*, 11 March. See https://www.cfr.org/backgrounder/taliban-afghanistan (accessed 8 September 2020).

Mathews-Aydinli, J. (ed.) (2017) *International Education Exchanges and Intercultural Understanding: Promoting Peace and Global Relations*. Basingstoke: Palgrave Macmillan.

Mathieu, X. (2019) Critical peacebuilding and the dilemma of difference: The stigma of the 'local' and the quest for equality. *Third World Quarterly* 40 (1), 36–52.

Mayring, P. (2000) Qualitative content analysis. *Forum: Qualitative Social Research* 1 (2). See https://www.qualitative-research.net/index.php/fqs/article/view/1089/2386 (accessed 12 December 2021).

McAlinden, M. (2018) English language teachers' conceptions of intercultural empathy and professional identity: A critical discourse analysis. *Australian Journal of Teacher Education* 43 (10), 41–59.

McEwan, B. and Sobre-Denton, M. (2011) Virtual cosmopolitanism: Constructing third cultures and transmitting social and cultural capital through social media. *Journal of International and Intercultural Communication* 4, 252–258.

Medgyes, P. (2012) The NNEST lens: Non-native English speakers in TESOL. *ELT Journal* 66 (1), 122–124.

Medley, R.M. (2016) Tension and harmony: Language teaching as a peacebuilding endeavor. In C. Hastings and L. Jacob (eds) *Social Justice in English Language Teaching* (pp. 47–64). Alexandria, VA: TESOL Press.

Miike, Y. (2017) Between conflict and harmony in the human family: Asiacentricity and its ethical-imperative for intercultural communication. In X. Dai and G.M. Chen (eds) *Conflict Management and Intercultural Communication* (pp. 38–65). London: Routledge.

Mitra, S. (2015) Communication and peace: Understanding the nature of texts as a way to resolve conceptual differences in the emerging field. *Global Media and Communication* 11 (3), 303–316.

Mollov, B. and Lavie, C. (2001) Culture, dialogue, and perception change in the Israeli-Palestinian conflict. *International Journal of Conflict Management* 12 (1), 69–87.

Montiel, C.J. (2001) Toward a psychology of structural peacebuilding. In D.J. Christie, R.V. Wagner and D.A. Winter (eds) *Peace, Conflict, and Violence: Peace Psychology for the 21st Century*. Englewood Cliffs, NJ: Prentice-Hall.

Morgan, B. and Vandrick, S. (2009) Imagining a peace curriculum: What second-language education brings to the table. *Peace & Change* 34 (4), 510–532.

Motha, S. (2014) *Race, Empire, and English Language Teaching: Creating Responsible and Ethical Anti-Racist Practice*. New York: Teachers College Press.

Moussu, L. and Llurda, E. (2008) Non-native English-speaking English language teachers: History and research. *Language Teaching: Surveys and Studies* 41 (3), 315–348.

Naples, N.A. and Méndez, J.B. (eds) (2014) *Border Politics: Social Movements, Collective Identities, and Globalization*. New York: New York University Press.

Narea, N. (2020) How Trump made it that much harder to become a US citizen. *Vox*, 3 September. See https://www.vox.com/2020/9/3/21408528/trump-naturalization-backlog-citizenship-voting (accessed 1 June 2021).

Nation, I.S.P. and Macalister, J. (2010) *Language Curriculum Design*. New York: Routledge.

Nation, The (2020) *Past in Perspective*. See https://nation.com.pk/17-Jan-2019/past-in-perspective (accessed 7 December 2019).

NCES (National Center for Education Statistics) (2002) *Selected Characteristics of Students, Teachers, Parent Participation, and Programs and Services in Traditional Public and Public Charter Elementary and Secondary Schools: 1999–2002*. See http://nces.ed.gov/ (accessed 16 September 2017).
Nawa, F. (2013) In Afghanistan, fathers barter daughters to settle drug debts. *The Atlantic*, 31 July. See https://www.theatlantic.com/international/archive/2013/07/in-afghanistan-fathers-barter-daughters-to-settle-drug-debts/278217/ (accessed 6 April 2020).
Nayak, M. and Suchland, J. (2006) Gender violence and hegemonic projects. *International Feminist Journal of Politics* 8 (4), 467–485.
Nazari, M., Miri, M.A. and Golzar, J. (2021) Challenges of second language teachers' professional identity construction: Voices from Afghanistan. *TESOL Journal*, 4 March. See https://doi.org/10.1002/tesj.587.
Nilsson, B. (2003) Internationalisation at home from a Swedish perspective: The case of Malmö. *Journal of Studies in International Education* 7 (1), 27–40.
Noack, R. and Gamio, L. (2015) The world's languages, in 7 maps and charts. *The Washington Post*, 23 April. See https://www.washingtonpost.com/news/worldviews/wp/2015/04/23/the-worlds-languages-in-7-maps-and-charts/ (accessed 8 May 2020).
Nolden, D. and Kostić, V. (2017) *Strengthening Resilience – Building Peace from Within*. Berlin: Berghof Foundation. See https://berghof-foundation.org/library/strengthening-resilience-building-peace-from-within (accessed 14 March 2021).
Norton, B. (2000) *Identity and Language Learning: Gender, Ethnicity and Educational Change* (1st edn). Edinburgh: Pearson Education.
Norton, B. and Toohey, K. (2011) Identity, language learning, and social change. *Language Teaching* 44 (4), 412–446.
NYSED (New York State Education Department) (2018) *Culturally Responsive-Sustaining Education Framework*. See http://www.nysed.gov/common/nysed/files/programs/crs/culturally-responsive-sustaining-education-framework.pdf (accessed 11 May 2021).
O'Dowd, R. (2018) From telecollaboration to virtual exchange: State-of-the-art and the role of UNICollaboration in moving forward. *Journal of Virtual Exchange* 1 (1), 1–23.
O'Dowd, R. (2021) Virtual exchange: Moving forward into the next decade. *Computer Assisted Language Learning* 34 (3), 209–224.
Okayama, C.M., Furuto, S.B. and Edmondson, J. (2001) Components of cultural competence: Attitudes, knowledge, and skills. In R. Fong and S.B. Furuto (eds) *Culturally Competent Practice: Skills, Interventions, and Evaluations* (pp. 89–100). Boston, MA: Allyn & Bacon.
Okoro, E. (2013) International organizations and operations: An analysis of cross-cultural communication effectiveness and management orientation. *Journal of Business & Management (COES&RJ-JBM)* 1 (1), 1–13.
O'Rourke, B. (2007) Models of telecollaboration (1): eTandem. In R. O'Dowd (ed.) *Online Intercultural Exchange: An Introduction for Foreign Language Teachers* (pp. 41–61). Bristol: Multilingual Matters.
Ortiz, F. (1947) *Cuban Counterpoint: Tobacco and Sugar*. New York: Alfred A. Knopf.
Österberg, C. and Lorentsson, T. (2011) *Organizational Conflict and Socialization Processes in Healthcare: A Case Study of Intercultural Organizational Conflict and Socialization Processes in Healthcare*. Riga: Lambert Academic.
Oxford, R.L. (ed.) (2013) *The Language of Peace: Communicating to Create Harmony*. Charlotte, NC: Information Age Publishing.
Oxford, R.L. (ed.) (2014) *Understanding Peace Cultures*. Charlotte, NC: Information Age Publishing.
Oxford, R.L., Gregersen, T. and Olivero, M.M. (2018) The interplay of language and peace education: The language of peace approach in peace communication, linguistic analysis, multimethod research, and peace language activities. *TESL Reporter* 51 (2).

Oxford, R.L., Olivero, M.M., Harrison, M. and Gregersen, T. (eds) (2021) *Peacebuilding in Language Education: Innovations in Theory and Practice*. Bristol: Multilingual Matters.

Paffenholz, T. (2014) International peacebuilding goes local: Analysing Lederach's conflict transformation theory and its ambivalent encounter with 20 years of practice. *Peacebuilding* 2 (1), 11–27.

Paris, D. and Samy Alim, H. (eds) (2017) *Culturally Sustaining Pedagogies: Teaching and Learning for Justice in a Changing World*. New York: Teachers College Press.

Paris, R. (1997) Peacebuilding and the limits of liberal internationalism. *International Security* 22 (2), 54–89.

Parsons, T. (1951) *The Social System*. London: Collier Macmillan.

Pennycook, A. (1994) *The Cultural Politics of English as an International Language*. London: Routledge.

Pennycook, A. (1998) *English and the Discourses of Colonialism*. London: Routledge.

Pentikainen, A. and Rizk, S. (eds) (2019) *Dialogue in Peacebuilding: Understanding Different Perspectives*. Uppsala: Dag Hammarskjöld Foundation.

Pettigrew, T.F. and Tropp, L.R. (2006) A meta-analytic test of intergroup contact theory. *Journal of Personality and Social Psychology* 90 (5), 751–783.

Phillipson, R. (1992) *Linguistic Imperialism*. Oxford: Oxford University Press.

Phillipson, R. (2009) *Linguistic Imperialism Continued*. New York: Routledge.

Phillipson, R. (2018) Linguistic Imperialism. In C. A. Chapelle (ed.) *The Encyclopedia of Applied Linguistics* (pp. 1–7). See https://doi.org/10.1002/9781405198431.wbeal0718.pub2.

Pierce, R. (2008) *Research Methods in Politics: A Practical Guide*. London: Sage.

Pousada, A. (2016) *Literacy as a Prerequisite for World Peace, Plenary Address, PRTESOL, 27 August*. See https://aliciapousada.weebly.com/uploads/1/0/0/2/10020146/literacy_as_a_prerequisite_for_world_peace.pdf (accessed 7 July 2020).

Pratt, M.L. (1991) Arts of the contact zone. *Profession* 1991, 33–40. See http://www.jstor.org/stable/25595469 (accessed 26 September 2020).

Puig Larrauri, H. and Kahl, A. (2013) Technology for peacebuilding. *Stability: International Journal of Security and Development* 2 (3), 61.

Pundak, R. (2012) More relevant than ever: People-to-people peacebuilding efforts in Israel and Palestine. *Palestine-Israel Journal of Politics, Economics, and Culture* 18 (2/3), 46.

Quraishi, N. (Dir.) (2015) *ISIS in Afghanistan*. Frontline film, 17 November. See https://www.wpbstv.org/isis-in-afghanistan-full-film-frontline/ (accessed 24 September 2020).

Rauschert, P. and Byram, M. (2018) Service learning and intercultural citizenship in foreign-language education. *Cambridge Journal of Education* 48 (3), 353–369.

Ravitch, D. and Viteritti, J.P. (2001) *Making Good Citizens: Education and Civil Society*. New Haven, CT: Yale University Press.

Remland, M.S., Jones, T.S., Foeman, A. and Rafter Arevalo, D. (2014) *Intercultural Communication: A Peacebuilding Perspective*. Long Grove, IL: Waveland Press.

Reychler, L. (2010) Peacemaking, peacekeeping, and peacebuilding. In *ISA (International Studies Association) Compendium on Peace Studies*. Oxford: Wiley-Blackwell.

Reychler, L. (2017) Peacemaking, peacekeeping, and peacebuilding. In *Oxford Research Encyclopedia of International Studies*. See https://oxfordre.com/internationalstudies/view/10.1093/acrefore/9780190846626.001.0001/acrefore-9780190846626-e-274 (accessed 4 June 2019).

Richards, J.C. (2002) *Curriculum Development in Language Teaching*. New York: Cambridge University Press.

Richards, J.C. and Farrell, T.S.C. (2011) *Teaching Practice: A Reflective Approach*. New York: Cambridge University Press.

Ricœur, P. (1992) *Oneself as Another*. Chicago, IL: University of Chicago Press.

Ritzen, Y. (2016) Largest refugee crisis in history. *Al Jazeera*, 20 June. See https://www.aljazeera.com/indepth/interactive/2016/06/refugee-crisis-160620083009119.html (accessed 24 September 2020).

Robana, A. (2005) Personal narratives as a peacebuilding tool: A study of Djerbien Jewish and Muslim co-existence. Capstone Collection no. 1568, School for International Training. See https://digitalcollections.sit.edu/capstones/1568 (accessed 14 February 2020).

Rogers, R., Malancharuvil-Berkes, E., Mosley, M., Hui, D. and O-Garro, G. (2005) Critical discourse analysis in education: A review of the literature. *Review of Educational Research* 75 (3), 365–416.

Rosenberg, M.B. (2003) *Life-Enriching Education: Nonviolent Communication Helps Schools Improve Performance, Reduce Conflict, and Enhance Relationships*. Encinitas, CA: PuddleDancer Press.

Rothman, J.R. and Sanderson, S. (2018) Language and peace: Using global issues in the English language classroom to create a more sustainable dialogue. *Forum for and by Teachers of English to Speakers of Other Languages* 51 (2), 53–76.

Rubio, F. (2007) *Self-Esteem and Foreign Language Learning*. Newcastle upon Tyne: Cambridge Scholars Publishing.

Said, E. (1978) *Orientalism*. New York: Vintage Books.

Sarathy, V. and Scheutz, M. (2016) Beyond grasping – perceiving affordances across various stages of cognitive development. *Conference: Proceedings of the Sixth Joint IEEE International Conference Developmental Learning and Epigenetic Robotics (ICDL)*. See https://www.researchgate.net/publication/310590077_Beyond_Grasping_-_Perceiving_Affordances_Across_Various_Stages_of_Cognitive_Development (accessed 18 November 2019).

Schäffner, C. and Wenden, A.L. (eds) (1995) *Language and Peace*. Farnham: Ashgate.

Schlosser, M. (2019) Agency. In E.N. Zalta (ed.) *The Stanford Encyclopedia of Philosophy*. See https://plato.stanford.edu/archives/win2019/entries/agency/ (accessed 15 June 2020).

Schmid, P.F. (2001) Comprehension: The art of not knowing. Dialogical and ethical perspectives on empathy as dialogue in personal and person-centred relationships. In S. Haugh and T. Merry (eds) *Empathy* (pp. 53–71). Ross-on-Wye: PCCS Books.

Schön, D. (1983) *The Reflective Practitioner*. New York: Basic Books.

Schug, J., Yuki, M. and Maddux, W. (2010) Relational mobility explains between – and within – culture differences in self-disclosure to close friends. *Psychological Science* 21 (10), 1471–1478.

Sengupta, S. (2018) What is the United Nations? Explaining its purpose, power and problems. *The New York Times*, 25 September. See https://www.nytimes.com/2018/09/25/world/americas/what-is-united-nations-facts.html (accessed 10 June 2019).

Slade, M.L., Burnham, T.J., Catalana, S.M. and Waters, T. (2019) The impact of reflective practice on teacher candidates' learning. *International Journal for the Scholarship of Teaching and Learning* 13 (2), art. 15. See https://doi.org/10.20429/ijsotl.2019.130215 (accessed 28 February 2021).

Smith, A.D. (1992) National identity and the idea of European unity. *International Affairs* 68 (1), 55–76.

Smith, J. (2019) Globalization of peace. In O.P. Richmond and G. Visoka (eds) *The Oxford Handbook of Peacebuilding, Statebuilding, and Peace Formation* (pp. 318–327). Oxford: Oxford University Press.

Soliya (2020) *Soliya*. See https://www.soliya.net/ (accessed 23 September 2020).

Songhori, M.H. (2008) Introduction to needs analysis. *English for Specific Purposes World* 4. See www.esp-world.info (accessed 7 July 2020).

Spitzberg, B.H. (1989) Issues in the development of a theory of interpersonal competence in the intercultural context. *International Journal of Intercultural Relations* 13 (3), 241–268.

Spitzberg, B.H. and Changnon, G. (2009) Conceptualizing intercultural competence. In D.K. Deardorff (ed.) *The Sage Handbook of Intercultural Competence* (pp. 2–52). Thousand Oaks, CA: Sage.

Spitzberg, B.H. and Cupach, W.R. (1984) *Interpersonal Communication Competence*. Beverly Hills, CA: Sage.

Spolsky, B. (2004) *Language Policy*. Cambridge: Cambridge University Press.

Stephan, W.G. and Finlay, K. (1999) The role of empathy in improving intergroup relations. *Journal of Social Issues* 55 (4), 729–743.

Stevens Initiative (2020) *Stevens Initiative*. See https://www.stevensinitiative.org (accessed 20 September 2020).

Stokke, C. and Lybæk, L. (2018) Combining intercultural dialogue and critical multiculturalism. *Ethnicities* 18 (1), 70–85.

Sunstein, C.R. (2002) The law of group polarization. *Journal of Political Philosophy* 10 (2), 175–195.

Suurmond, J.M. (2005) Our talk and walk: Discourse analysis and conflict studies. Clingendael Institute Working Paper no. 35. The Hague: Netherlands Institute of International Relations 'Clingendael'. See https://www.clingendael.org/sites/default/files/pdfs/20051000_cru_working_paper_35.pdf (accessed 27 November 2018).

Swales, J. and Feak, C. (2012) *Academic Writing for Graduate Students*. Ann Arbor, MI: University of Michigan Press. (Original work published in 1994.)

Swan, A., Aboshiha, P. and Holliday, A. (2015) *(En)countering Native-speakerism Global Perspectives*. New York: Palgrave MacMillan.

Tajfel, H. and Turner, J.C. (2004) The social identity theory of intergroup behavior. In J.T. Jost and J. Sidanius (eds) *Political Psychology: Key Readings* (pp. 276–293). New York: Psychology Press.

Tamimi Sa'd, S.H. (2017) Foreign language learning and identity reconstruction: Learners' understanding of the intersections of the self, the other and power. *CEPS Journal* 7, 13–36.

Taylor, A. (2014) The Soviet war in Afghanistan, 1979–1989. *The Atlantic*, 4 August. See https://www.theatlantic.com/photo/2014/08/the-soviet-war-in-afghanistan-1979-1989/100786/ (accessed 1 September 2020).

Tella, S. (2005) Multi-, inter- and transdisciplinary affordances in foreign language education: From singularity to multiplicity. In J. Smeds, K. Sarmavuori, E. Laakkonen and R. de Cillia (eds) *Multicultural Communities, Multilingual Practice: Monikulttuuriset Yhteisöt, Monikielinen Käytäntö* (p. 67–88). Turku: Annales Universitatis Turkuensis B 285.

TESOL & UN (1990) TESOL and the United Nations: A new partnership. *TESOL Newsletter* 24 (5), 31.

Texas Global (2020) *Global Virtual Exchange Initiative*. See https://global.utexas.edu/special-initiatives/virtual-exchange (accessed 6 April 2020).

Thorne, S. (2010) The intercultural turn and language learning in the crucible of new media. In S. Guth and F. Helm (eds) *Telecollaboration 2.0: Language and Intercultural Learning in the 21st Century* (pp. 139–165). New York: Peter Lang.

Ting-Toomey, S. and Kurogi, A. (1998) Facework competence in intercultural conflict: An updated face-negotiation theory. *International Journal of Intercultural Relations* 22 (2), 187–225.

Ting-Toomey, S. and Oetzel, J.G. (2001) *Managing Intercultural Conflict Effectively*. Thousand Oaks, CA: Sage.

Tinkler, A. and Tinkler, B. (2013) Teaching across the community: Using service-learning field experiences to develop culturally and linguistically responsive teachers. In V.M. Jagla, J.A. Erickson and A.S. Tinkler (eds) *Transforming Teacher Education through Service-Learning* (pp. 99–117). Charlotte, NC: Information Age Publishing.

Torgan, A. (2016) Acid attacks, poison: What Afghan girls risk by going to school. *CNN*, 17 March. See https://www.cnn.com/2012/08/02/world/meast/cnnheroes-jan-afghan-school/index.html (accessed 6 September 2020).

UN (United Nations) (1945) *United Nations Charter*, 24 October. See https://www.un.org/en/about-us/un-charter (accessed 31 May 2021).
UN Secretary-General. (2012) Peacebuilding in the aftermath of conflict: Report of the Secretary-General. *United Nations Digital Library*. See https://digitallibrary.un.org/record/740644?ln=en#record-files-collapse-header (accessed 14 December 2021)
UN (United Nations) (2010) *UN Peacebuilding: An Orientation*. See https://www.un.org/peacebuilding/sites/www.un.org.peacebuilding/files/documents/peacebuilding_orientation.pdf (accessed 21 December 2019).
UNESCO (United Nations Educational, Scientific and Cultural Organization) (2019) *Through Education, UNESCO Clears the Path for Peace*. See https://en.unesco.org/70years/education_clears_path_for_peace (accessed 7 July 2020).
UNHCR (United Nations High Commissioner for Refugees) (2019) *Figures at a Glance*. See https://www.unhcr.org/en-us/figures-at-a-glance.html (accessed 24 September 2020).
UNICEF (2016) *Education and Healthcare at Risk*. See https://www.unicef.org/afghanistan/media/201/file/afg_report_eduhealthattack2016eng.pdf (accessed 8 May 2020).
UNICollaboration (n.d.) *Cross-Disciplinary Organisation for Telecollaboration and Virtual Exchange in Higher Education*. See https://www.unicollaboration.org/ (accessed 10 May 2020).
USAID (US Agency for International Development) (2011) *People-to-People Peacebuilding: A Program Guide*. See https://www.usaid.gov/sites/default/files/documents/1866/CMMP2PGuidelines2010-01-19.pdf (accessed 24 September 2020).
USAID (US Agency for International Development) (2018) USAID call for proposals People-to-People Peace Program. *Intercultural Leaders*, 16 March. See https://interculturalleaders.org/an_opportunity/usaid-call-for-proposals-people-to-people-peace-program/ (accessed 24 September 2020).
van Dijk, T.A. (2000) New(s) racism: A discourse analytical approach. *Ethnic Minorities and the Media* 37, 33–49.
van Leeuwen, T. (2008) *Discourse and Practice: New Tools for Critical Discourse Analysis*. New York: Oxford University Press.
van Lier, L. (2000) From input to affordance: Social interactive learning from an ecological perspective. In J.P. Lantolf (ed.) *Sociocultural Theory and Second Language Learning: Recent Advances* (pp. 245–259). Oxford: Oxford University Press.
van Meurs, N. and Spencer-Oatey, H. (2007) Multidisciplinary perspectives on intercultural conflict: The 'Bermuda Triangle' of conflict, culture and communication. In H. Kotthoff and H. Spencer-Oatey (eds) *Handbook of Intercultural Communication* (pp. 99–122). Berlin: De Gruyter Mouton.
Villamizar, A.G. and Mejía, G. (2019) Fostering learner autonomy and critical reflection through digital video-journals in a university foreign language course. *Reflective Practice* 20 (2), 187–200.
Virkama, A. (2010) From othering to understanding: Perceiving 'culture' in intercultural communication, education and learning. In V. Korhonen (ed.) *Cross-Cultural Lifelong Learning* (pp. 39–60). Tampere, Finland: Tampere University Press.
Vulpe, T., Kealey, D., Protheroe, D. and MacDonald, D. (2001) *A Profile of the Interculturally Effective Person*. Ottawa: Centre for Intercultural Learning, Canadian Foreign Service Institute.
Walker, A. (2019) Culturally relevant pedagogy, identity, presence, and intentionality: A brief review of literature. *Journal of Research Initiatives* 4 (3), art. 11. See https://digitalcommons.uncfsu.edu/jri/vol4/iss3/11.
Warschauer, M. (ed.) (1996) *Telecollaboration in Foreign Language Learning*. Manoa: Second Language Teaching and Curriculum Center, University of Hawai'i at Manoa.
Wei, M. and Zhou, Y. (2021) International faculty and international students in universities: Their roles in fostering peace across languages and cultures. In R.L. Oxford,

M.M. Olivero, M. Harrison and T. Gregersen (eds) *Peacebuilding in Language Education: Innovations in Theory and Practice* (pp. 146–161). Bristol: Multilingual Matters.

Weiss, G. and Wodak, R. (eds) (2003) *Critical Discourse Analysis: Theory and Interdisciplinarity*. New York: Palgrave MacMillan.

Wenden, A.L. (2007) Educating for a critically literate civil society: Incorporating the linguistic perspective into peace education. *Journal of Peace Education* 4 (2), 163–180.

WFP (World Food Programme) (2020) *Essential Needs Guidelines*, 30 June. See https://www.wfp.org/publications/essential-needs-guidelines-july-2018 (accessed 22 June 2020).

Whitney, D.K. and Trosten-Bloom, A. (2003) *The Power of Appreciative Inquiry: A Practical Guide to Positive Change*. San Francisco, CA: Berrett-Koehler.

Wiggins, S. (2009) Discourse analysis. In H.T. Reis and S. Sprecher (eds) *Encyclopedia of Human Relationships* (pp. 427–430). Thousand Oaks, CA: Sage.

Wilson, I. (2017) Exchanges and peacemaking: Counterfactuals and unexplored possibilities. In J. Mathews-Aydinli (ed.) *International Education Exchanges and Intercultural Understanding* (pp. 21–40). Cham: Palgrave Macmillan.

Wiseman, R.L. and Koester, J. (eds) (2001) *Intercultural Communication Competence*. Newbury Park: Sage.

Witte, A. and Harden, T. (eds) (2011) *Intercultural Competence: Concepts, Challenges, and Evaluations*. Oxford: Peter Lang.

Wodak, R. (2004) Critical discourse analysis. In C. Seale, G. Gobo, J.F. Gubrium and D. Silverman (eds) *Qualitative Research Practice* (pp. 197–213). London: Sage.

Wodak, R., de Cillia, R., Reisigl, M. and Liebhart, K. (2009) *The Discursive Construction of National Identity* (A. Hirsch, R. Mitten and J.W. Unger, trans.). Edinburgh: Edinburgh University Press. (Original work published 1999.)

Wong, S.C.H. and Bond, M.H. (1999) Personality, self-disclosure and friendship between Chinese university roommates. *Asian Journal of Social Psychology* 2, 201–214.

Zembylas, M. (2014) Affective, political and ethical sensibilities in pedagogies of critical hope: Exploring the notion of 'critical emotional praxis'. In V. Bozalek, B. Leibowitz, R. Carolissen and M. Boler (eds) *Discerning Critical Hope in Educational Practices* (pp. 11–25). New York: Routledge.

Index

Note: References in *italics* are to figures, those in **bold** to tables; 'n' refers to chapter notes.

action and research 36
affordances 64
Afghanistan
   2021 167, 169
   causes of conflict 125–126
   conflict and societal norms 131–133
   demand/need for English 24, 122–124
   educational contexts 57–58, 133–136
   effects of conflict 118
   history and lives of Afghan participants 54–58
   human rights 132
   resources 127–130
   societal norms 131–132
   teaching of English 78
   US-based 'people-to-people peacebuilding' program 2, 26–28
agency, defined 115
agency and emotion 164–166
agency and power 159–161
   activities: agency beyond classroom, beyond virtual intercultural borderlands 162–164
   activities: agency in classroom and virtual intercultural borderlands 161–162
AI (Appreciative Inquiry) 10
Aijazi, O. 109
al Qaeda 56
Alias, A.M. 17
Allport, G.W. et al. 45
Alred, G. et al. 15
Altman, I. 106
Amnesty International 38, 134
Anzaldúa, G. 52, 67
Appleby, R. 164
Appreciative Inquiry (AI) 10
Ashworth, M. 7–8

assumptions 76, 83, 104, 131–132
Auberbach, E.R. 100
autoethnography 68
Avruch, K. 11

Bakhtin, M. 24
Baldwin, J. 40
Belz, J. 62
Bennett, M.J. 15, 97, 105
Bhabha, H.K. 52, 69
Biden, Joe 56
Bin Laden, Osama 56
Blackledge, A. 24
Bohm, D. 95, 96
Boot, M. 56
borderlands 53, 61–71
   intercultural borderlands 15, 61
   see also virtual intercultural borderlands of online exchange
Boulding, E. 34, 35–36, 37, 39
Boulding, K.E. 13, 25, 34–35, 37, 48
Boutros-Ghali, B. 38
Bramsen, I. 164–165
Brantmeier, E.J. 15, 61, 66–67
Brookings Institute Doha 16
Broome, B.J. and Collier, M.J.
   access to resources 152–153
   contextual framework 53, 66
   peacebuilding and intercultural communication 11–12, 18–20, **21**, 22, 25, 28, 41, 66, 159
   personal dimension 42, 72, **73**, 73–75, 77, 82, 84, 87, 92
   relational dimension 45, 46, 93, **94**, 94, 100–101, 102, 103, 109, 110
   structural dimension 47, 48, 49, 116, 117, **117**, 118, 126, 127, 131, 133, 136, 137, 139, 142, 150

Burde, D. 57
Byram, M. 42–43, 45–47, 48, 68, 105, 111, 128

Callahan, C. 52
causes of conflict, participants' understandings of
    conflict and societal norms 131–133
    differential access to resources: English/'native speakers' 129–130
    differential access to resources: technology 127–129
    social actors and causes of conflict 125–127
CCA *see* critical cultural awareness
CDA *see* critical discourse analysis
chaos 1–2
chapters overview 29–31
child protection 139–141
children 91, 132–133
Chiluwa, I. 25
China 91, 132
Chinese students 60
Cierpisz, A. 122
civil society 39
Coll, S. 56
Collaborative Online International Learning (COIL)
    Institute for Globally Networked Learning in the Humanities 62
Collier, M.J. *see* Broome, B.J. and Collier, M.J.
Collins, R. 164
communicative competence 8, 44
communicative peace 8
conflict 25, 167
    differential access to resources 127–130, 131–133
    landscapes of conflict 5–6, 76
    mediation 11, 139
    social actors and causes of conflict 125–127
    and societal norms 131–133
    understandings of effects of 117–124
    see also causes of conflict, participants' understandings of
'conflict competencies' 16
conflict resolution 34
Conole, G. 64
contact hypothesis 45
contact zones 68
context(s) 51, 142

Afghanistan, history and lives of our Afghan participants 54–58
    and our research 51–53
    US-based graduate TESOL programs and our participants 58–61
    virtual intercultural borderlands of online exchange 61–71, 95–96
Cossey, K. 63–64
COVID-19 63, 167
critical cultural awareness (CCA) 48, 68, 122, 128, 129, 166
critical discourse analysis (CDA) 10–11, 23–25
critical praxis 148, 152
cross-cultural communication 40
cross-cultural research 52
Croucher, S.M. et al. 52
Crozet, C. et al. 69–70
cultural competence 48
cultural dimension of person to person peacebuilding 19, 37, 50n5
cultural violence 33
culture, teaching of 70

DAESH *see* ISIS (Islamic State of Iraq and the Levant)
Darhower, M. 64–65, 66
de Sousa, G.U. 70
Deardorff, D.K. 14, 16–17, 26, 42, 43–44, 48, 85, 100, 106, 111·
Dervin, B. 51
DeTurk, S. 102
Dewey, J. 147, 148
dialogue 95–96, 102
difference 15–16, 102–105
Digital Education Action Plan 63
digital sojourners 42
Dingledine, R. 28
diplomacy 36, 50n2
discourse analysis 25
discursive processes 25–26
Dorronsoro, G. 55
Dyke, M. 64

educational exchange programs 13–14
effects of conflict, understandings of 117–122
    demand for English 122–124
Elosúa, M.R. 45
emotional stability 76
empathy 110–113, 137
English

access to 129–130
   demand for as effect of conflict 122–124
English as a foreign language (EFL) 31n1
English as an additional language (EAL) 31n1, 58–61
English as an international language (EIL) 31n1
English for academic purposes (EAP) 31n1
Erasmus 63
ethnorelativism 129
European Commission 63
'Experimental Digital, The' 63

Fairclough, N. 23, 24, 113
Fantini, A.E. et al. 131
Ferlazzo, L. 161, 162
Fischer, H. 63–64
Floyd, George 167
fostering person to person peacebuilding while teaching 146–147
   agency and emotion 164–166
   agency and power 159–164
   differential access to resources 152–154
   exploring identity, leveraging peacebuilding 154–156
   reflection, writing and the reflective practitioner 147–152
   concluding remarks 166–168
Freire, P. 10, 148, 152

Galtung, J. 11, 13, 18, 33–34, 35, 36, 37, 38, 48, 49, 103
gender 35, 131–132, 133–136
genocide 38
genre analysis 163
Gibson, J.J. 64, 65
Giddens, A. 25, 115–116, 124
Gkonou, C. et al. 8
Gomes de Matos, F. 8, 9–10, 17, 162
Goodman, D.J. 48–49, 122
Goodwin, A.L. 112
Gould, J. 51
Grant-Hayford, N. 111
Greater Good Science Center (GGSC) 157
group identity 82–83, 85
Guaman Poma de Ayala, Felipe 67–68

Gudykunst, W.B. 40, 45, 85
Gulliver, P.H. 11

Habermas, J. 103
Hahn, A. 12
Hall, E.T. 39–40, 104
Hansen, L. 97
Harjanne, P. 64, 65
Heleta, S. 16–17
Hodges, S.D. 110
Hofstede, G.J. 106, 131
honesty 104
Huang, M. 38
Hull-Sypnieski, K. 161, 162
human rights 12, 19, 38, 55, 132

identity
   activities: exploring identities 156–159
   exploring identity, leveraging peacebuilding 154–156
   expressions of 52
iEARN 63
Im, E. et al. 52
in-groups and out-groups 81, 82–85, 89, 101, 155–156, 157
inclusion 133–136
integrative power 35
interaction 34, 35
interaction ritual (IR) chains 164–165
intercultural borderlands 15, 61
   see also virtual intercultural borderlands of online exchange
intercultural communication 29, 62
   defined 25, 40
   and person to person peacebuilding 11–13, 32–33, 35
intercultural communication competence 39–40, 68
   across peacebuilding levels 40–41
   attitudes/knowledge/awareness 40
   personal dimension 41–44
   relational dimension 44–47
   structural dimension 47–49
   conclusion 49–50
intercultural competence 16–17, 131
intercultural language teaching 70
intercultural understanding 17
International and Intercultural Communication Annual, The 40
international educational exchange programs 13–14

International Journal of Intercultural Relations, The 40
International Security Assistance Force (ISAF) 12
'international students' 59
IR (interaction ritual) chains 164–165
Iraq 75, 76
ISIS (Islamic State of Iraq and the Levant) 56, 60, 125

Jackson, N. 54
Jakar, V.S. 9
Johnson, J.L. 52
Journal of Conflict Resolution 34
Journal of Peace Research 33

Kahl, A. 99
Karlberg, M. 25
Karn, J.M. 17
Khan, A. 57
Khan, D. 54
Kim, Y.Y. 45
King, M.L. 9
Klein, K. 110
Kolb, D.A. 147
Kostić, V. 156, 158
Kruger, F. 8, 9, 17, 162
Kumaravadivelu, B. 60, 80

Laclau, E. 97
landscapes of conflict 5–6, 76
language curriculum development 163
language teaching and person to person peacebuilding 7–11
Larson, D. 7, 8
learner agency 65
Lederach, J.P.
 cultural dimension 50n5
 defining peacebuilding 6, 36–37
 identity and power 159
 peacebuilding and intercultural communication 13, 18–20, **21**, 22, 28, 39, 41, 49, 50n5, 66, 147, 148
 personal dimension 37, 42, 72–75, **73**, 76, 83, 85, 92, 150, 151–152
 relational dimension 37, 45, 46, 47, 50n4, 93–94, **94**, 95, 96, 97, 98, 100, 101–102, 104, 105, 106, 107, 109, 110, 113, 114
 structural dimension 37, 47, 116, **117**, 133
 virtual intercultural borderlands 69
Lederach J.P. et al. 4, 19, 31n2
Leeds-Hurwitz, W.L. 39–40
liminal states 67
linguistic imperialism 122, 124
literacy 68, 120, 129, 134
Lo Bianco, J. et al. 52, 69–70
Lybæk, L. 110–111

Macalister, J. 67
McEwan, B. 52
MacKenzie, T. 161–162
Macrina, A. 28
materials 163–164
Mathews-Aydinli, J. 13–14, 17, 26
Mathewson, N. 28
media discourses 136–138
mediation 11, 139
Mejía, G. 152
Méndez, J.B. 66, 67
Milofsky, A. 9
miscommunication 12
Mitra, S. 25
Mohammad Zahir Shah 54
Motha, S. 69, 80
Mouffe, C. 97
Mujahideen 55

Naples, N.A. 66, 67
Nation, I.S.P. 163
'native speakerism' 60, 61, 79–80, 81, 130
native speakers 129–130
NATO 56, 60, 123
Nazari, M. et al. 57–58, 60–61
NGOs 123, 124
Nigeria: Boko Haram 25
NNEST (non-native English speaking teachers) 80
Nolden, D. 156, 158
Nonviolent Communication (NVC) 9–10

O'Dowd, R. 61, 62, 63
Oetzel, J.G. 12
Omar, Mullah 55
online project with Afghan English learners 2, 26–27
'openness' (self-disclosure) 76

Index 193

out-groups *see* in-groups and out-groups
Oxford, R.L. et al. 8–10, 17

Paffenholz, T. 50n3
Pakistan: Inter-Services Intelligence directorate (ISI) 55
Paris, R. 50n2
participants' understandings of causes of conflict
　conflict and societal norms 131–133
　differential access to resources 127–130, 131–133
　social actors and causes of conflict 125–127
participants' understandings of effects of conflict 117–122
　demand for English as effect of conflict 122–124
PDPA (People's Democratic Party of Afghanistan) 54
peace
　defined 125
　negative and positive 3, 35
　ways to contribute to 138–142
peace education 8–9
peace linguistics 9–11
peacebuilding 29, 66
　critical discourse analysis (CDA) 23–25
　deductive content analysis 22–23
　defined 6–7, 11, 36–38, 50n3
　exploring identity, leveraging peacebuilding 154–156
　frameworks 18–22, **21**
　methods, projects, participants 22
　conclusion 49–50
　see also person to person peacebuilding; personal dimension of peacebuilding; relational dimension of peacebuilding; structural dimension of peacebuilding
peacebuilding: understandings of 32–33
　perspectives from practice 35–38
　research perspectives 33–35
peacebuilding in practice: UN example 38–39
peacekeeping 33, 50n1
peacemaking 33
Pennycook, A. 79, 124

'people-to-people peacebuilding' program 26
People's Democratic Party of Afghanistan (PDPA) 54
person to person peacebuilding
　cultural dimension 19, 37, 50n5
　defined 6–7
　and intercultural communication 11–13, 32–33, 35
　and language teaching 7–11
　purposes, aims and focus of this book 3–4
　see also personal dimension of peacebuilding; relational dimension of person to person peacebuilding; structural level of person to person peacebuilding; US-based 'people-to-people peacebuilding' program
person to person peacebuilding and intercultural communication 11–13
　in practice 13–14
　theory and empirical research 15–18
personal dimension of intercultural communication competence 41–44
personal dimension of peacebuilding 19, 20, **21**, 37, 41–44, 72–74, 110, 137–138
　changes in beliefs about self, others and the world 90–92
　changes in beliefs/attitudes about others 81–87
　changes in beliefs/attitudes about the world 87–90
　changes in beliefs/attitudes about themselves 75–81
Phillip III, King of Spain 67
Phillipson, R. 122–123, 124
Poder, P. 164–165
political education 48
Pousada, A. 134
poverty 34
power 25, 35
　and agency 159–164
　defined 10, 34
　integrative power 35
　use or sharing of power 107–110
power distance 108–109

Pratt, M.L. 52, 67–68, 69
Puig-Larrauri, H. 99

Ramadan 112–113
reflection, writing and the reflective practitioner 147–149
　activities: guided reflection, modeling, sharing 149–152
refugees 5
relational dimension of intercultural communication competence 44–47
relational dimension of peacebuilding 19, 20, **21**, 37, 44–47, 93–95, **94**, 109
　closeness and distance 105–107
　growing nature of relationships through dialogue 95–96
　maximizing mutual understanding: empathy 110–113
　resistance: poorly functioning communication 113–114
　structuring relationships: embracing the difference 102–105
　structuring relationships: similarities 96–102
　use or sharing of power 107–110
religion 101
　interreligious dialogue 101, 102–103
　intrareligious dialogue 101, 102
Remland, M.S. et al. 13
research and action 36
resistance 75–77, 94, 113–114, 142–145
resources, differential access to 152–154
　activity: access to resources 153–154
　conflict and societal norms 131–133
　English and 'native speakers' 129–130
　technology 127–129
Richardson, Lewis 34
Robana, A. 17
Rogers, R. et al. 23
Rosenberg, M.B. 10, 162
Rothman, J.R. 8–9, 148, 156

Sanderson, S. 8–9, 148, 156
savoirs 42–43, 46, 48
Scheyer, V. 111
Schmid, P.F. 111
Schön, D. 147
self-confidence 80–81, 150–151

self-disclosure ('openness') 76
self-esteem 80–81
self-perception 76–77
skills 47
Slade, M.L. et al. 147–148
smiling 96–97
Smith, A.D. 126
Smith, J. 153
Sobre-Denton, M. 52
social actors 125–127
social justice 138–142
social penetration theory 106
societal norms 131–132
sojourners 42
Soliya 62–63
South Korea 60, 131–132
Soviet Union 54–55
Spencer-Oatey, H. 12
Stevens Initiative 63
Stokke, C. 110–111
structural dimension of intercultural communication competence 47–49
structural dimension of peacebuilding 19, 20, **21**, 37, 47–49, 115–117, **117**
　demand for English as an effect of conflict 122–124
　resistance 142–145
　structural discourses: individuals and groups 136–138
　understandings of causes of conflicts 125–133
　understandings of effects of conflicts 117–124
　understandings of inclusion 133–136
　ways to contribute to social justice and peace 138–142
　conclusion 145
structuration theory 115–116
structure, defined 115
Suurmond, J.M. 25
Syria 60

Taliban 55–56, 125, 169
Taylor, D.A. 106
teacher agency 65
teacher education 8
teaching *see* fostering person to person peacebuilding while teaching

technology 96–97, 127–129, 167
telecollaboration 62
Tella, S. 64, 65
terrorism 5–6, 56, 158
TESOL (teaching English to speakers of other languages) 2, 7–8
  and peace education 8
  US-based TESOL programs 58–61
  see also US-based 'people-to-people peacebuilding' program
theory building 151
Third Space 69
Thorne, S. 62
Ting-Toomey, S. 12
Tor browser 27–28
transculturation 68
transformative change 148–149
Trosten-Bloom, A. 10
Trump, D. 56, 143

Ukraine 60
UNESCO 57, 134, 139
UNICollaboration 63
United Nations (UN) 32, 55
  Brahimi Report 38
  criticisms of 38
  peacebuilding 38–39
  and TESOL 7–8
United States
  in Afghanistan 56
  Central Intelligence Agency (CIA) 54–55
  resistance 142–144
US-based graduate TESOL programs 58–61

US-based 'people-to-people peacebuilding' program 2, 26–28
USAID (United States Agency for International Development) 6–7, 123

van Leeuwen, T. 24, 77–78, 123, 143
van Lier, L. 65
van Meurs, N. 12
videoconferencing 1, 2, 4, 15, 26, 53, 62, 95
Villamizar, A.G. 152
violence 33, 34, 35
virtual intercultural borderlands of online exchange 61
  conceptualizaing the virtual intercultural borderlands 66–71
  growing nature of relationships 95–96
  understanding affordances and constraints 64–66
  virtual exchange and existing models 61–64

Walker, A. 156
Wei, M. 17–18
Weiss G. 23–24
Whitney, D.K. 10
Wilson, I. 14
Wodak, R. et al. 23–24, 87, 130
women 35, 55, 131–132, 133–136
World Learning 63

Zahir, King 54, 55
Zhou, Y. 17–18

For Product Safety Concerns and Information please contact our EU Authorised Representative:

Easy Access System Europe

Mustamäe tee 50

10621 Tallinn

Estonia

gpsr.requests@easproject.com

www.ingramcontent.com/pod-product-compliance
Lightning Source LLC
Chambersburg PA
CBHW070609300426
44113CB00010B/1472